Ecospectrality

Environmental Cultures Series

Series Editors:

Greg Garrard, University of British Columbia, Canada
Richard Kerridge, Bath Spa University

Editorial Board:

Frances Bellarsi, Université Libre de Bruxelles, Belgium
Mandy Bloomfield, Plymouth University, UK
Lily Chen, Shanghai Normal University, China
Christa Grewe-Volpp, University of Mannheim, Germany
Stephanie LeMenager, University of Oregon, USA
Timothy Morton, Rice University, USA
Pablo Mukherjee, University of Warwick, UK

Bloomsbury's *Environmental Cultures* series makes available to students and scholars at all levels the latest cutting-edge research on the diverse ways in which culture has responded to the age of environmental crisis. Publishing ambitious and innovative literary ecocriticism that crosses disciplines, national boundaries and media, books in the series explore and test the challenges of ecocriticism to conventional forms of cultural study.

Titles available:
Bodies of Water, Astrida Neimanis
Cities and Wetlands, Rod Giblett
Civil Rights and the Environment in African-American Literature, 1895–1941, John Claborn
Climate Change Scepticism, Greg Garrard, George Handley, Axel Goodbody, Stephanie Posthumus
Climate Crisis and the 21st-Century British Novel, Astrid Bracke
Colonialism, Culture, Whales, Graham Huggan
Ecocriticism and Italy, Serenella Iovino
Fuel, Heidi C.M. Scott

Literature as Cultural Ecology, Hubert Zapf
Nerd Ecology, Anthony Lioi
The New Nature Writing, Jos Smith
The New Poetics of Climate Change, Matthew Griffiths
This Contentious Storm, Jennifer Mae Hamilton
Climate Change Scepticism, Greg Garrard, Axel Goodbody, George B. Handley and Stephanie Posthumus

Forthcoming Titles:
Reclaiming Romanticism, Kate Rigby
Teaching Environmental Writing, Isabel Galleymore
Radical Animism, Jemma Deer
Cognitive Ecopoetics, Sharon Lattig
Eco-Digital Art, Lisa FitzGerald
Environmental Cultures in Soviet East Europe, Anna Barcz
Weathering Shakespeare, Evelyn O'Malley
Imagining the Plains of Latin America, Axel Pérez Trujillo Diniz
Ecocriticism and Turkey, Meliz Ergin

Ecospectrality

Haunting and Environmental Justice in Contemporary Anglophone Novels

Laura A. White

BLOOMSBURY ACADEMIC
LONDON • NEW YORK • OXFORD • NEW DELHI • SYDNEY

BLOOMSBURY ACADEMIC
Bloomsbury Publishing Plc
50 Bedford Square, London, WC1B 3DP, UK
1385 Broadway, New York, NY 10018, USA
29 Earlsfort Terrace, Dublin 2, Ireland

BLOOMSBURY, BLOOMSBURY ACADEMIC and the Diana logo
are trademarks of Bloomsbury Publishing Plc

First published in Great Britain 2020
This paperback edition published in 2021

Copyright © Laura A. White, 2020

Laura A. White has asserted her right under the Copyright, Designs
and Patents Act, 1988, to be identified as Author of this work.

For legal purposes the Acknowledgments on p. viii–ix constitute an
extension of this copyright page.

Cover design: Paul Burgess / Burge Agency
Cover image © Shutterstock

All rights reserved. No part of this publication may be reproduced or transmitted
in any form or by any means, electronic or mechanical, including photocopying,
recording, or any information storage or retrieval system, without
prior permission in writing from the publishers.

Bloomsbury Publishing Plc does not have any control over, or responsibility for, any
third-party websites referred to or in this book. All internet addresses given
in this book were correct at the time of going to press. The author and publisher
regret any inconvenience caused if addresses have changed or sites have
ceased to exist, but can accept no responsibility for any such changes.

A catalogue record for this book is available from the British Library.

A catalog record for this book is available from the Library of Congress.

ISBN: HB: 978-1-3500-9156-6
PB: 978-1-3502-4324-8
ePDF: 978-1-3500-9157-3
eBook: 978-1-3500-9158-0

Series: Environmental Cultures

Typeset by Integra Software Services Pvt. Ltd.

To find out more about our authors and books visit www.bloomsbury.com
and sign up for our newsletters.

Contents

Acknowledgments	viii
Introduction: Holding Open the Door of Haunting	1

Part 1 Materializing Environmental Threats

1. Urban Hauntings: On Ghosts and Garbage in *GraceLand*	27
2. Spectral Toxicity in Michelle Cliff's *No Telephone to Heaven*	53

Part 2 Materializing Environmental Knowledges

3. Haunted Histories, Animate Futures: Recovering Noongar Knowledge through Kim Scott's *That Deadman Dance*	81
4. Mapping Modes of Inhabitance: Haunting, Homing, and the Cartographic Imagination in Henrietta Rose-Innes's *The Rock Alphabet*	103
5. Life in the Graveyard: Architectures of Survival and Extinction in Arundhati Roy's *The Ministry of Utmost Happiness*	131
Conclusion: Plotting Just Futures in the Company of Ghosts	159
Notes	166
Bibliography	194
Index	207

Acknowledgments

My academic interest in hauntings was activated more than a decade ago during a pair of graduate seminars I took with William V. Spanos. While specters were not the overt focus of either course, they vividly appeared as Spanos spoke with passion about the politics of vision and the violence of erasure. This initial contact with specters culminated in a seminar paper about vision and spectrality in Rushdie's *Midnight's Children*, but then I turned away from ghosts as I immersed myself in environmental approaches to literature. The possibilities for connecting these threads did not visit me until several years later. True to the habit of ghosts, though, specters kept returning to demand my attention, and so in various ways this book represents my response to hauntings.

I am grateful for the support that I have received at Middle Tennessee State University. When I arrived at MTSU ten years ago, my transition was facilitated by the warmth and kindness of English Department Chair Tom Strawman. I have since been sustained by the understanding and encouragement of chairs Maria Bachman and Steve Severn. Thanks to College of Liberal Arts Dean Karen Petersen and the Dean's Writing Group for creating a haven for writing. The opportunity to teach and participate in the Women's and Gender Studies program shepherded by Vicky MacLean has provided welcome camaraderie and intellectual support. I have profound appreciation for the generosity of my colleague Allen Hibbard who shares and strengthens my commitment to Anglophone literature, and I am deeply indebted to my mentor, Mischa Renfroe, for all of the patience, good advice, and good wine. I feel lucky to have had the chance to share my developing ideas about hauntings with groups of talented and insightful undergraduate and graduate students. Special thanks go to my graduate research assistant Alexis Constantine for her adept assistance with tracking down sources and formatting the manuscript.

An earlier version of Chapter 3 was first published in *Commonwealth Essays and Studies* ("Unsettling Oceania," 41.1, Autumn 2018). I would like to thank the SEPC (Society for the Study of Commonwealth Countries/Société d'Etude des Pays du Commonwealth) for permission to reprint the material, and I would like to thank the editor of that special issue, Salhia Ben-Messahel, and the journal editor, Christine Lorre-Johnston, for their assistance.

I owe thanks to David Avital at Bloomsbury for his guidance and his patience and to Lucy Brown for her thoughtful assistance.

Finally, my family might not share my academic interest in hauntings, but their love and support made my work possible. Deepest gratitude to all the members of the White/Modzik/Finn clan for letting me talk about ghosts and letting me take the time to write about them. My partner, Kevin, most of all, has had to live with my ghosts, and I could not have made it through this process without him. Thank you.

Introduction: Holding Open the Door of Haunting

We live in spectral times, when toxic residues of past wars emerge in bodies of new generations, when "electronic graveyards" testify to the material persistence of electronic products that have been discarded and replaced by newer models, and when de-extinction projects attempt to restore life to species that vanished hundreds or thousands of years ago. Our world is a haunted world in the sense that past human actions, systems of governance, and structures of knowledge refuse to stay neatly contained in the past: they reemerge to shape the material environments of the present, but they also persist in less concrete ways as they continue to influence how we understand the world, conditioning what we register as the past, what counts as an environmental issue, or what is accepted as knowledge. The return of refused matter and repressed knowledge to active awareness creates experiences of disorientation and discomfort, but these returns also activate possibilities for understanding connections and consequences that endure in spite of practices and narratives that have collaborated to erase them.

Creative writers have the potential to help contemporary humans negotiate these possibilities by offering a mediated space where readers can listen to and learn from ghosts. Their depictions move beyond immediate surfaces—images of dumped garbage or melting glaciers—to engage the complex dynamics through which environmental conditions emerge over a range of temporal and spatial scales. Environmental scholars have lamented the difficulties of devising representational strategies capable of conveying the urgency of threats that take generations to unfold and the legitimacy of threats that can be so minute, so immense, or so dispersed that they evade detection by the human eye.[1] Representational challenges in turn impact what Tonya Davidson, Ondine Park, and Rob Shields have termed "scales of engagement,"[2] and scholars suggest that a disconnect between human-centered scales and environmental realities leads to alienation and feelings of futility that discourage humans from undertaking personal change or political action.³ Literary hauntings powerfully respond to these varied challenges of scale. As a force that operates between the visible and the invisible, the corporeal and the incorporeal, haunting combats obstacles of scale by facilitating movement; specters open possibilities for perception by traveling across boundaries used to separate time, space, and species. They resurface across centuries and continents, not only putting vast scales into intimate contact, but also making minute scales perceptible, for instance manifesting traces of toxins that would evade visual detection. They bring the limits of visual epistemologies to awareness, validate nonvisual senses such as listening, and cultivate affective engagement, providing readers with an alternative way of knowing that relocates the human in relation to varied scales of interdependence and makes the claims of a range of human and nonhuman others tangible.

To demonstrate how narrating hauntings transforms the terrain of the novel, and with it, possibilities for environmental justice, *Ecospectrality* dwells with the specters that haunt five contemporary Anglophone novels. None of these novels are traditional ghost stories, but they all bring readers into contact with specters that emerge from distinctive multispecies communities. Each text conjures specters to tell stories that document specific histories, cultural imaginaries, and material conditions, but the movement of specters also allows writers to reveal connections between local and planetary scales and between present and past. This movement confronts ways that environmental threats traverse human-constructed borders of nation as well as ways that environmental responsibilities extend across geographic and generational boundaries. In other words, narrating hauntings enables writers to respond to the spectral demands of our times, challenging material, epistemological, and narrative practices that draw power from exclusionary borders and facilitating contact with a range of temporal, spatial, and species others that can then become included in formulations of justice. Embracing the potentiality of specters to make multi-scalar movement and multispecies communities comprehensible, this study counters the contention that novels are ill-suited to represent the current realities of environmental crises; it proposes that literary hauntings provide writers with tools to portray the spectral realities of contemporary capitalist development and environmental inequalities that involve ongoing interactions between the visible and the invisible, the absent and the present, the living and the nonliving.

Literature as Haunted Ground

Ecospectrality draws attention to the circulation of specters and the positive potential this movement holds to make environmental threats, histories, and knowledges tangible. Elaborating this concept, I seek to build on scholarship about spectrality from a range of fields and to differentiate ecospectrality from other related approaches to literary hauntings. First, as opposed to models of the ecogothic that take a Euro-American tradition of haunting as their point of departure, my exploration starts with the texts of Anglophone writers, examining a range of culturally situated experiences of haunting. This positioning deliberately seeks to counter any notion that Anglophone engagement with ghosts and hauntings is a simple derivative of the Euro-American gothic. Scholars have done valuable work exploring the concept of a postcolonial gothic, including analyzing ways that anxieties about colonial contact, especially fears about racial others and about threatening foreign landscapes, have been constitutive of the gothic and inform imaginations of monstrosity in vital ways.[4] While the writers in this study acknowledge and interact with the Euro-American gothic tradition to varying extents, they equally turn to the duppies of Jamaica, the animating language Western Australia's Noongar people, or the vanishing vultures of India as guides for narrating haunting. Drawing from a range of local knowledges as well as academic theories of spectrality, this study recognizes multiple traditions and significations of haunting that reach beyond gothic haunted house tales. In addition to the returning spirits of deceased humans, the specters that populate this study include living humans that are rendered socially invisible, nonhuman matter that haunts human bodies, and repressed knowledges that register the presence and agency of nonhuman matter in the world.

As important as expanding the territory of haunting beyond gothic tropes (which some of these writers do also engage), ecospectrality also invites analysis of affective registers that differ from other manifestations of literary haunting. As opposed to encounters with spirits or landscapes that generate nostalgia, paralysis, or fear, ecospectral encounters use disorientation and disruption of borders of time and space to make environmental threats tangible and to transmit environmental wisdom. Distinct from conceptions of ecogothic, ecohorror, and ecophobia which foreground fear and hatred directed at nature[5] and opposed to models of haunting that aim at the resolution of the past and the exorcism of ghosts,[6] ecospectrality seeks to mobilize the productive potentialities of haunting, with the consequence that instead of attempting to avoid or silence ghosts, texts that demonstrate ecospectrality seek to live with specters in the unstable time/spaces they open, offering this contact as an invitation to inhabit the current moment with awareness of a multitude of coinhabitants.

A specific literary example might help to illustrate the range of hauntings that occurs within a single Anglophone novel and the ways that an ecospectral approach seeks out different elements from an ecogothic reading. Indra Sinha's *Animal's People* has drawn substantial attention from ecocritical scholars. While some have noted the spectral quality of the work and the ways the novel engages issues of visibility, it is not typically categorized as a ghost story.[7] However, specters circulate across multiple levels including the landscape, the human body, and the text itself. The novel chronicles the impacts of an industrial disaster that releases toxic gas on the fictional city of Khaufpur, echoing the devastation that happened in the city of Bhopal, India, following a gas release from the Union Carbide pesticide plant in December 1984. The factory is a physical location where spirits of the dead return to demand redress: "crying out in rage against their murderers ... Give us justice, screams the blood."[8] This traditional haunting of a physical space by deceased human spirits interacts with a range of other hauntings, though. A woman explains to a visiting doctor: "Our wells are full of poison. It's in the soil, water, in our blood, it's in our milk,"[9] registering the ways that the physical residues of chemicals impose effects across generations and constitute a haunting that also dislocates boundaries between the human and nonhuman. The body of the central character, Animal, is multiply haunted; as it visibly manifests the effects of the poison through his twisted spine that forces him to walk on all fours, it constantly brings "that night" to presence, and Animal also remains conceptually haunted by the ideal of the able body that travels with him as an invisible second self "who's straight, stands upright and tall ... thinks, speaks, and acts, but it's invisible."[10] Finally, the novel itself is a haunted space, which Sinha skillfully highlights through his references to other texts. His range of references to Western texts from his "uncanny summoning of the *Oresteia*" to his verbal play with James Bond (whose catch phrase Animal repeats as Namispond Jamispond during his own spy missions) mingle with his incorporation of Indian aesthetic traditions, pointing to ways that the imperial inheritance of the novel can be adapted to chronicle interactions between cultural traditions that range across borders of time and space, while at the same time demonstrating the participation of literary works in circulating figurations of time or individuality that inform conceptions of justice.[11]

These diverse hauntings evoke a range of emotional reactions that go beyond fear or contempt; in fact, they invite the conversation and complex interaction that characterize cohabitation. While Animal does vent his frustrations at the factory ghosts at one point, challenging them, "who the fuck do you think you are, to threaten me with your reedy fucking complaints," he does not seriously endeavor to silence any of the many ghosts that share his world.[12] Instead, his remark shows his familiarity with specters and positions them among the multitude of other inhabitants of the city clamoring for justice, affirming that spectrality constitutes part of Animal's everyday reality. Living with specters does not mean ignoring their disruptive potential or the horrors of the past violences that they bring to light. It does mean validating their presence and perspective and letting their insights shape decisions. It requires learning to listen to their demands. Animal learns about listening as a way of knowing from many sources, including the classical musician, Somraj. Somraj teaches Animal:

> If you know how to listen you can hear music in everything. Then he says that according to the old writers, peacocks, goats, and even the grey herons which sometimes we'd find dead beside the Kampani's lakes, these creatures too sing notes of the scale, and if you listen carefully, you can hear the same notes in many other things which you wouldn't expect such as the creaking of bicycle wheels.[13]

Referencing classical musical works such as the raga Deshkar, Somraj brings ghosted knowledge of how to listen to Animal's attention and also into the Western form of the novel. Animal, in turn, shares this capacity with readers as a way of tuning in to hauntings: "Listen, how quiet, it's. No bird song. No hoppers in the grass. No bee hum. Insects can't survive here. Wonderful poisons the Kampani made, so good it's impossible to get rid of them, after all these years they are still doing their work."[14] Attention to sound and silence becomes a way to make ongoing impacts of the poisoning tangible, and Sinha not only alternates the silences of poisoned landscapes with the screams of ghosts, but he adds the voices of nonhuman characters which allows them to figure in demands for justice. Animal's ability to listen transforms a medical specimen of a damaged fetus preserved in a jar into a friend that has his own distinct perspective on events, and Sinha's narrative strategies immerse readers in these perspectives that challenge the primacy of the living human, such as when readers occupy the perspective of Jara for several pages before learning that she is a dog. Focusing on listening as a way of knowing and attending to the range of voices that Sinha makes audible expands models for thinking about justice to include those not visibly present and those beyond the human, distinguishing ecospectrality from approaches to haunting that emphasize a fear of ghosts and seek to put those ghosts to rest.

As this brief example attests, my attention to spectrality will be wide ranging, allowing for consideration of the returns of deceased and absent humans, but also including the surfacing of nonhuman presences within human bodies and environments and returns of repressed ways of knowing and narrating. How does this approach articulate with other recent scholarly attention to environmental hauntings? It encourages greater attention to connections among types of haunting, frameworks of knowledge, and political and economic relations of power. For instance, Amitav Ghosh's discussion of the representability of environmental threats leads him to note an uncanny aspect of environmental threats that "is not the same as the uncanniness of the supernatural: it is different precisely because it pertains to nonhuman forces and beings. The ghosts of literary fiction are not human, either, of course, but they are certainly represented as the projections of humans who were once alive."[15] Similarly turning to the language of haunting, Timothy Morton elaborates an understanding of contact between the human and the nonhuman: "Ecological awareness is coexisting, in thought and in practice with the ghostly host of nonhumans."[16] He clarifies that this includes "the 'nonhuman' aspects of ourselves,"[17] and it means accepting the supernatural not as abstraction or metaphor, but as "part of the actual world."[18] Building on this work, I propose that instead of assigning literary ghosts to realms of fantasy or primitive superstition that have no bearing on contemporary environmental realities, critics might open space for ghosts and other specters to testify to experiences of material and epistemological violence. Literary ghosts vividly return readers to specific scenes of injustice, but analyzing these ghosts with attention to spectrality more broadly as a movement across borders, not only between life and death, but also between human and nonhuman, visible and invisible, allows patterns of injustice to emerge, and it implicates ways of thinking that rely on borders as a connecting feature between sites of injustice. Studying forms of spectrality in concert, thus, provides a way of approaching entanglements between ways of organizing human-nature relationships conceptually, economically, and politically, inviting consideration of how divisions of human and nonhuman articulate with a privileging of visible evidence and linear modes of storytelling and how these serve economic and political interests by positioning certain humans as separate from nonhuman nature and isolated from consequences and limits.

Further, spectrality offers a conceptual model and a vocabulary to account for experiences of contemporary humans confronting suppressed awareness of human–nonhuman interpenetration; while it shares ground with other ecocritical models that attempt to account for movement across scales and connectivity across species, it carries the advantage of providing a way to understand this movement in relationship to multiple pasts, encouraging accountability for histories of violent erasure and recognition of the persistence of alternative ways of knowing that have long validated human–nonhuman connection. Therefore, by following a range of manifestations of spectrality, this study suggests that the specter as an aesthetic device serves to represent the realities of connections across borders of generations, nations, and species that evade other forms of representation and/or that have been actively repressed in other forms of storytelling; it provides a way of understanding dependencies and responsibilities while also insisting on reckoning with the material and epistemological histories that have led to contemporary environmental damage and inequality. Attention to a range of specters requires a critical practice of reading for traces as they emerge in characters' bodies, in the landscapes with which characters' lives unfold, and in the narrative forms that writers develop, and it invites ecocritical practice to respond to absences, traces, and permeability of material and conceptual boundaries, adapting methods in response to awareness not only of the interdependencies of human and nonhuman, but also of specific histories of exploitation and repression that have actively screened these connections from awareness.

Turning to literature instead of to the material land distinguishes my project from analyses of haunted landscapes in work such as the recent collection *Arts of Living on a Damaged Planet*. Focusing on the literary, however, does not downplay the need for direct engagement with the material world; rather, it acknowledges the roles of imagination and narrative in human relationships with that world. This approach accords with much work in postcolonial ecocriticism and the environmental humanities that recognizes the role that stories can play in mediating between humans and environments,[19] in this case reflecting culturally situated experiences of living with and as specters and using narratives to circulate these experiences to readers. Scholars warn that in order to effectively address the challenges posed by contemporary environmental threats "some adjustment [must be] made to the ways in which we think about the relations among time, space, and species".[20] Literary hauntings, specifically those presented in Anglophone novels, do not turn away from the challenges impacting the material world; they offer rich possibilities for undertaking the conceptual adjustments needed to plot environmentally just futures in which humans acknowledge their debts and responsibilities to a range of human and nonhuman others.

Spectral Re-turns

In formulating a concept of ecospectrality that emphasizes haunting as a force for environmental justice, the hauntological scholarship of Jacques Derrida and Avery Gordon has been vital to my thinking. Providing an introduction to their *Spectralities Reader*, Blanco and Peeren explain that Derrida's "suggestion that rather than being expelled, the ghost should remain, be lived with, as a conceptual metaphor signaling the ultimate disjointedness of ontology, history, inheritance, materiality and ideology, has been widely taken up."[21] In fact, their collection documents how Derrida's work provided a spark for a spectral turn in which "certain features of ghosts and haunting—such as their liminal position between visibility and invisibility, life and death, materiality and immateriality, and their association with powerful affects like fear and obsession—quickly came to be employed across the humanities and social sciences to theorize a variety of social, ethical and political questions."[22] What is also notable about their 2013 collection is the absence of thinking about ecological ghosts at that time; while the essays collected represent the breadth of work theorizing ghosts and some do address issues of place, they do not engage with the environmentalist potential of ghosts. On the other hand, a current spectral re-turn is taking up the potential of ghosts to confront suppressed environmental violences; while this work has forcefully articulated an imperative to "get back to the pasts we need to see the present more clearly,"[23] my project emphasizes the double nature of the ghost proposed by Derrida: the ghost as both revenant that returns the past to attention and arrivant that announces possible futures.

While Derrida and Gordon do not address the environmental potentialities of ghosts, their insistence on letting ghosts remain provides a strong framework for thinking about them as agents of social justice that can be usefully extended to address environmental concerns and nonhuman histories. Derrida begins his influential exploration, *Specters of Marx*, by asserting:

> It is necessary to speak *of the* ghost, indeed *to the* ghost and *with* it, from the moment that no ethics, no politics, whether revolutionary or not, seems possible and thinkable and *just* that does not recognize in its principle the respect for those others who are no longer living or for those others who are not yet there, presently living, whether they are dead or not yet born.[24]

Derrida emphasizes interaction with the ghost; speaking not just of the ghost but to it and with it supports an understanding of justice that extends beyond the visible and the present, making justice include the interests of those who are dead or not yet born by making them part of a conversation. Gordon similarly links a collapse of divisions of time to conceptions of justice: "Haunting raises specters, and it alters the experience of being in time, the way we separate past, present, and the future. These specters or ghosts appear when the trouble they represent and symptomize is no longer being contained or repressed or blocked from view."[25] Literary texts provide a way to allow specters to appear, to escape the forces that have been blocking them from awareness, and to move across the divisions of past, present, and future that collaborate in blocking them from speaking with readers. These models posit hauntings not as individual psychological phenomena, but as social, political, ethical encounters, as meeting points across divisions of time and space where "we might locate a profound and durable practice of thinking and being and acting toward eliminating the conditions that produce [the social violences] in the first place."[26] In this conception of haunting, times touch one another to enable action; this interaction allows ghosts "to help you imagine what was lost that never even existed" and to reveal "that it could have been and can be otherwise."[27] Key to these formulations of spectrality is the way that the reemergence of past violence and the emotional impacts it generates create a disruption that it also an opening, a possibility for imagining alternatives and acting in response to injustice.

In this way, ghosts offer a conduit for contact and responsibility across generations, allowing for an approach to the future that avoids the pitfalls that Donna Haraway identifies in her formulation of "staying with the trouble." Haraway encourages dwelling with the challenges of the present as opposed to an "abstract futurism and its affects of sublime despair and its politics of sublime indifference."[28] The futures she rejects are those marked by a groundless hope that technology or God will come to the rescue or a resignation to destruction because it is too late to create any change.[29] In these futures, human action and responsibility play no part. Gordon's thinking, on other hand, links haunting to possibilities for change that cut across temporal divides. In this way, the future figures not in an abstract sense that absolves individuals of the need to act, but as direct result of current positions in relation to other generations and species, actually inviting the response-ability that Haraway seeks. Haraway, referencing Isabelle Stengers, proposes that "decisions must take place somehow in the presence of those who will bear their consequences."[30] Haunting answers to that "somehow"; specters put contemporary humans in touch with multiple species and multiple generations that bear the impacts of current decisions.

Specters of Justice

My formulation of ecospectrality foregrounds ways that literary texts can reconfigure divisions between past, present, and future and reflect lived experiences of relationships that extend across temporal and species divides. Such a conception builds on thinking about temporalities and justice from both postcolonial scholarship and environmental justice scholarship and also holds potential to enrich both fields. Articulating points of connection as well as obstacles to joining the disciplines of postcolonial and ecocritical studies, Rob Nixon identifies relationship with the past as one of the points of tension. He suggests that postcolonial scholarship enacts a commitment to recover suppressed pasts, while environmental literature and criticism have participated in erasing histories of colonized people by circulating myths of empty lands; environmental literature also tends to subordinate historical contexts in order to celebrate "timeless, solitary moments of communion with nature."[31] In choosing to develop a model of ecospectrality through examination of Anglophone literary texts, I demonstrate how this obstacle can become a strength, as using Anglophone texts as a starting point contributes to a necessary expansion and refinement of thinking about environmental literature. As cross disciplinary work has proceeded, it has revealed how Western ecocritical assumptions about what constitutes environmental literature were based on limited texts and perspectives. DeLoughrey and Handley directly challenge the exclusion of postcolonial scholars from ecocritical genealogies in their foundational work of postcolonial ecocriticism, *Postcolonial Ecologies: Literatures of the Environment*, while their earlier work with Renee Gosson analyzing *Caribbean Literature and the Environment* and work such as Byron Caminero-Santangelo's *Different Shades of Green: African Literature, Environmental Justice, and Political Ecology* illustrate rich veins of environmental thinking that complicate reductive notions of environmentality based on Western ideals of pristine wilderness. Such work highlights the ways that human-shaped spaces ranging from plantations to cities are environments that demand scrutiny, and they reinforce the idea that human histories such as histories of imperialism have always also been environmental histories that have impacted nonhuman communities as well as human ones.

As this scholarship illustrates, explorations that proceed from the intersections of postcolonial and ecocritical studies have rich tools at their disposal for approaching submerged human and nonhuman histories. Particularly, the need to address the pain and trauma of the past without losing track of the ability to continue to act to shape the present and the future has long characterized postcolonial thinking. Frantz Fanon's exhortation to "the native poet" in *The Wretched of the Earth* is:

> It is not enough to try to get back to the people in that past out of which they have already emerged; rather we must join them in that fluctuating movement which they are just giving shape to.... We must not therefore be content with delving into the past of a people in order to find coherent elements which will counteract colonialism's attempts to falsify and harm. We must work and fight with the same rhythm as the people to construct the future and to prepare the ground where vigorous shoots are already springing up.[32]

Rather than exclusively marking the devastations of precolonial cultures and the trauma inflicted by colonial violence, Fanon encourages artists to participate in a return to the past that can support action in the present—and he figures this collaboration in terms of cultivating the ground where shoots are springing up—returning attention to colonization as planting of material and cultural seed and figuring material and artistic responses as acts of cultivating human–nonhuman flourishing. He posits an attitude to the past that refuses to look exclusively at the past in a way that resonates with Derrida and Gordon's theorizing of haunting as communication with the past that can inspire work for alternative futures.

In light of such connections, it is not surprising that scholars have taken Derrida and Gordon's formulations of haunting as tools for approaching the violences of colonialism, slavery, war, and neocolonial domination. For example, in her study of African diaspora literature, Hershini Bhana Young contends that ghosts provide a valuable response to "the difficulty of articulating the affective imprints of racial injury and grief... with injury that revolves around absence and loss, around a submerged archive of memory,"[33] and she figures haunting as a way to access "resurfaced stories" that can "point toward a new kind of scholarship that is fundamentally concerned with redress, with honoring the cultural and spiritual memories of colonized peoples."[34] Young suggests that models of haunting are well suited to dealing with the impacts of violence that elude visibility and quantification and thus resist models of accounting for damage that are based on visual evidence and numerical data. Hauntings insist on the recognition of absence and repression as kinds of loss, and Young reinforces a conceptualization of haunting as a force that makes those losses tangible in ways that have the potential to shape different outcomes: "Ghosts signal our inheritance of the past and the necessity to act responsibly to change the future."[35]

Positing ghosts as agents of environmental justice, then, builds on an established tradition of deploying spectrality to help readers imagine losses that are difficult to visualize. I emphasize this continuity to align my analyses of hauntings with postcolonial ecocritical projects that seek to highlight connections between imperial pasts and neocolonial presents and that track consequences for communities that include material impacts on humans and nonhumans as well as on ways of knowing. While the burgeoning of postcolonial ecocriticism has allowed for increased analysis of the intersections between imperial exploitation of land and peoples and helped to highlight vital currents of environmental thinking developing outside the Global North, I remain keenly aware that scholars must resist the dangers of homogenizing distinctive colonial histories, landscapes, and strains of environmental thought and practice. As Caminero-Santangelo rightly notes, "Ecocriticism and postcolonialism run the risk of becoming imperial forms of discourse precisely when they assume the universality of frameworks that are, in actuality, the product of particular geographical and/or social positions—for example, environmentalism of the affluent (in the case of ecocriticism) or poststructuralism (in the case of postcolonialism)."[36] He clarifies that neglecting the situatedness of knowledge would undermine postcolonial ecocriticism: "It will risk betraying its resistance to colonizing forms of representation and its commitment to true dialogue among different narratives of nature and culture."[37] While I am proposing ecospectrality as a broad framework that can apply across cultures and reveal patterns of oppression, loss, and recovery, the framework and the practice of applying it to texts simultaneously demand careful attention to specific sociocultural, epistemological, and material contexts. In other words, specters haunt all of the texts in my study and all of the texts in some ways confront issues of visibility and repression, but each text also presents a distinctive configuration of material conditions and local knowledges; each text manifests a particular set of environmental challenges and a particular set of material, intellectual, aesthetic and affective resources. By weaving together readings of texts from five different physical and cultural locations, my project attempts to highlight a potential to combine culturally situated analysis and comparative thinking across traditions in support of the dialogue among different narratives of nature and culture that Caminero-Santangelo identifies as crucial for postcolonial ecocriticism.

An ecospectral approach also carries important implications for theorizing justice, and I want to tease out connections between concepts of redress and justice forged by postcolonial scholars of spectrality such as Young and chart connections to environmental justice scholarship. The environmental justice framework emerged in the United States to call attention to ways that issues of race and class impact access to environmental resources and exposure to environmental threats. Scholars such as Joan Martinez-Alier criticized early theorizations of environmental justice for failing to engage with issues beyond the United States. Since its emergence, environmental justice scholarship has expanded to address some of these concerns, as scholars beyond the United States have adapted the model to local contexts and deployed it to frame transnational issues such as waste disposal, trade agreements, and climate change. Some scholars and activists remain reluctant to identify with a method developed in the West, fearing that such a move may contribute to centralizing Western environmental models and depicting other environmentalisms as derivative.[38] In its developing global forms, though, environmental justice has begun to build more nuanced understandings of justice. As David Scholsberg notes, notions of distributive justice, of the distribution of environmental benefits and risks, impose a limited notion of justice that is insufficient to deal with global issues. He points out that environmental justice movements at the global scale "offer a much more broad definition of justice which includes conceptions of, and demands for, recognition, participation, and capabilities for both individuals and communities."[39] Justice includes much more than access to benefits; "recognition for cultures, traditions, and ways of economic, social and religious life" becomes crucial to achieving justice and exploring how beyond access, justice models need to account for the functioning and flourishing of communities that extend across generations.[40] Incorporating aspects of cultural recognition and long-term community thriving, this expanded understanding of justice requires thinking beyond those beings and those consequences that are visibly present, returning attention to the representational challenges posed by environmental threats.

How can aspects that resist visual documentation such as transgenerational community functioning come to matter in calculations of justice? This question prompts me to revisit Young's contention that hauntings "point toward a new kind of scholarship that is fundamentally concerned with redress, with honoring the cultural and spiritual memories of colonized peoples."[41] Here it seems important to note the way that she positions redress—as an honoring of the cultural and spiritual memories of colonized peoples. As in Sinha's novel that interrogates understandings that reduce justice to the law, the combination of postcolonial hauntlogy and environmental justice scholarship pushes conceptions of justice beyond legal frameworks of compensation; indeed it questions how legalistic paradigms impose limits on more meaningful and wide-reaching justice. Scholarly work can participate alongside artistic work in this redress, in recovering knowledge and using it to imagine alternative futures. Extending Young's proposition, *Ecospectrality* argues that hauntings can provide a way to retrieve suppressed knowledges, enacting justice as recognition, but also rejecting the idea that justice must remain narrowly focused on recompense for past wrongs and moving with environmental justice scholars to imagine long-term flourishing of human and nonhuman communities as a crucial aspect of justice.

Specters of Literary Form

As it investigates how literary hauntings might work in the service of global environmental justice, this study focuses on Anglophone novels that depict historical and contemporary social conditions, but that also challenge conventions of the realist novel in a range of ways. The choice of texts deliberately responds to existing debates about literary form within ecocriticism and engages with current debates about realism in global novels. First, including attention to narrative strategies answers contemporary calls for ecocritics to engage more deeply with issues of form, and it addresses broader concerns that novels are ill-suited to represent current environmental realities, drawing attention to how such claims ignore the innovative strategies that writers are developing to represent temporal and spatial scales beyond those typically depicted in realist novels.

While many scholars working in the environmental humanities accept the crucial role of narratives in "advanc[ing] understanding of the specificity of ecological concerns as well as anticipatory visions for the future,"[42] the narratives selected for study and the critical methods deployed generate debate. One debate has centered around early ecocriticism's celebration of realist aesthetics, with scholars such as Nancy Easterlin and Dana Phillips arguing that the privileging of realist representation in Anglo-American ecocriticism reveals a misguided belief that mimetic strategies allow for better understanding of environmental problems and are more likely to produce environmentalist reactions. In response, Easterlin encourages greater attention to human cognitive processes,[43] while Phillips urges more careful engagement with literary theory and ecology.[44] Although the development of postcolonial ecocriticism has supported shifts in ecocritical practice including greater openness to literary theory and a broader definition of environmental literature that reaches beyond realist nature writing, a failure to critically engage with issues of form still impacts this field. For instance, Ursula Heise has noted: "Postcolonial as well as ecocritical analyses have often tended to assess creative works most centrally in terms of whether they portray the realities of social oppression and environmental devastation accurately, and what ideological perspectives they imply."[45] In *The Storyworld Accord: Econarratology and Postcolonial Narratives*, Erin James emphasizes a similar point: that a preference for realism extends into postcolonial ecocriticism not only by encouraging study of realist texts, but also by influencing methods of reading, so that even when antirealist texts are foregrounded, their interpretation emphasizes the texts' depiction of social and environmental realities while neglecting its formal strategies.[46] In response, she cultivates a practice of econarratology and demonstrates ways that narrative theory can support greater ecocritical engagement with issues of form.

While I turn to James's work as inspiration, I also want to reinforce in my own way her contention that ecocritical engagements with form can benefit from narratological insights and from postcolonial theorizing about and artistic experimentation with the form of the novel. Edward Said brought attention to the imperial heritage of the novel and encouraged analysis of how the form of the British realist novel reinforces capitalist, imperialist ideologies of progress: its linear plot structure often conforms to individual human life spans and uses endings to enforce existing social hierarchies by incorporating a character into the social order or killing off those who cannot be accommodated.[47] Drawing on their own specific experiences, scholar-writers such as Ngugi wa Thiongo and Edourard Glissant have explored the inheritance of the novel form and have powerfully argued that although the novel originated as a European form that ideologically reinforced imperialism, in the hands of postcolonial writers, it can be adapted to reflect other temporal rhythms and other ways of organizing human relationships with the environment.[48] Although such experiments with form and intersections between form and material histories have been insufficiently studied by ecocritics, even postcolonial ecocritics, scholars who are focusing on form are beginning to reveal how such attention can enrich ecocritical analyses.[49] As DeLoughrey, Didur, and Carrigan explain their attentiveness to form in *Global Ecologies*, they contend: "We see such generic negotiations as offering incisive critiques of how mainstream environmental narratives are framed, drawing attention to the power relations and structural inequalities they all too frequently occlude, and contributing to the creation of alternative modes of articulation and analysis in line with the tradition of postcolonial thought and writing."[50] I seek to contribute to this growing understanding of ways that narrative forms reflect and contest environmental knowledge by pursuing a specific focus on the narrative devices that portray haunting and attempting to situate haunting not as a break with reality but as a strategy for representing specific material and epistemological relationships with the world that capitalist narratives have obscured or actively repressed.

My approach to form is also influenced by current debates about realism, particularly in relationship to global and Anglophone novels. Recently, literary critics have been investigating how generalizing claims about realism and reductive oppositions between realism and modernism might be preventing productive analysis of ways that contemporary Anglophone writers continue to draw on and adapt realist conventions, blending efforts to represent social conditions with experiments in form.[51] As he analyzes the critical debates that emerged around realism in the United Kingdom in the late nineteenth century and in the United States in the mid-twentieth century, Jed Esty proposes that realism debates correspond with moments of geopolitical change, leading him to wonder what kinds of change current realism debates presage.[52] Employing a historical materialist approach, the scholars of the Warwick Research Collective also link questions of form to moments of sociopolitical change. Instead of focusing on the debates that surround realism, however, their project focuses directly on literary texts and involves "seek[ing] an explanation for the apparent proliferation of forms of irrealist narrative and catachresis at particular moments of systemic crisis, above all as experienced in the (semi-)peripheries of the world system."[53] These scholars highlight the value of moving beyond sweeping elevations or dismissals of realism[54] to consider how representational strategies interact with one another as well as how they reflect social positioning and participate in social change.

Esty cautions that scholars might not have the distance necessary to fully comprehend the shifts in global politics and literary practice that are currently underway, but his work also encourages careful examination of ways that debates about form reflect anxieties about political and social change, including the role of literature in such change,[55] an issue that I would like to pursue in more direct conversation with concerns about realism in particular and the novel more broadly as inadequate to the representational challenges posed by current environmental threats such as climate change. For instance, writers such as Ghosh have expressed qualms about nonrealist fictional depictions of contemporary environmental conditions, contending that literature that employs fantastic strategies is not taken seriously as literature and is instead consigned to genre categories. He ominously predicts: "As the waters rise around us, the mansion of serious fiction, like the doomed waterfront properties of Mumbai and Miami Beach, will double down on its current sense of itself, building ever higher barricades to keep the waves at bay."[56] The privileging of realist texts by scholars from ecocritics to narratologists supports Ghosh's claim about the exclusive neighborhood of literary fiction, but instead of perpetuating a limiting notion of the literary, scholars can help to counter this trend, dismantling the barricades that confine literary fiction. Expanding attention to narrative strategies is a move that is partially underway in ecocritical scholarship, and it joins similar innovations by narrative theorists, for instance, those working in the emerging field of unnatural narratology. As Brian Richardson argues, antimimetic[57] narrative strategies "have been largely ignored by most existing narrative theories," not only as an oversight but as an exclusion, and he demands expansion of theory to account "for all narratives, not a limited subset" that follow mimetic models.[58] A collaborative article undertaking an explanation of the field asserts that "scholars working within the tradition of unnatural narrative argue that narratives are interesting precisely because they can depict situations and events that move beyond, extend, or challenge our knowledge of the world," and they clarify that unnatural narratives "may move beyond real-world notions of time and space, thus taking us to the most remote territories of conceptual possibilities."[59] By engaging more rigorously with nonmimetic and antimimetic texts as well as texts that blend mimetic and antimimetic components, ecocritics might help to challenge the notion that such depictions do not cast light on lived experiences and cannot influence understandings of real-world threats.

While I wish to borrow tools from narratology and inspiration from unnatural narratology's effort to expand paradigms to account for a range of representations, I also seek to complicate consideration of ways that texts "move beyond real-world notions of time and space," suggesting that the construction of real-world time and space is complexly entangled with questions of ideology that Richardson begins to tackle. Such discussions would benefit from greater attention to ways that depictions of the real reflect cultural and material situatedness. For instance, studying novels by Amos Tutuola and Ben Okri, Esther Peeren documents how coexistence with spirits plays a part in Nigerian reality so that "neither in the occurrence of *abiku* [a child who dies and is reborn to the same mother repeatedly] nor in its cure is the notion of living *with* ghosts seen as particularly different from living with other people,"[60] and she cites the work of anthropologist Misty Bastian who argues, "for the people involved the spirits form part of everyday reality and cannot therefore be dismissed as 'only abstractions and mystifications.'"[61] These examples provide specific illustration of Phillips's claim that "realism is idiomatic. It works only when interlocutors share assumptions about what is ordinary and the proper way to describe it."[62]

What shapes assumptions about the ordinary is not only a matter of cultural belief, but also a matter of socioeconomic positioning. The Warwick Research Collective examines ways that writers from parts of the world that have been underdeveloped by capital are responding to conditions by generating new literary forms, contending that it is in these specific locations where "the pressures of combined and uneven development find their most pronounced or profound registration—including in the sphere of culture, where new forms are likely to emerge, oriented (and uniquely responsive) to these pressures."[63] They turn their attention to strategies that writers develop to represent their experiences of combined and uneven development, highlighting how their situation at the conjunction of abstract, immaterial forms of capitalization and embodied histories and presents of imperialist extraction and exploitation create a social reality that blends material and immaterial means of production, that conditions people to the simultaneity of the visible and the invisible, and that is reflected in an aesthetics that "might then be presented as corresponding not to any deprecation of realism, but to a refinement of it, under the specific circumstances of combined and uneven development."[64] Without directly invoking the figure of the specter, these scholars describe the socioeconomic reality of those living on the (semi-)peripheries of capitalism in spectral terms, as involving daily negotiations between the abstract and invisible and the painfully corporeal and visible, positing that the literary modes that they develop to represent these experiences could be understood not as a rejection of realism, but as an expression of their situated experiences of reality. Similarly, I am suggesting that Anglophone novels deploy spectral content and form to reflect lived realities of capitalist development and resulting environmental inequalities and to incorporate ways of knowing that account for ongoing interactions with deceased ancestors and the animate voices of nonhuman matter; their narration of spectral experience does not necessarily convey a rejection of realist representation, but instead invites further attention to how definitions of and debates about realism participate in adjudicating whose experience of the world counts as real and the consequences those judgments carry for how we perceive and respond to social and environmental crises.

Haunting the Anthropocene

Ecospectrality offers terminology and concepts for thinking the current dynamics of time, space, and species that clearly intersect with, but also provide alternatives to, currently dominant discourses of the Anthropocene.

Since Paul Crutzen's popularization of it beginning in 2000, the term that identifies a new geological era characterized by the influence of humans on the environment has gained widespread currency in popular and academic discourses. Environmentally oriented scholars have raised questions about the impacts of this way of thinking our current times, raising powerful questions about the concept of the human that the term enshrines. Mary Louise Pratt speculates in the Coda to *Arts of Living on a Damaged Planet*, "These naturalist revenants remind us that the Anthropocene chronotope leaves humans, modern, Occidental humans, at the center of the narrative. Its story is still all about an 'us.'"[65] The problem that Pratt identifies is not that we are telling stories about an "us," a collective group, but in the way these stories reinscribe a restricted sense of community and an exceptionalist construction of the human. Donna Haraway underscores the irony of the name "Anthropocene" for a time when biological sciences, environmental philosophies, arts, and humanities are raising profound challenges to ideas of bounded individuals,[66] while Stacy Alaimo points to material feminisms and posthuman feminisms as challenging the disembodied, rational man that the Anthropocene seems to enshrine.[67] As Neimanis, Asberg, and Hedren clarify, "Discourses of the Anthropocene risk overwriting important differences among human populations and covering over uneven power distributions both in terms of responsibility for and vulnerability in the face of environmental problems."[68]

These scholars stress that more is at stake than just a name; the concept can reinforce reductive understandings of the human and limiting epistemologies that have collaborated in causing environmental damage. Alaimo turns to examples from popular and scientific discourse to demonstrate how the term reflects a specific way of thinking: "the epistemological position of the 'God's-eye-view' that Donna Haraway critiqued in 'Situated Knowledges' dominates many of the theoretical, scientific and artistic portrayals of the Anthropocene,"[69] a claim that she supports by providing multiple examples of ways that visual tropes and tactics such as zooming out are deployed in attempts to visualize planetary scales, but at the cost of making "nonhuman agencies and trajectories" invisible[70] and perpetuating the detached vision of the imperial eye that places viewers outside the scene and removed from any consequences.[71] Alaimo concludes that these images "ask nothing from the human spectator; they make no claim; they do not involve or implore,"[72] and I suggest that, in contrast, hauntings activate a powerful counternarrative for conceptualizing current temporalities and relationships. Instead of relying on a distant eye to make global dependencies perceptible, hauntings allow direct contact and shifting between scales so that local particularities and nonhuman trajectories need not be sacrificed to grasp planetary scales. Moving across borders with ghosts involves the reader, creating an affective encounter that does make insistent claims on humans who become transformed from spectators to participants.

Making a claim on audiences requires implicating them intellectually, emotionally, and ethically. Narratives have that power. Many environmental humanities and ecocritical scholars recognize this power: "An essential ingredient of the process by which humans make sense of crises in public life—or feel inspired to work towards solutions—is stories: narratives we tell ourselves in order to find our bearings."[73] Some have charged creative writers to craft new forms that can help us face the shifting realities of environmental precarity, and I would suggest that they are (and have been) doing just that. Haraway coins an alternate term, "the Chthulucene," to recognize ways that alternative possibilities already exist in our current times and are another story, another way of knowing that we could embrace: "the Chthulucene is made up of ongoing multispecies stories and practices of becoming-with in times that remain at stake ... Unlike the dominant dramas of Anthropocene and Capitalocene discourse, human beings are not the only important actors in the Chthulucene, with all other beings simply able to react. The order is re-knitted: human beings are with and of the earth."[74] Here, Haraway joins the discourses of Anthropocene and Capitalocene, but some important differences do distinguish them. Scholarship about the Capitalocene brings necessary attention to the historical development of capitalism as a shaping force of attitudes and practices that underlie current environmental and sociopolitical crises. Scholars such as Jason W. Moore also succeed in emphasizing the role of capitalism without reinforcing a separation of human from nonhuman forces. In fact, while he offers a different term than Haraway—he concentrates on cultivating a concept of *oikeios*—he similarly endeavors to confront the separation of human and Nature and account for processes of co-creation and interdependence, and he advocates for "developing a language, method, and a narrative strategy that puts the *oikeios* at the center," validating the importance of alternative concepts and stories because "power, production, and perception entwine; they cannot be disentangled because they are unified, albeit unevenly and in evolving fashion."[75] Such attention to the role of stories in reflecting and contesting the material ordering of relationships amplifies the important role available for ecocritics: creative writers are tapping into alternative stories that surround us, recovering repressed knowledge and charting alternative futures; as critics and scholars we can advance this project by opening the door to the mansion of fiction to new texts and experimenting with new strategies of reading.

The image of an open door has been haunting me as I compose this introduction. I was struck by the image as it was used by Arundhati Roy in *The Ministry of Utmost Happiness*, the text that will be my focus in Chapter 5. As her characters build a community in a graveyard, they speculate about how they are able to "h[o]ld open the doors between worlds (illegally, just a crack) so that the souls of the present and the departed could mingle, just like guests at the same party."[76] The welcoming attitude of a door opening to facilitate a party provides a stark contrast to depictions of dark castles or eerie cemeteries where death and ghosts are threats to be avoided. I encountered similar language again in Thom Van Dooren's work including *Flight Ways* and the introduction to *Extinction Studies: Stories of Time, Death, and Generations* composed with Deborah Bird Rose and Matthew Chrulew, where they affirm the power of stories to hold space open for others across time and species. They assert that stories "can hold open possibilities and interpretations and refuse the kind of closure that prevents others from speaking or becoming... [they] can help us to inhabit *multiply*-storied worlds in a spirit of openness and accountability to otherness."[77] Narratives of haunting hold space open for a wide range of others, allowing for ways of thinking human connection and kinship across borders and disrupting narrow definitions of the human without rejecting the idea that human perspectives, ways of understanding, and storytelling practices matter. The image of holding open a door between worlds offers a beautiful and instructive way to think about the gift offered by literary texts; they hold a door open for us to mingle with ghosts, creating an experience of time and space that allows us to reconsider our habitation and our responsibilities to the distant and diverse others who are guests at the same party. My formulation of ecospectrality is offered in this spirit as an effort to contribute to the project of opening possibilities.

Thinking with Ghosts: Overview of Chapters

Partially through experiments with form and partially through content, the texts assembled here all comment on the powers of language and the ability of narrative to help humans comprehend contemporary environmental threats and expand conceptions of environmental justice. While issues overlap and echo throughout the project, the first part foregrounds ways that specters allow comprehension of environmental threats that evade the eye, and the second part explores possibilities to recover environmentalist knowledges that have been driven to the margins.

The opening chapter begins to apply the concept of ecospectrality through a close reading of Chris Abani's novel *GraceLand*. Providing a vivid portrait of the slums of Lagos, Nigeria, Abani mobilizes ghosts to expose how promises of capitalist development rely on keeping inconvenient pasts, peoples, and places invisible. As he reveals the ghosts of the city and documents their enduring presence, he indicts superficial responses to urban poverty such as slum clearances that only address the immediate and the visible surfaces. Examining the content of Abani's novel as well as its form that oscillates across time and space, I argue that Abani forges a spectral narration that allows the marginalized living, the dead, and the nonhuman to demand a voice in planning environmental futures. By opening my study with a focus on slums, garbage, and road conditions as urgent environmental issues facing Nigerians, I foreground intersections between social inequalities and environmental threats that constitute the core of environmental justice scholarship and activism, establishing a foundation for considering different conceptions of environmental justice in the different local contexts that I study in each chapter.

The first chapter ends by engaging questions about resolution, especially interrogating the possibility that the resolution of an individual human plot could adequately address questions of environmental justice, and the second chapter embarks by centering attention on the link between novels and the concept of the individual, bounded human. In *No Telephone to Heaven*, Michelle Cliff's central character, Clare Savage, travels from Jamaica to the United States to England and throughout Europe before returning to Jamaica. Her movement calls attention to a variety of borders and classifications as she searches for a sense of racial and national identity, and that aspect of the novel has been well studied. My reading problematizes the focus on Clare as individual, drawing attention to Cliff's narration of collective and permeable bodies. Cliff documents the movement of toxins and joins the movement of toxins with the circulation of ghosts, delivering a comprehensive critique of ways that binary categories conceal movement across categories and across bodies. Doing so, she patterns her novel according to the spectral rhythms of transcorporeal networks that confound ideas of individual identity or linear journeys, and she demonstrates how environmental justice demands notions of community that reach across generations and species.

Transitioning into Part Two, the study begins to explore how ecospectrality functions in relation to repressions and recoveries of environmental knowledges. Chapter 3 takes as its focus Kim Scott's novel *That Deadman Dance* and analyzes how Scott vividly reimagines encounters between British settlers, American whalers, and Western Australia's Indigenous Noongar people to demonstrate how Noongar knowledge became discredited and repressed by Western settler narratives. Setting his work during this early colonial contact, Scott complicates traditional narratives of conquest, and he uses the novel to stage a haunting, to return Noongar vocabulary and ontology to presence in the lives of contemporary readers. I locate Scott's novel in relation to his language recovery and community activism projects to reinforce his contention that local communities must remain at the center of knowledge recovery projects, but from this position of power, local communities can share recovered knowledge, circulating stories to support social and environmental justice in contemporary Australia and beyond.

Henrietta Rose-Innes shares Scott's interests in linguistic and epistemological dispossession, and her novel *The Rock Alphabet* becomes the ground for encountering repressed knowledges in Chapter 4. The novel includes a complex investigation of connections between language and mapping, suggesting that maps, like other forms of communication, participate in systems of power, but also like other forms of communication, maps can be subjected to different interpretive strategies that can transform their meaning. This chapter uses Paul Carter's provocative questions, "Can we live with our maps differently? Could we inhabit our histories differently?,"[78] to structure an exploration of how Rose-Innes presents the consequences that different mapping and interpretive practices carry. She creates characters who exemplify different ways of relating to maps to develop a contrast between detached, classificatory reading practices that are associated with stagnancy, isolation, and death and embodied, imaginative practices that are tied to playfulness, life, and community. Rose-Innes positions these epistemologies as inheritances that the current generation must confront, and she suggests that a playful relationship with maps can facilitate a process of homing, of learning to live in relationship with multiple generations and species in communities where death nourishes future generations and ghosts remain to guide current inhabitants.

In the final chapter, I explore Arundhati Roy's intertwined interests in architecture, writing, and ghosts and use this exploration to shape a reading of her latest novel *The Ministry of Utmost Happiness*. Some reviewers have struggled with the form of Roy's work, questioning whether a work that includes so many characters and employs such an expansive plot really deserves to be called a novel. In response, I foreground the ways that her adaptation of novelistic conventions provides a powerful illustration of how the novel can accommodate the scales of environmental threats that move across time, space, and species. Specifically, I focus on the space of the graveyard and consider how Roy uses it to provide entrances and exits for the plot, creating a structure for the novel that emphasizes return and repetition as keys for imagining the mutual flourishing of a multispecies, multigenerational community. Instead of presenting the graveyard as a gothic space of horrors that disrupts the comforts of home, she creates it as a home that welcomes guests human and nonhuman, living and no longer living, to share the space of death and use it as a chance to connect and communicate. Using the graveyard and other physical spaces as connective devices, Roy illustrates how the novel and the images of community that it advances can be detached from ideas of origins that bolster damagingly exclusive notions of belonging and re-formed around awareness of interdependencies, creating a narrative enactment of the proposition that she articulates in her nonfiction writing: recovering repressed awareness of connections and refusing to allow expert discourses to divide life into isolated compartments is vital to environmental justice.

I conclude the study by pursuing one powerful possibility these texts offer to help transform how we can imagine the future—a narrative shift in which the figure of the ghost serves as an alternative to the child and the nuclear family that are often mobilized in popular environmental campaigns. While the child and the family are invoked to create a point of emotional connection and personal implication in environmental decisions that might seem abstract, they also reinforce limited understandings of inheritance and responsibility. Ghosts and spectral narration invite more radical caring and allow us to imagine kinship and community across generational, geographic, and species borders. The variety of specters that appear in Anglophone novels provide paths for imagining alternative futures by demanding that these futures reckon with the inequalities of our pasts and presents. I invite you to join me in cultivating an ability to listen to them so that together we can take up their demands and work to make it otherwise ...

Part One

Materializing Environmental Threats

1

Urban Hauntings: On Ghosts and Garbage in *GraceLand*

I am trying to move beyond political rhetoric to a place of ethical questioning. I am asking us to balance the idea of our complete vulnerability with the complete notion of transformation of what is possible.
Chris Abani, "TED Video: Telling Stories from Africa"

No justice is possible without this relation of fidelity or of promise, as it were, to what is no longer living or not living yet, what is not simply present.
Jacques Derrida, "Spectrographies"

Ghosts haunt the pages of Chris Abani's novel *GraceLand* (2004), yet they have remained largely invisible in critical analyses of the novel.[1] Critics have thoughtfully examined Abani's depictions of Lagos, Nigeria, and the slum community of Maroko, exploring ways that Abani uses the coming of age story of his central character, Elvis Oke, to interrogate Nigeria's urban development policies.[2] However, consigning ghosts to the margins of the conversation ironically replicates the politics of (in)visibility that Abani identifies as inflicting social and environmental injustices in the name of urban development. Elvis is the living protagonist of the novel, but his maturation journey involves a process of learning to navigate a position on the margins of visibility, a position that has been shaped by histories of violence that extend beyond the living present. Mixing ghostly content and formal strategies that allow times, places, and perspectives to touch, Abani illuminates how the social and environmental injustices posed by slums and the government response of slum clearance are perpetuated by visual models that support capitalist practices and narratives of development by privileging the visible, the present, and the living. At the same time, his extensive engagement with spectrality offers an alternative way of conceptualizing the city that holds the potential to transform thinking about justice by undermining the dominance of capitalist models of vision and providing a way to include the interests of the marginalized living along with the nonhuman and the nonliving.

Abani's attention to the intertwined social and environmental challenges posed by slums makes his work consonant with environmental justice scholarship that has challenged mainstream Western definitions of environments that have tended to privilege landscapes devoid of human inhabitants. Environmental justice approaches reaffirm the idea that environmental activism should involve more than protecting flora and fauna and preserving land apart from humans; it should also attend to the flourishing of multispecies communities, including urban environments. While early environmental justice scholarship highlighted ways that improved environmental conditions for some communities often rested on displacing environmental threats to other communities, frequently those of racial and ethnic minorities,[3] urban justice scholarship has continued to build on these observations to analyze ways that "the displacement of environmental risks from affluent settlements, and the failure to displace them from deprived settlements, places a disproportionate burden on internationally disadvantaged groups such as urban slum dwellers."[4] With almost one billion humans, or one in eight currently living humans, living in slum conditions,[5] the complex local and global dynamics that shape these conditions demand the urgent attention of scholars across a range of disciplines.

Scholars working in the discipline of geography analyze ways that slums constitute a "spatial manifestation of various forms of social and economic exclusion,"[6] while environmental theorists bring necessary attention to connections between temporal and spatial scales as well as to the linked impacts of slums on humans and nonhumans. Questions of visibility have captivated environmental scholars, especially the challenges of representing temporal and spatial scales on which nonhuman things operate. They argue that environmental threats often involve "things that are massively distributed in time and space relative to humans," which means that they are not consistently visible to humans or easily represented in images.[7] This lack of visibility can lead humans to question the existence of such threats or to feel detached from them. Similar to environmental threats such as climate change and toxicity that Timothy Morton theorizes as hyperobjects, slums possess surface aspects that are visible to human observers, but also include multiple effects that are dispersed through time and space. Because surface aspects of slums are easily conveyed in images, these pictures can come to dominate and restrict understandings of slums, blocking awareness of long-term consequences that reach far beyond the borders of any image. For instance, a picture of a child standing on planks over dirty water and piles of trash provides concrete, visual evidence of environmental conditions in the present. It does not, however, help viewers to grasp the diverse impacts that radiate from this moment: toxins that lurk in the pile of rubble can infiltrate the child's body and transmit health effects that last for generations, the water that runs through the settlement can distribute impacts of pollution through layers of soil and miles of territory, the child may suffer from lack of access to educational opportunities, the piles of garbage now visible have displaced native plants that used to live on this ground, and slum housing has dislodged other modes of inhabitance. Such a list exemplifies a fraction of the social and environmental impacts of slums; the difficulty of visually representing the massive and minute scales on which these processes operate contributes to superficial understandings of and responses to these threats. As a result, urban development scholars stress the need to confront the issue of scale, and they conclude "without a better multi-scaled strategy it is hard to see how the urban environmental challenge can be met."[8]

Strategies for confronting the impacts of slums must include but also reach beyond representational challenges to interrogate the ideological consequences of privileging vision and presence, and some scholars are working to draw such consequences into the conversation. For instance, sociologist Avery Gordon investigates how visually dominated models impact human understandings of social injustices, arguing that industrial capitalism thrives on "epistemologies of blindness" that keep social violence and subjugated knowledge out of view.[9] Developing the concept of slow violence to demand recognition for processes that unfold on scales that resist visualization, Rob Nixon also includes attention to what he calls "the layered invisibility that results from insidious [environmental] threats, from temporal protractedness, and from the fact that the afflicted are people whose quality of life—and often whose very existence—is of indifferent interest to the corporate media."[10] These scholars unmask ways that manipulations of visibility collaborate to support capitalist interests by denying certain populations and consequences presence so that they cannot demand limits on consumption, extraction, and development; part of this politics of vision also involves discrediting or repressing alternative ways of knowing that validate absences or register the agency of the nonhuman. Nixon acknowledges the power that visual models have had even within Western environmental thinking as he quotes Aldo Leopold's claim that "we can be ethical only toward what we can see,"[11] and he identifies the somewhat paradoxical challenge posed by slow violence as an imperative to make slow violence visible, while also disrupting the primacy granted to vision. But what does it mean to make violence visible and challenge visual models at the same time? I suggest that it means decoupling physical vision from capitalist constructions of vision that have equated the visible with presence and knowledge in order to limit ethical responsibility to that which is immediately perceptible to the human eye. It means exposing erasures as acts of violence that depend on these specific capitalist constructions of vision that devalue and disclaim the invisible, the absent, and the nonliving. However, it does not require a total rejection or demonization of vision; rather it invites a relocation of vision in relationship to other senses and a (re)connection with other ways of knowing that validate circulations across the visible and the invisible and register ways that the absent, invisible, and nonliving exert effects.

Like many other environmental humanities scholars, Nixon affirms that artists are uniquely equipped to address such complexities, and I contend that the literary hauntings that Abani deploys in *GraceLand* help to address the multifaceted impacts of visual epistemologies because they are able to reveal the erasure of living populations and the denial of long-term environmental consequences as acts of violence, but also to provide an alternative to visual models by narrating the persistence of specters. By drawing on narrative traditions that validate the presence of ghosts, Abani is able to craft a representation of Lagos that moves across times and spaces and connects the living and the nonliving, demonstrating how environmental justice demands that humans respond ethically to others beyond those we can see. In short, by refusing to offer an alternative that ends with bringing the people and forces denied visibility into view, Abani's spectral narrative addresses the complexities of making the consequences of capitalist models of vision knowable without inadvertently reinforcing this limited construction of vision.

From the opening pages of the novel, Abani encourages attention to ways that sensory perception shapes human relationship with the city, yet he also shows how these perceptions reflect socioeconomic positioning. For instance, the novel begins with a detailed and cinematic description of Elvis's bedroom that becomes contextualized as the narrator pans out to locate this room within a house, within the slum of Maroko, in the city of Lagos. After depicting Elvis within these frames, Abani reveals that Elvis "hadn't known about the poverty and violence of Lagos until he arrived. It was as if people conspired with the city to weave a web of silence around its unsavory parts. People who didn't live in Lagos only saw postcards of skyscrapers, sweeping flyovers, beaches and hotels."[12] This narration skillfully moves readers through multiple scales, bringing Elvis's sensory immersion in a community where he can't escape the smells of others' food or the sounds of others' music into contact with a panoptic view of skyscrapers, beaches, and hotels that enforces invisibility on the slums of Lagos. Sequencing events so that readers get the distant postcard view of the thriving city after they have encountered Elvis's embodied experience of Maroko, Abani challenges the authority and primacy of this official version of the city, demanding attention to issues of perspective and power. Positioning the postcard alongside the description of life in the slum community disrupts its authority to define the city, while also identifying its role in erasing Elvis's experience; it circulates a static picture of prosperity that keeps poverty out of view, and as a result, out of the discussion and awareness of those who do not reside in the city's slums.[13] Juxtaposing different ways of knowing the city, Abani demands attention to ways that socioeconomic positioning influences what becomes visible, as those who can afford to maintain the distance required for a panoptic view of the city are insulated from mental and tactile contact with the polluted land and stagnant, waste-filled water that surround Elvis.

Abani locates this interrogation of viewing positions in relation to a history in which physical force has been deployed to preserve the official image of the city and keep impoverished inhabitants and inconvenient pasts out of awareness. While the initial description of the postcard suggests vaguely that "people" conspire to keep the violence and poverty of Lagos from view, Abani proceeds to implicate the government of Nigeria in efforts to preserve a postcard image of Lagos as an attractive center of business and tourism. Slums such as Maroko threaten that image, and rather than addressing issues of urban poverty and related environmental concerns of access to clean water, waste disposal, pollution, erosion of land, and displacement of people, the government responds by acting to defend the postcard facade. In a historical study of Maroko, Agbola and Jinadu trace this tactic for dealing with Nigeria's urbanization back to the 1920s when slum clearances were enforced by the Lagos Executive Development Board. They identify a continuity in urban housing policy, reporting, "the pre-independence and immediate post-independence clearances in Nigeria were marked by a series of eviction cases in the 1980s and this culminated in the large-scale Maroko eviction of 1990 where some 300,000 people were forcibly evicted."[14] Nigeria's creative writers have played a part in documenting the devastation imposed on inhabitants by these evictions. In fact, poet and critic Odia Ofeimun has identified a Maroko corpus that, in addition to his own poems, includes drama by Wole Soyinka, poetry by Ogaga Ifowodo and J.P. Clark, and a novel by Maik Nwosu.[15] Since the 1990 eviction, displaced residents have continued to pursue legal action, seeking compensation and recognition of the eviction as a human rights violation. At the same time, slum evictions have continued throughout Nigeria, and the Maroko corpus has continued to expand with novels such as Abani's *GraceLand* and Jude Dibia's *Blackbird*, suggesting that the legacy of violent exploitation surrounding Maroko continues to speak to contemporary Nigerians despite the government's efforts to impose "a web of silence." Agbola and Jinadu observe that "it is now generally agreed that forced eviction represents a dimension of urban violence,"[16] and Abani contributes to the literary engagement with Maroko's history by using his novel to convey an understanding of slum demolitions as staged images that operate to obscure the continuing impacts of urban poverty. His novel insists that urban poverty constitutes a spatially and temporally expansive threat that is not adequately understood or addressed by representations (and urban planning and development policies) that confine themselves to the immediately visible surfaces of the present picture.

GraceLand confronts readers with the demolition of Maroko as the government's effort to resolve problems posed by slums, but as with his use of the postcard image, Abani's strategy of nesting this depiction within the temporally and spatially expansive story of Nigeria that his spectral narration enables disrupts any illusion of closure that the dominant narrative of urban progress attempts to impose and conveys a lesson: that visually dominated models of the city can only result in superficial responses, creating spectacles rather than solutions. Elvis's father, Sunday, voices objections to the government's insufficient response to the housing conditions in Lagos's slums. Contesting eviction orders, Sunday proclaims, "No! And den we will move to another location and set up another ghetto. Instead of dem to address unemployment and real cause of poverty and crime, dey want to cover it all under one pile of rubbish."[17] Sunday exposes the demolition of Maroko as a visual trick, an aesthetic remedy that diverts attention from complex social and economic problems that exceed the present moment. Refusing to let these deeper issues be concealed by a pile of rubble, Sunday's comments force attention to divisions between rich and poor as well as the challenges of providing adequate employment, access to resources, and security for Nigeria's population. These issues are abstract and temporally expansive, and Sunday implores leaders to address these problems rather than manipulating the immediately visible by bulldozing Maroko. However, creating a spectacle serves the interests of Lagos's leaders; the destruction of the "pus ridden eyesore" that is Maroko[18] allows for problems of poverty and access to resources to become concretized in an image: pictures of waste strewn streets and ramshackle houses are material and immediate, and replacing one image of squalid houses with another image of a cleaned, emptied landscape creates the illusion that problems have been addressed. This substitution of images arrests time as well as space; it imposes a sanitized future over a disclaimed past, flattening the history of inhabitance in Maroko, thus preventing sustained engagement with issues of urban poverty and making lasting environmental justice unthinkable.

Sunday's protest against the demolition of Maroko presents similar arguments to those found in environmental and urban justice discourses; however, what distinguishes Abani's intervention from other literary representations and from other discourses of justice is his mobilization of haunting as a way to stage contact with the repressed histories and erased inhabitants of the city so that they can demand their own justice. To demonstrate the transformative potential of Abani's spectral representations of Lagos and the ways that it responds to the limitations of visually dominated narratives of capitalist development, I will first explore his engagement with the social violences that make certain populations invisible, subjecting them to environmental threats and alienating them from the "literacy, political rights and civil liberties [that] are strongly associated with reduced environmental burdens, particularly at low-income levels."[19] In this case, ghostly status strips living humans of their presence and refuses them recognition by the state, but Abani demonstrates that these are not the only specters of Lagos. After examining the processes through which material and discursive practices collaborate in endeavors to bury and repress unwanted presents, I explore how Abani puts these living specters into contact with a range of other ghosts and ghost stories to demonstrate the role of literary texts and spectral narrative strategies in allowing for contact and understanding, facilitating the transmission of knowledge across time and space and returning unresolved violences to presence to demand that they figure in formulations of justice.

Touching Spectrality: The Living Ghosts of Lagos

At the same time that Abani makes Elvis central by casting him as the protagonist of his novel, he reveals the dynamics through which Elvis becomes a ghost as he moves through the city of Lagos. Elvis's spectrality reflects his socioeconomic position in the city, and rather than evoking a language of haunting to indicate supernatural qualities, the novel grounds the ghostly representation of Elvis in relationship to historical details about the political and economic development of Lagos and the forces that operate to make certain populations invisible. Abani has described his own experiences growing up in Nigeria in terms of haunting,[20] and he reflects on ways that hauntings shape his fiction as well, saying "my characters...are the people who we would normally try to erase from our daily lives."[21] Achille Mbembe frames such processes of social erasure in spectral terms, proposing that African states impose forms of violence that create ghostly populations in the human world: "Forms of social existence in which vast populations are subjected to conditions of life that confer upon them the status of living dead (ghosts)."[22] Elvis occupies such a position, and Abani explores its complexities and contradictions by showing how Elvis's embodiment makes him subject to environmental threats of the slums and to physical violence at the hands of state actors, at the same time that his social and economic position in the city dematerialize him. In *Specters of Marx*, Derrida proposes a formulation of the specter as "a paradoxical incorporation, the becoming-body, a certain phenomenal and carnal form of the spirit. It becomes, rather, some 'thing' that remains difficult to name: neither soul nor body, and both one and the other."[23] Abani shows how this formula applies in an inverse way for slum inhabitants like Elvis, who become reduced to things as their corporeality paradoxically makes them vulnerable to violence while their embodiment is obscured to prevent the naming of violence as such.

Abani's narration reflects Elvis's process of becoming-spectral by following interactions between Elvis's body and the city. The embodiment of characters and the way it influences narrative perspective and understandings of relationships between character and setting has not been a primary focus for narratologists, but scholars such as Daniel Punday insist that the effects of embodiment deserve greater attention. For instance, Punday suggests that a corporeal approach to setting would consider interactions with spaces that "shape and constrain character movement" along with "what it means to occupy a space and to move between barriers frequently ignored by the traditional narratological interest in setting as symbol or atmosphere."[24] While a focus on character embodiment enables careful scrutiny of how bodies and spaces interact, Punday also turns to the work of Elizabeth Grosz to suggest that how bodies are conceptualized should also factor into the analysis. He considers how visual models of embodiment carry consequences such as promoting a sense of the bounded individual that stops at the border of the skin, while models based on touch reconfigure skin as a point of contact rather than a boundary marker, facilitating consideration of ways that "bodies engage in an ongoing exchange."[25] The framework of corporeal narratology offers tools for analyzing Elvis's contradictory experiences of embodiment, and in turn, the example of Elvis emphasizes the need for conceptual models that can account for ways that different modes and experiences of embodiment function within narrative.

For instance, when Elvis tries to enter the postcard city, he becomes invisible, a ghost rather than a fully fleshed body. The language of haunting is repeatedly deployed to characterize Elvis and his relationship with urban spaces beyond Maroko. Early in the novel, the narrator reports that in his career as an aspiring dancer and Elvis Presley impersonator, Elvis spends time "haunting markets and train stations, invisible to the commuter or shopper as a real ghost."[26] He metaphorically becomes a ghost to the city dwellers who look through him, ignoring his frantic dance and erasing his material body, blocking his Elvis performance, his hunger, and his poverty from their view and their consciousness. Abani also reveals conceptual links across forms of invisibility as he chronicles how the construction of Elvis's body as ghost overlaps with his construction as garbage. Elvis's friend, Redemption, teaches Elvis about the city, and secures him various legal and illegal jobs. At his job dancing with wealthy night-club patrons, Redemption explains to Elvis, "you are disposable and dey will never care about you,"[27] warning Elvis that in the space of the club, he is only a laboring body that is indistinguishable and replaceable: he is garbage. Other critics have noted the recurrent images of decay and refuse and have argued that these physical depictions of the city serve as allegory for political corruption or metonymy for the postcolonial nation-state.[28] I propose that Abani links the language of garbage to the language of ghosts to expose how metaphors participate in ways of understanding the city; they operate to keep people and places invisible, denying their value and masking their material existence to remove them from consideration in planning urban futures.

The conjunction of ghosts and garbage evolves from Abani's earliest description of Elvis. As he stares into the puddles in "the swamp city of Maroko," Elvis regards his own face in the water, "floating there like a ghostly head in a comic book."[29] After he scrutinizes his appearance, he concludes, "Shit... I look like shit," and as he moves away from the puddle "one thought repeated in his mind: What do I have to do with all of this?"[30] The novel poses this question early and proceeds to unravel some answers: What Elvis has to do with all of this, with the swamp city dissociated from the "rich suburbs of the west" with their "beautiful brownstones set in well landscaped yards,"[31] is that both Elvis and the slum community constitute unwanted remainders. Scanlan explains that "garbage is leftover matter. It is what remains when the good, fruitful, valuable, nourishing and useful has been taken... the creation of garbage is the result of a separation—of the desirable from the unwanted; the valuable from the worthless."[32] Both ghosts and garbage constitute remainders, indeterminate leftovers whose haunting presence troubles the idea of easy separation of useful from waste, of living from dead, and both force attention to the endurance of matter despite changes in form. While the rhetorical packaging of matter as garbage reflects the desire to enforce division and disclaim association with or responsibility for such matter, the matter remains and demands recognition, which leads Scanlan to proclaim: "Garbage is the ghost that haunts presence."[33] In Abani's novel, Elvis and the other human and nonhuman inhabitants of Maroko are the garbage, the remainders of Lagos's capitalist development projects, that continue to haunt the static postcard image of a prosperous Lagos.

The metaphorics of ghosts and garbage convey Elvis's position on the boundaries of awareness, and in the novel, similar language is applied to other groups that the dominant culture would like to ignore and erase from view: for instance, "the transvestites that haunted the car parks of hotels favored by rich locals and visiting whites."[34] Their invisibility in this specific raced and classed space makes them vulnerable to physical violence, as Elvis continues to observe, "like them, he would be a target of some insult, or worse, physical beatings, many of which were meted out by the police, who then took turns with their victims in the back of their vans."[35] In this scene, Abani uncovers ways that social invisibility intersects with corporeality, suggesting that denying presence creates conditions for material violence, accentuating the physical vulnerability of bodies that have no recourse to state protection and showing how social invisibility can create the conditions of living death that Mbembe describes.

Attention to characters' experiences of embodiment and ways that bodies can be experienced differently in different constellations of material and social space helps to reveal tensions within visual models that seek to position bodies as bounded entities that can be expelled from the useful parts of the city, while also trading on the permeability of these bodies. For example, in Part Two of the novel, a chapter that begins with the demolition of Maroko and the death of Elvis's father concludes with a portrait of Elvis, who is absent for the demolition because he is in the custody of the Colonel being tortured. Abani vividly depicts Elvis's experience of his body through pain, as he is covered with a chemical paste that burns his skin before he is whipped, and the pain serves as confirmation of his existence: "As long as he was in pain, he was still human."[36] To Elvis, his pain assures him of his humanity, while the claim also functions ironically to highlight the failure of his torturers to register him as a fellow human, their ability to conceive of his sensing body only as a device through which they can secure the power they desire. Abani links the destruction of the slum and the assaults on Elvis's body to underscore how invisibility enables a range of violent practices that the state uses to maintain its power. He also connects these local manipulations of visibility to global scales through incidents like the work that Elvis does with Redemption moving body parts. While Elvis is horrified to learn what he has been transporting, Redemption explains "American hospitals do plenty organ transplant. But dey are not always finding de parts on time.... Dis world operate different ways for different people. Anyway, de rich whites buy de spare parts from the Arabs who buy from wherever they can,"[37] exposing a global network that thrives on the paradoxical invisibility of populations that can be capitalized for their corporeal components. By joining discursive conceptualizations of ghosts and garbage to the material treatment of living bodies that have been assigned these labels, Abani records wide-ranging consequences of invisibility, and yet he also insists on the failure of these methods to fully erase the material existence of discarded people and things. Always, on the edge of awareness is the shadow of a presence; Redemption claims "try as dey might, we won't go away,"[38] attesting to a materiality that persists beneath the metaphors and the practice of violent repression.

Attention to Elvis's spectral embodiment underscores the imperative for urban planning to account for the existence of populations that are consigned to invisibility. Environmental justice scholars argue for participatory justice, for the inclusion of perspectives of the poor and the marginalized, claiming "a majority of the local population is often excluded from any mainstream development interventions or sustainability planning. Without meaningful partnership and engagement, development efforts cannot reach their full potential."[39] Abani's novel illuminates the consequences of social invisibility, including excluding populations from participation in planning urban futures, but his treatment of spectrality also puts the forced invisibility of marginalized living populations into relationship with other forms of haunting that serve to bring repressed histories and alternative knowledges to awareness. In this way, he confirms the need to go beyond restoring erased populations to visibility, using spectral narration to recover and validate an alternative way of understanding the city in terms of long-term connections across time, space, and species.

Learning to Live with the Ghosts of Lagos

Elvis's personal experiences of spectrality occur along with other types of hauntings including interactions with deceased spirits who bring unresolved histories and repressed knowledge into understandings of the city. Chronicling the position that the living and nonliving ghosts of Lagos share between the visible and the invisible, the corporeal and the incorporeal, Abani also complicates the conceptualization of ghosts as tortured remainders advanced by Mbembe. While acknowledging how Elvis's paradoxical embodiment makes him vulnerable to violence, Abani also locates transformative potential in spectrality, narrating ways that ghosts can disrupt dominant paradigms and help imagine just futures. Instead of figuring haunting exclusively in terms of the pain and oppression of forced invisibility, he deploys haunting to document the endurance and coexistence of multiple ways of knowing and to register the value of people and knowledges that have been figured as garbage. Discussing his own experiences, Abani has affirmed that "everything in Nigeria is about haunting. It's about ghosts. The dead are everywhere and they won't stay dead," but he also identifies a role for art in confronting these ghosts: "my work asks if it is possible, if this absence, this malevolent place, can enfold and nurture and be reclaimed through prose and poetry, to turn into possibility."[40] The spectral narration he devises in *GraceLand* enables him to circulate the ghosts of violent pasts in ways that open new futures, for instance, using the presence of specters to create a perspective on the growth of Lagos that complicates celebratory narratives of progress. Choreographing interactions between these different types of spectrality, Abani interrogates ways that dominant paradigms collaborate to discredit the marginalized living as well as others denied full presence such as the dead, the unborn, and the nonhuman. His narration of Elvis's interactions with the city materialize ghosts and ghost stories, permitting Abani to create a portrait of the city that includes spatial and temporal scales beyond the immediately visible and to use this multi-scalar awareness to shape demands for justice that go beyond visible surfaces.

While the framework of corporeal narratology elucidates Elvis's contact with the city in the present, understanding the injustices of the city demands a long-term perspective that addresses ways that spaces and epistemologies touch across temporal boundaries. Punday's argument that thinking about bodies in terms of touch rather than vision enables awareness of interactions and interdependencies can be expanded to analyze ways that Abani puts times, spaces, and knowledges next to one another so that they touch. From the epigraphs that frame each chapter by juxtaposing anthropological and mythological representations of Igbo rituals of the kola nut to the organization of chapters that set 1983 alongside moments from the 1970s, Abani orchestrates contact across borders. This tactic accords with Cajetan Iheka's insight that African literary texts demonstrate an "aesthetics of proximity." Iheka contends that African writers use spatial nearness to convey their understanding of connections between human and nonhuman worlds, and he urges literary critics to accept proximity as an analytical tool that can combat anthropocentric readings of texts that miss the richness of interspecies interactions that African texts hold.[41] His focus remains on spatial proximity, while the framework of ecospectrality offers a chance to consider spatial, temporal, and epistemological proximity in concert. Environmental justice demands not only understanding how humans share proximity with the nonhuman in the present; it requires understanding how conditions of injustice have emerged over time and will impose effects that radiate across time and species. It also demands accounting for temporal components of power contests between ways of knowing and complicating environmental paradigms that ignore ways that alternatives to figurations of human separation from the nonhuman have been repressed to allow for capitalist hegemony and ongoing exploitation of land and people. Examining how Abani uses specters to reflect the touching of spaces, times, and epistemologies supports comprehensive thinking about human interdependence with the nonhuman, and it exemplifies the powerful role that narratives play in shaping ways of registering and responding to the demands of others.

The content of Abani's novel foregrounds ghost stories to validate their role in responding to violence and injustice. He recounts the oral transmission of ghost stories to portray Lagos as an environment that ghosts inhabit alongside the living and to put ghost stories into contact with Western realist conventions as contemporaneous ways of knowing and narrating the city. While Esther Peeren argues that Derrida's formulation of living with ghosts does not account for the ways that spirits are part of the everyday worlds of many Nigerians,[42] in the case of Elvis, he does, in fact, need to learn to live with ghosts. Elvis is engaged in a process of learning how to survive in Lagos that involves navigating the material dangers of the city as well as formulating a framework that can make sense of his experiences, and the roads of Lagos provide an example of how Elvis confronts intersecting temporalities and multiple ways of knowing.

While lack of water access and sewage disposal pose obvious urban dangers, as Mike Davis reveals, roadways are a frequently overlooked environmental hazard that present one of the largest health threats slum-dwellers must combat.[43] Abani uses vivid realist narration to document the threat that roads pose to Lagos's inhabitants in the present; pedestrians often cross the wide, busy roads instead of using the overhead bridges, which leads to a horrific rate of traffic deaths, so that it is almost expected when the bus that Elvis is riding crushes the body of a pedestrian that has been hit by another car. Elvis seems to be the only passenger troubled by this event that the others have accepted as part of routine road travel.[44] A man on the bus explains to Elvis that the bodies remain on the roads because the government has enacted a fine on dying while crossing roads illegally, making it expensive for families to claim their dead, and the state does not remove the bodies because government ambulances are busy, being used for private gain.[45] Economic and political conditions create a system in which dead human bodies litter roads like garbage, and the descriptive narration presents the stark material and social conditions of the present landscape of the city within which Elvis is learning to live.

The death of humans on roadways is a material factor of life in the city that distant postcard images obscure, but going beyond the manipulation of visibility in the present, Abani incorporates ghost stories to put the roads into larger spatial and temporal contexts and to illustrate how ghosts can provide city residents with a way of making sense of the violent conditions of daily life. Elvis is not aware of local beliefs in road ghosts until another bus passenger brings them to his awareness. Everyday practices of storytelling allow ghosts to enter the novel and become one of Elvis's resources for comprehending his urban inhabitance:

> An old man on the bus had told him that the spirits of the road danced around the buses trying to pluck plump offerings, retribution for the sacrilege of the road, which apparently, when it was built, severed them from their roots, leaving them trapped in an urban chaos that was frightening and confusing. Elvis never knew whether these spirits inhabited a particular road or all roads, or what they looked like. But the old man's story sounded so plausible it had stayed with him.[46]

The ghost story introduces a way of knowing the city beyond its visible surfaces. The old man's story does not include a physical description of the spirits, and Elvis struggles to imagine their appearance, but despite the lack of visible evidence, the ghost story has its own substance; it touches Elvis, and it stays with him. It accompanies him as he travels on city buses, and it shapes his concept of the road, forming part of his way of knowing Lagos. Contrary to the postcard image that packages roads in terms of speed and progress and remains detached from the past, the road ghosts introduce temporal resonances in which the past is not finished and silent; it actively interrogates the present so that the transformation of human relationship with the land through urbanization continues to register physical and emotional impacts on the contemporary city. The displaced spirits hungry for retribution manifest a malevolent remainder of past destruction of culture and modes of inhabitance, and they also convey a counter-story of the city's infrastructure, incorporating experiences of pain, loss, and anger that echo across spatial and temporal boundaries.

To deal with the spatial contexts first, the circulation of ghosts and ghost stories allows Abani to demonstrate how the city is entangled with, rather than radically distinct from or superior to, the country. As AbdouMaliq Simone discusses, the city has been figured as a space of reason and coherence in binary opposition to the bush as a space of "primordial attachments, spirits and fascinations,"[47] but Abani challenges these oppositions. Analyzing Mieville's *The City and the City,* Simone argues that the city's inhabitants sense the presence of the rural in the urban "but cannot take in both of them in any clear-cut simultaneous apprehension. As many African urban residents are fond of saying, urban life is returning to the bush—a place of inhabitation where humans are not in charge and engage only reluctantly for the powers of description."[48] Simone suggests that city-dwellers both fictional and actual feel connections between rural and urban life, but lack the ability to clearly understand and articulate these links. Abani's novel uses the presence of ghosts to offer readers a way to apprehend the intermingling of city and country spaces and epistemologies. Elvis comes to the city from the village of Afikpo, but Abani does not present ghosts as part of a backward, rural outlook that Elvis must outgrow in the city. Rather, the stories of road ghosts emerge in the city and are presented to the reader in the first chapter, disrupting chronological order and giving the urban ghosts primacy. The second chapter acquaints readers with the country, allowing us to trace continuities between the road ghosts and the ghost stories Elvis's grandmother tells him about how criminals were buried alive and had stakes driven into their heads which became fruit trees, stories that impacted Elvis so that he "couldn't walk past the trees without feeling the ghosts of the criminals reaching out to him."[49] Ghosts provide residents in both spaces with ways of understanding their own habitation in relation to the living and the dead, the present and the past, the near and the distant. Ghosts dissolve binaries and borders, revealing overlap and interaction between distant territories and confounding the strict temporal divisions of progress that assign the rural and the spectral to a past that must be decisively completed and left behind.

In terms of reaching across temporal contexts, as Elvis moves through Lagos in 1983, he traverses a ghostly city of half-completed projects and an abandoned strategic plan that was rejected by the military rulers who returned to power that year.[50] Road ghosts bring awareness to ways that the current spatial layout of Lagos and current economic inequalities extend beyond visible remains. In addition to this recent past, as Danica Savonik mentions in her discussion of automobility in urban Nigeria, roads also deliver haunting reminders of a lengthy history: they manifest a past of colonial exploitation, the physical shaping of the city and the construction of roads to legitimate promises of colonial progress and facilitate growth of the oil economy, and a continuing legacy of economic inequalities within the nation and beyond, as neocolonial extraction and foreign investment in development plans continue to shape the city. Savonick proposes that "these melancholy spirits that live in 'frightening and confusing' chaos neither memorialize nor pave over Lagos's colonial history; instead, they layer histories of colonial violence into contemporary infrastructures."[51] I suggest a slightly different way to conceptualize the presence of these spirits. Unlike the model of the palimpsest which postcolonial writers and critics have deployed to imagine relationships with the past, a model of spectrality allows for a sense of dynamic interplay among multiple times and spaces; it refuses the palimpsest's premise that times can be separated and organized into distinct, stratified layers, and it allows attention to points of overlap and contradiction, the messy territory where pasts touch the present and demand recognition of repressed stories and ways of knowing. These points of contact also manifest coexisting possibilities that remain available in the present, paths that could be followed to different futures.

Abani demonstrates these alternate possibilities when he chronicles how ghosts participate in the lives of current residents. The reports of the road ghosts establish the city as an environment inhabited by specters, but Abani also narrates scenes in which specters act alongside human inhabitants, offering multiple competing ways to interpret contemporary reality. For instance, as Sunday refuses to move from his house during the slum clearance, he is joined by the ghost of his dead wife, Beatrice, and a spirit leopard, the totem of his family. Abani allows for the possibility that these are hallucinations of Sunday, a habitual drinker, but also validates the possibility that these specters accompany and counsel Sunday. Such a possibility is consistent with the continuing presence of Beatrice in the narrative; although she dies when Elvis is eight years old, Abani allows Beatrice's voice and knowledge to remain present in the novel. He weaves her journal entries into most chapters of the novel, chronicling her awareness of the living landscape through recipes and medicinal notes about plants, enabling this knowledge accumulated over generations to remain present to interrogate the official postcard view of the city.

Abani uses Beatrice's appearance to Sunday to introduce an alternative narrative of the slum clearance that disrupts binaries of life and death, presence and absence. During the slum clearance, Sunday is shot by a police officer and crushed by a bulldozer, but Abani records that "ending" in counterpoint with a spectral version in which Sunday "roared, leapt out of his body and charged at the policeman, his paw delivering a fatal blow to the back of the policeman's head. With a rasping cough, Sunday disappeared into the night."[52] Instead of death meaning an end for Sunday, death becomes a transformation; he moves across borders between animal and human, life and death, presence and absence as he leaves his human body behind and disappears into the night. Several chapters later, Elvis returns to the scene of the slum clearance and finds his father's body as well as the body of the police officer that "looked like he had been mauled by some large predator."[53] As Elvis muses that there are no large predators in the area and that rats could not have inflicted this damage, he "sat there in the rubble and tried to figure out what had really happened."[54] Elvis, like readers, witnesses visual evidence of damaged bodies and crushed houses, but must decide how to formulate a satisfactory answer about "what had really happened." To comprehend what his eyes have seen, he needs a narrative, and this scene allows Abani to stress that visual perception alone does not provide the answer; vision still relies on acts of interpretation.

The novel uses Elvis's personal quest for answers to dramatize the consequences of competing ways of knowing and narrating Lagos. It puts two interpretations of events into contact: in the discourse of development, the government Cleans the Nation, erases Sunday and a complex history of habitation, and absorbs the slum of Maroko into a linear narrative of urban progress that removes traces of past violence and poverty from view. However, by forging a spectral counter-narrative that refuses to code death as closure and by enabling spirits and knowledge to circulate freely across time and space (including across sections of his novel), Abani reveals how that development narrative relies on visual manipulation to foreclose ongoing considerations of justice, and he implies that spectral narratives can support expanded notions of social and environmental justice that include accountability beyond the living present. In this way, he not only affirms the coexistence of different ways of knowing, but also underscores the material consequences of which narratives hold sway.

The spectral alternative that Abani crafts extends from the content of these ghost stories to the structure of the novel itself. He refuses spatial figurations of the past as behind or beneath the present, instead devising strategies that allow the past and its ghosts to coinhabit and move alongside the current moment. The novel is unevenly divided into two parts with the first part of the novel comprising roughly two-thirds of the tale. In Part One, chapters alternate between Elvis's adventures in the city in 1983 and key moments from his childhood in the village of Afikpo from 1972 to 1980. In Part Two, the movement between chapters becomes spatial rather than temporal, as the chapters narrate events that happen exclusively during 1983. Climatic events recorded in these chapters include the bulldozing of Elvis's home in Maroko, the death of his father, Sunday, and the death of his mentor, the King of the Beggars, and chapters shift focalization, as Elvis is physically absent for all of these events. Readers access these events first without Elvis, and then again as he becomes aware of what transpired while he was being tortured in prison. The structure of the novel, then, replicates an experience of haunting through which characters and readers gain knowledge as times, spaces, ways of knowing, and strategies of narrating come into contact.

The novel's structure vividly enacts haunting as a way of knowing and demonstrates how figuring time as a series of spectral returns can disrupt authoritative narratives that seek to censor the past and refuse its claims on the present. Organizing chapters to move between 1983 and 1972–80 allows Elvis's childhood to run alongside and interact with his current life in the city rather than providing an explanatory backdrop or a sense of a past that has been left behind. In one case, in 1983, Elvis confronts his father about memories of violence that his family has clearly tried to assign to the past. He brings repressed events to awareness when he questions his father about the murder of his cousin Godfrey and the rape of his cousin Efua. His father denies that these events happened, trying to erase them from the family history, but Elvis testifies to the aspects that he experienced: "'Innocent came to my room a few nights after the murder.' Elvis said, pausing after the word 'murder.' That was something, to call it that, but what else was it? he thought. 'I gave him food and he seemed very afraid. He mentioned Godrey, then fled in terror.'"[55] Similarly, when his father asks him what he really knows about the rape of Efua, saying, "You can't know for sure, unless it happened to you," Elvis calmly and simply replies, "He raped me too."[56] These traumatic moments of violence surface in the present through dialogue, and the narration also includes a brief moment of Elvis reflecting on his choice of words, calling attention to the importance of the terms he has chosen; he has claimed power to recognize these acts of violence as crimes: murder and rape. During this conversation, though, Sunday challenges Elvis's knowledge of the events, arguing that the testimony of Innocent and Efua cannot constitute definitive knowledge, that only direct experience, only presence, could equal knowledge and grant him the authority to label these crimes.

In the following chapter, Abani returns readers to the event of Elvis's rape in Afikpo, 1980, narrating the incident a second time, this time as a scene in the present. What was first brought to the reader's awareness through a single retrospective statement, "he raped me too," now unfolds as a lived experience that includes sensory details of the attack, Elvis's thoughts and feelings during it, and his conversation with his cousin in the aftermath. The chapter does not serve the traditional functions of flashback that narratologist Gerard Genette identifies of filling in information omitted from an earlier part of the story or introducing an event that was deliberately sidestepped, since readers already know that the event occurred. Genette explains that some analepses create a return that "retroactively confers on the past episode a meaning that in its own time it did not yet have... either by making significant that which was not so originally or by refuting a first interpretation and replacing it with a new one."[57] Abani's movement through time allows readers to inhabit the event as it was first experienced, but only after it has already been designated as rape; thus, this return does not retroactively assign meaning or refute an earlier interpretation. It validates Elvis's initial interpretation by revisiting the events and allowing readers to confirm the designation of rape and murder; it resists Sunday's effort to deny or bury the events by putting readers directly into their presence, but it also does more than simply affirm the equation of knowledge and presence. The narration demonstrates that even when the labels and the stories that would have identified the past events as crimes were repressed, these experiences continued to exert effects; they were still part of Elvis's reality. The spectral return confirms his naming of the acts as crimes, but this naming and narrating does not put an end to the effects; it registers their ongoing movement and allows them to be lived with. In scenes such as this, spectral narration resembles other forms of analepses, but it is also a distinct type of return that serves the interests of social and environmental justice, in part by creating contact across times and places that positions responsibilities to others as extending in multiple directions rather than having an end.

The way that haunting conveys a refusal to resolve and absolve the past is captured in Avery Gordon's postulation: "Haunting is one way in which abusive systems of power make themselves known and their impacts felt in everyday life, especially when they are supposedly over and done with (slavery, for instance) or when their oppressive nature is denied (as in free labor or national security)."[58] The specters that visit Elvis span the personal and national, cultural and political, incorporating Innocent's experiences as a child soldier in the Biafran War along with cultural ideals of masculinity and honor that shape Sunday's reactions to Elvis, and by expanding the reach of the novel to touch all of these, Abani recognizes them as contributing to the current conditions of inequality in Lagos. Abani's spectral narration connects these threads, as he puts multiple temporalities and geographies into contact to call attention to the ways violence is repressed, both by attempting to relegate it to the past and by refusing to name it as violence. The spectral form that Abani devises stretches the conventions of the novel and modifies traditional uses of flashback, refusing to assign the past to an anterior position and instead allowing it full force to share in defining the meaning of justice in the present, in his own way expressing Derrida's proposition that "no justice is possible without this relation of fidelity or of promise, as it were, to what is no longer living or not living yet, what is not simply present."[59]

On Recycling and Resolution

Registering the invisibility of impoverished Lagosians as a form of urban violence and refusing to be distracted from long-term consequences by immediate spectacle are part of addressing the injustice that Abani uncovers, but at the end of the novel, Elvis remains on the threshold of visibility as he responds to a new name and prepares to leave Lagos. Some critics have expressed dissatisfaction with the novel's conclusion, lamenting that both Elvis and Abani seem to be fleeing from Lagos and retreating from the complex political, social, and environmental issues that global slums present.[60] Attention to Abani's use of ghosts and his crafting of a spectral form provides a different way of interpreting the novel's resolution. Certainly, Abani does not offer easy solutions to problems of urban poverty and environmental injustice. However, he does contribute to critiques of global capitalism by complicating celebratory narratives that leave slum inhabitants to their own resourcefulness. And just as he rejects slum clearances as inadequate responses, he refuses narrative resolutions that create an illusion of closure by imposing superficial change. In fact, crafting an ending for his novel that refuses to arrest the circulation of effects is entirely consonant with his deployment of a spectral structure throughout.

First, Abani's novel contributes to investigations of connections between capitalism and waste that have been pursued by a range of scholars including Zygmunt Bauman who casts light on wasted human lives and environmental scholars such as Maria Mies and Veronika Bennholdt-Thomsen who expose ecological effects of modern garbage disposal. These scholars concur that a growing capitalist economy demands increased waste production, which means that the global capitalist market has an interest in keeping the human and environmental consequences of garbage concealed. Bauman asserts, "We dispose of leftovers in the most radical and effective way: we make them invisible by not looking and unthinkable by not thinking."[61] Abani's novel challenges readers to look and to think with a perception tuned to specters, with the consequence that we must reevaluate the processes that create material waste and wasted humans. Mies and Bennholdt-Thomsen elucidate how granting visibility to garbage holds the potential to transform attitudes and behaviors: "if waste is again seen as part and parcel of our life processes, which cannot be dumped 'somewhere', but which has to be reinserted into the regenerative cycles of distinct ecosystems on which communities depend, then also the production process as well as the circulation of goods will have to change."[62] Abani's novel makes a valuable contribution to this broader critique of capitalism by using ghosts to provide readers with a way of understanding waste in terms of both its erasure and its reabsorption into regenerative cycles.

GraceLand demonstrates that the impoverished residents of Maroko possess creative abilities that enable waste to be re-purposed within the community, but Abani also insists that such recycling is not a satisfactory answer to problems of urban poverty. As Simone explains, people can redefine garbage by finding new uses for discarded objects:

> There must be a willingness to extricate particular things and materials from conventional uses ... Objects must be converted into functions and locations to which they are unfamiliar, and this stems from a process where people are able *to see differently*—that is, anticipate the realization of a project through assembling bits and pieces of things that don't seem to belong, that may seem out of place.[63]

Abani suggests that such awareness is already part of the ways of seeing, knowing, and living for residents of Maroko. The novel opens with a description of Elvis's bedroom, beginning with a shuttered window that is propped open with an old radio battery. The narrator leads readers' eyes through Elvis's room where objects have been converted to new functions and locations:

> A piece of wood, supported at both ends by cinder blocks, served as a bookshelf. On it were arranged his few books, each volume falling apart from years of use. By the window was a dust-coated desk, and next to it a folding metal chair, brown and crisp with rust ... A wooden bar secured diagonally between two corners of the room served as a closet.[64]

The objects are weathered and worn, but they are not garbage; they have value because Elvis has the capacity to imagine ways they can be put to use. However, this ability is present at the start of the novel as is Elvis's awareness of it; Abani includes the resourcefulness of impoverished citizens as part of the living conditions in the city, not as a solution to problems of poverty and inequality or an epiphany that Elvis moves readers toward. With its depiction of urban recycling, the novel starkly demonstrates that leaving the poor to these innovations does not solve problems of economic and environmental injustice, reinforcing claims that "grassroots responses alone cannot coordinate the structural dimensions of urban development."[65]

Additionally, Abani clarifies that recycling is related to but distinct from relocation by chronicling various instances in which waste moves without being reused or revalued. For instance, the Nigerian government and investors reimagine Maroko as valuable real estate instead of wasteland. However, unlike the objects in Elvis's room and the components of the molue buses that show how discarded objects can be fit to new uses, the bulldozing of Maroko simply shifts unwanted remainders into the shadows without reconsidering their worth. This kind of movement supports global capitalism by keeping waste out of view and out of mind, and Abani's engagement with the ambivalence of movement—a process which at times collaborates with capitalist concealment and at other times brings new possibilities to light[66]—provides a lens for reading the novel's ending that might help to address some critical complaints about the unsatisfying resolution.

The close of the novel intensifies the ambivalence of movement because leaving Lagos does not solve the problems Elvis has raised, but his motion does expand awareness of the scales of connections in which slums participate. Throughout the novel, the global circulation of ghosts illuminates scales of urban poverty which often resist representation; the novel documents the movement of culture through music and film and literature, but it also chronicles complex economic circuits through which move specters: drugs, body parts for illegal organ transplants, and anonymous laboring bodies. As he prepares to leave Nigeria, Elvis is reading James Baldwin's *Going to Meet the Man* and reflecting on a scene that describes lynching and castration. Elvis's reading habits guide readers of Abani's novel[67]; they help to make tangible the planetary scope of haunting. Elvis's reading activates an image of America not as a paradise or retreat from his problems, but as a land haunted by violence and racism; the destination that Elvis evokes is traversed by ghosts of colonialism and slavery in ways that ally it with rather than distinguish it from the nation that he is leaving. Pairing Elvis's physical movement with other kinds of physical, cultural, and economic flows, Abani reveals that the politics of visibility he has been interrogating extend far beyond Maroko or Nigeria. While specific local spaces provide the physical setting within which Elvis's body moves, throughout the novel, all of these other kinds of movement that characterize global flows of capital and culture have participated in shaping that local present. Having Elvis's body move into contact with new physical settings does not exorcise ghosts or place him beyond the reach of haunting; it brings contact with additional ghosts and reinforces the need for narratological tools that can address interactions between bodies and spaces that exceed the visible surfaces of present proximity.

The movement of Elvis's body, then, is only the most visible form of movement happening as the novel draws to a close, and this movement does not impose resolution, but challenges the concept of the end (both as goal and as finality). Analyzing the last scenes of the novel, Ashley Dawson suggests that "spatial egress is substituted for temporal progress" so that at the novel's end Elvis "achieves mobility and the promise of settled community"[68] while Hilary Dannenberg concludes that "the novel stresses Elvis's disorientation and his lack of ability to construct a coherent whole out of the multiple spaces and experiences of his life."[69] While these critics disagree about Elvis's potential to achieve a fixed position, both proceed from the assumption that settled community and settled identity are desirable goals and end points for a journey. However, I suggest that Abani more comprehensively challenges the strategy of using the progress of an individual human journey to signify meaningful social change.

"Nothing is ever resolved, he thought. It just changes," Elvis muses as he prepares to board a flight to the United States at the end of the novel.[70] Like the movement of garbage to keep it from view, like the movement of the displaced slum dwellers from Maroko into the slum under the flyover, global migration simply shifts matter without resolving underlying issues. It is not an end in terms of a remedy; it is a temporary fix that shifts bodies and manipulates surfaces without addressing structures of inequality. The way that ghosts continue to accompany Elvis as he prepares for his departure emphasizes this point and comments on the need for different kinds of justice. As he waits for his plane, Elvis admits that he remains "haunted by the specter of the Colonel"; he cannot ignore his memories of his cousin, Efua, or Redemption's accusations about his selfish attitude toward her; additionally, "nearly every night, in his dreams, he saw Sunday's ghost wandering aimlessly searching for his house and Madame Caro's buka, long gone under the tyrannical wheels of the bulldozers," and the King not only haunts Elvis; he has become a public icon whose story is circulating through the media as well.[71]

By ending with attention to the continuing presence of ghosts, Abani implicates the conventions of the novel, particularly the bildungsroman, suggesting that resolving an individual journey as a way to contain anxieties about social order is another way of manipulating surfaces. The novel concludes with Elvis's voice responding to the boarding call for his flight to America; he answers, "Yes, this is Redemption."[72] The details of this response have important implications. First, by using the phrasing "this is Redemption," rather than having Elvis proclaim "I am Redemption," Abani invokes expectations for a proclamation of identity as a resolution to a personal journey, as a signal that individual identity has been confirmed and reconciled to social expectations. However, Abani subverts that expectation and substitutes a process, redemption, for a fixed state of identity. Further, by calling attention to the host of ghosts that still surround Elvis, the reference to redemption raises questions about differences between redemption and justice. Redemption refers to "the action of freeing a prisoner, captive, or slave by payment," or to "deliverance from sin and damnation."[73] Both of these meanings refer to outcomes for an individual who is rescued from perilous physical or spiritual circumstances. Closing on this note, Abani highlights a dissonance between the individual plot and the scales of environmental justice, showing how a plot restricted to the individual might lead to redemption, but not to justice that includes the multiple generations that the novel has brought into contact. His attention to ghosts even during this departure scene reminds readers that it is not only Elvis's story and the injustices that he has experienced that demand resolution.

Through the inclusion of ghosts and ghost stories, Abani suggests that urban processes of change include Elvis Oke, but they also extend far beyond him. In her foreword to Gordon's *Ghostly Matters*, Radway explains that Gordon "is not so naïve as to believe that agency is a matter of simply recovering an individual will or intention to act, however. Rather, she implies, radical political change will come about only when new forms of subjectivity *and* sociality can be forged by thinking *beyond* the limits of what is already comprehensible."[74] Following this line of thinking, radical change must include more than the personal transformation of Elvis Oke; it requires a re-conception of relationships of subjectivity and sociality, an ability to understand the individual within relationships that extend massively through time and space. In this regard, Elvis's travel at the end of the book does not suggest fixity or resolution, but offers an opportunity to explore "the complete notion of transformation of what is possible."[75] Read as an effort to transform what is possible, the novel's ending does not record the failure of Elvis to assimilate into society or the failure of the postcolonial city as other critics assert, but the inability of the individual plot to provide a satisfactory response to the injustices posed by slums. It points to the need to reconsider the claim that novels are not equipped to represent the scales of contemporary environmental threats, and asks us instead to consider how conventions of the novel can be reconfigured to disrupt their role in advancing limited constructions of vision that grant priority to presence. Withholding the satisfaction of a clear resolution that lays the specters of environmental injustice to rest, Abani empowers these specters to continue making demands on his readers, as they persist across borders and advocate for justice, which is not an end, but an ongoing process.

2

Spectral Toxicity in Michelle Cliff's
No Telephone to Heaven

> *We are afflicted not only by social conditions but by the ways we think them.*
> Timothy Morton, *Humankind: Solidarity with Nonhuman People*

> *I come out of a colonial tradition in which we are taught that the "novel" was defined in such and such a way—a rigid definition. We come from an oral tradition that encompasses the telling of history, dreams, family stories, and then we also have the European idea of what the novel is.*
> Michelle Cliff, "Journey into Speech: A Writer between Two Worlds"

In *No Telephone to Heaven*, Michelle Cliff powerfully challenges a foundational fiction of military industrial capitalism: that humans can neatly enforce boundaries to divide land and categorize people. Literary critics have noted ways that Cliff interrogates borders and binaries as her character, Clare Savage, struggles with oppositions between male and female, white and black, present and absent, native and foreign. However, Cliff's novel holds more radical potential than most critics have credited to it. In addition to Clare's travels from Jamaica to the United States to England and throughout Europe, other types of movement structure the novel. Cliff chronicles the penetration of bodies by toxins, displaying ways that toxins operate in the mode of haunting, and she links the movement of toxins to the circulation of other ghosts, demonstrating how these transits that happen on less traditionally visible scales reveal the permeability of corporeal, national, and temporal borders. At first glance, the Agent Orange that has poisoned Clare's lover, the ex-soldier Bobby, might seem geographically and conceptually distant from bauxite mining and aluminum refining in Jamaica, and both might seem minor background details in a novel that narrates Clare's negotiation with the multiple facets of her heritage and her desire to become "whole."[1] However, these links constitute a vital part of

Cliff's novel that has been neglected because of the tendency to focus on Clare as an individual protagonist. Foregrounding the movement of toxins and other ghosts repositions Clare within circuits of transcorporeal and transgenerational movement, an interpretive move that enhances understanding of Cliff's comprehensive critique of binaries and borders. Such borders serve the interests of capitalism as they radically restrict consideration of responsibilities and dependencies, but Cliff's novel demonstrates how haunting can bring discredited and repressed experiences to awareness in order to demand social and environmental justice that acknowledges responsibilities to those beyond the immediate and the visible. By adapting the novel to advance alternatives to the self-contained individual, Cliff shows that the novel as a form does not need to be abandoned in the fight for social and environmental justice.

Haunting the Borders of the Individual

The Western realist novel typically follows an individual human protagonist, focusing on the temporal scale of the biological human life span and separating the human from the nonhuman, which is positioned as background. Circulating images of the bounded individual, the novel helps to normalize this depiction, equating this conception with reality and concealing its status as a culturally specific way of conceiving the human. Investigating the pressure for novelists to focus on an individual protagonist, Amitav Ghosh suggests that the genre convention reflects and supports capitalist ideology. In a discussion of John Updike's review of Abdul Rahman Munif's *Cities of Salt* which found fault with the work for not focusing on a single protagonist, Ghosh contends that the focus on the individual "is not by any means an essential element of the novel," a claim which he extends by arguing that the preference for the individual journey displays how capitalist ideology impacts both literary form and material practices, as he notes "the acceleration in carbon emissions and the turn away from the collective are both, in one sense, effects of that aspect of modernity that sees time (in Bruno Latour's words) as 'an irreversible arrow, as capitalization, as progress.'"[2] Beyond connecting capitalist ideology and aesthetic form, he implicates cultural constructions of time and the human in environmental destruction. Inserting Cliff's novel into this conversation helps to illuminate how the novel has not been exclusively tied to the conceptualization of the human as bounded individual nor has it been restricted to an exclusive focus on the human, despite critical pressures to adhere to this pattern. Writers have been adapting the form of the novel to reflect different experiences of reality, and my analysis will proceed by exploring how Cliff's novel complicates ideas of the individual, bounded human, how it crafts a structure of conjuring that confounds linear ordering, and how it supports radical conceptions of environmental justice as a result.

Previous analyses of Cliff's novel have been confined by the expectation that a novel must follow an individual human protagonist; this has encouraged critics to approach the novel as a quest for individual identity, starting with a basic assumption that some scholars directly state and others imply: "The protagonist of *No Telephone to Heaven* is Clare Savage."[3] Clare does hold an important role in the narrative, but Cliff also denies Clare centrality in important ways—from leaving her unnamed in a collective human group that shares primacy with the forest in the opening chapter to continuing the narrative after her death. The way that Cliff imagines Clare as enmeshed in the lives of a range of human and nonhuman others and the way that she detaches the novel's time frame from an individual human life span also accords with a broader tradition of Caribbean writers who have looked not to the individual human as the structuring unit, but to the land itself.

Because colonialism destroyed the history of Caribbean peoples and alienated them from sources of information about the past, Caribbean writers have turned to the land as a source of historical memory.[4] Writers such as Edouard Glissant, Wilson Harris, Jamaica Kincaid, and Olive Senior have created a vibrant literature (including fiction and theory) that relies on the land to provide traces of occluded histories, and more broadly to structure an understanding of time and provide temporal rhythms for their writing. The forest, the garden, and the sea provide these writers with models for representing scales and rhythms that differ from the Western realist novel's bounded human progressing through linear time. For instance, Glissant describes an understanding of collective identity in which the human and the land share agency: "The collective 'We' becomes the site of the generative system, and the true subject,"[5] and this collective "We" includes the land as participant and partner: "Describing the landscape is not enough. The individual, the community, the land are inextricable in the process of creating history. Landscape is a character in this process."[6] Discussing the conventions of the novel, Wilson Harris expresses a similar conviction that Caribbean writers must develop their own strategies to reflect local understandings of human relation with the land:

> May I emphasize again that the life of the *earth* is not *fixed*; it is not a description of *fixed* mountains or valleys divorced from the characters that move on it. The life of the earth needs to be seen *in fiction* as sensitively woven into the characters that move upon it, whose history, may I say, reflects a profound relationship to the earth.[7]

In their own ways, these writers voice an imperative for creative writers to devise narrative strategies to reflect lived experiences of interdependence that challenge the capitalist separation of human and the land that conventions of the novel confirm. Foregrounding a collective we rather than an individual I, representing the dynamics of relationship between humans and the land rather than confining the land to the background, and recording the agency and creativity of the land rather than depicting it as inert or passive require adapting conventions to accommodate the realities of human connection and nonhuman agency.

Cliff experiments with form in ways that similarly draw on the land as a source of inspiration, but she also demands attention to ways that representations mediate relationships between Caribbean writers and the land. As she describes in the epigraph to this chapter, she operates at the intersection of multiple legacies, having inherited a rigid definition of the novel through British colonial education at the same time that she is heir to oral traditions and their patterns for recounting histories and dreams. As Helen Tiffin notes, colonial education influences more than knowledge of formal genre conventions; it also impacts how Caribbean writers perceive the land since this education valorized English landscapes and the literatures that depicted them while figuring the Caribbean landscape as "richly but degeneratively tropical, frightening, fecund, even pathological."[8] Cliff addresses this impact of colonial education, wondering, "When our landscape is so tampered with, how do we locate ourselves?"[9] Some Caribbean artists respond by reconnecting with the land itself; Harris, for instance, provides a powerful account of his awakening to the land's agency during an expedition in 1942,[10] but both Tiffin and Cliff provide the important reminder that writing strategies also emerge in relation to the form and content of previous representations which must factor into the discussion to avoid creating a romanticized, essentializing notion of pure connection with the physical land.

Cliff deploys ghosts and conjuring to address the challenges of reflecting the profound, multifaceted connection between human characters and the earth and to displace the individual human as the ordering unit for the novel. While some critics have entertained the argument that *No Telephone* is a collective novel,[11] the collective in these discussions remains tied to human concerns of forging personal and national identity in postcolonial contexts, and the land remains consigned to a position as "background" to Clare's journey or becomes a symbolic mother with whom Clare can reunite.[12] Attending to the movement of toxins and other specters, however, reveals that the collective that Cliff imagines includes nonhuman beings from living animals and trees to chemical residues to decaying matter to duppies or spirits. In this way, she stretches the boundaries of the novel, including dynamic human characters, but complicating the notion that the novel is bound to chronicle individual human journeys.

The circulation of ghosts helps shift attention from Clare as individual protagonist and reveal how the land can provide an alternative conception of time that exceeds the human life span. The opening chapter of the novel presents the land of Jamaica, specifically the forest, as a haunted place. It begins with an epigraph that introduces the word ruinate, "the distinctive Jamaican term used to describe lands which were once cleared for agricultural purposes and have now lapsed back into ... 'bush.'"[13] Ruinate characterizes the forest as a bearer of historical traces and as historical agent; a ruinate forest records past configurations of the land, including a past of human efforts to shape the land to support human economic and aesthetic goals, but at the same time it collapses divisions of past and present as it enfolds previous iterations into the new growth of the forest. In the ruinate forest, the human no longer holds the power to design space and order time. The narrator reports, "The forest had obliterated the family graves, so that the grandmother and her husband, and their son who died before them were wrapped by wild vines which tangled the mango trees shading their plots, linking them further to the wild trees, anchoring their duppies to the ground."[14] In this passage, human efforts to assign matter to its proper place, to bury the dead and inscribe their fixed location and meaning through a headstone, are undone by the continuing motion of the land. Rather than being connected to the land through the fixity of human language and memorial rituals designed to keep the dead in their allotted time and place, the human remains become a material component of the evolving landscape. The land incorporates the remains, literally entangling them in the growth of the forest community so that death is reconfigured as part of the ongoing life of the forest, and the duppies, or spirits of the dead, remain linked to this place. Introducing human inhabitants as ghostly remainders that haunt a land that has its own power and its own history denies the individual human primacy as narrative subject. It dislocates the human life span as the unit of measurement, encouraging greater attention to shared attributes and linked histories of human and nonhuman matter.

The forest is presented as a collective composed of multiple members and agencies, but Cliff's imagining of the collective also involves more than leaving the idea of the individual in place and assembling multiple individuals. Glissant observes that the landscape is "not saturated with a single History but effervescent with intermingled histories, spread around, rushing to fuse without destroying or reducing each other."[15] As in Glissant's description, Cliff's narration of the forest presents intermingled histories and agents that fuse without destroying or reducing each other and that counter the idea that parts have to unify to compose a single master narrative, a single History. In an ecocritical context, Timothy Morton considers the relationship between parts and wholes, and he develops a concept of solidarity in terms of "discrete yet deeply interrelated beings."[16] Similar to Glissant's image of intermingling histories that can fuse without destroying one another, Morton carefully theorizes solidarity to distinguish it from romanticized notions of community, stressing the need to locate shared experiences and interests despite difference, rather than ignoring or collapsing difference. He argues that "allowing for others to exist in some strong sense, joining their ways of accessing things or at least appreciating them, just is solidarity. Solidarity requires having something in common," and he goes on to clarify that "we could reimagine what 'to have in common' means"[17] to avoid the problems of essentializing or turning wholes such as community into transcendent concepts, radically different from and greater than the sum of their parts.[18]

Cliff develops a style of narration that conveys an understanding of the forest in these terms of "discrete yet deeply interrelated beings": "The forest had already moved in—long-time—around the house, edging the verandah. Mahogany. Broadleaf. Mosquito wood. Shadbark. Silk-cotton. Guango. Cashew. Lignum vitae. Ebony. Wild pine."[19] The named parts and the division of each name into its own sentence recognize the continuing existence of distinct trees despite the existence of the larger entity that is the forest. Cliff's narration reveals how this collective includes the plants that are visible in the present moment, but also how the present members rely on and record a history that extends beyond the present:

> As the land cleared, it turned black—blackness filled with the richness of the river and the bones of people in unmarked graves... They found, in the process of clearing the land, things that had been planted long before—before even the grandmother—which had managed to survive the density of the wild forest. Cassava. Afu. Fufu. Plantain.[20]

Cliff describes the soil to reflect collectivity and connectivity across temporal borders, as the richness of the soil has been created over generations, nourished by the river and decaying sea life as well as by the bones of unknown and unnamed humans, and the plants that emerge reveal a history of human interaction with the land that extends beyond the genealogy of which the humans are aware; the plants are a haunting reminder of a history of human dependence on the land written directly on the land in ways that challenge and extend the oral family history, reaffirming that the collective includes more than the currently living plants and humans. Yet even as they share identity as part of the forest, the bones and the soil, the plants and the trees retain distinctiveness and compose their own stories; they are not merged into a homogenized whole.

Beginning her novel with this complex introduction to the collective of the forest, Cliff signals the need to reconsider human positions within collectives as well. Clare surfaces as a human character who appears across the novel, but Cliff waits until the novel's fourth chapter to reveal that Clare was one of the rebels on the back of the truck in the first chapter and that she was the girl who had sex with Paul who then went home to find his family murdered in chapter 2. The reader recognizes Clare's presence and learns Clare's name in retrospect, which forces the reader to travel back to make connections, rather than sequencing the plot according to the forward motion of linear progress. With this choice, Cliff compromises with expectations of the novel, offering a human character who connects the incidents of the plot, but at the same time making readers attend to ways that human life remains bound up in the stories of others that interject on one another and refuse to conform to a linear trajectory. At the point in the novel when she reveals Clare's presence throughout the earlier events, Cliff repeats the stylistic move she had made to characterize the forest as collective. The narrator first reports, "There are many bits and pieces to her, for she is composed of fragments,"[21] and then reveals, "She is the woman who has reclaimed her grandmother's land. She is white. Black. Female. Lover. Beloved. Daughter. Traveler. Friend. Scholar. Terrorist. Farmer."[22] The passage conveys the idea that Clare herself is a fragmented multitude, composed of many parts that remain distinct even as they interact to form a collective recognized as Clare. While other critics note this passage as crucial in describing Clare's process of postcolonial identity formation, neglecting the parallels to the depiction of the forest reinscribes the priority and separation of human identity rather than pursuing the entangled sense of collectivity that Cliff advances. It is not simply that the forest as collective parallels the human as collective; the forest and the human are implicated in one another. The description of the forest reveals how it has been built through interactions between human and nonhuman lives and deaths. The resistance of the forest to human ordering not only parallels the human rebel movement, but participates with it in testifying to past exploitation through the traces left on the land and in resisting exploitation by pursuing its own growth and designs that present material obstacles to its colonization and conceptual challenges to human categories. Figuring Clare not only as a participant in social collectives such as the nation or the rebel group, but representing the human itself as a product of multispecies collectivity, Cliff opens possibilities to recognize that the potential for solidarity does not stop at the species border.

The Specter of Permeable Bodies

The spectral movement of toxins further complicates conceptions of the individual human protagonist by powerfully illustrating how individual bodies are not discrete, bordered territories. Like other specters, toxins operate in a mode of haunting, erupting at the edges of visibility to demand recognition. While it is characteristic for specters to traverse binaries between life and death, and presence and absence, toxins take on this spectral quality, announcing their presence by crossing boundaries, especially of the skin, the outer surface that covers humans, animals, plants, and soil. By narrating the movement of toxins, Cliff demands attention to ways that collectivities are more than assemblies of bodies that remain separate and enclosed. For instance, while the forest is composed of plants, trees, soil, and animals that retain distinctive identities, toxins force a shifting of scales and perspectives that reveals that even the units that we identify as discrete entities are themselves collectivities which form across and through visible surfaces. Stacy Alaimo develops the concept of transcorporeality to account for movement across borders and describe "interconnections, interchanges and transits between human bodies and nonhuman natures."[23] Alaimo acknowledges that her work builds on other similar formulations such as Linda Nash's "ecological body" that emphasizes the human body as participant in fluxes and flows profoundly shaped by the nonhuman environment,[24] and Nancy Tuana's "viscous porosity" that accounts for ways that "boundaries between our flesh and the flesh of the world we are in and of are porous" and mediated by various physical and social membranes such as skin, prejudgments, symbolic imaginaries, and habits.[25] These models challenge concepts of a distinctly bounded human, and they emphasize the need to think through intra-actions across human and nonhuman bodies and across discursive and material borders. However, by focusing heavily on spatial dynamics, these formulations might unintentionally confine thinking to present movement. For this reason, theorizations of spectrality might supplement thinking about transcorporeality by adding greater attention to temporal dynamics.

Derrida's formulation of the specter that I discussed in the previous chapter in relation to Elviss's embodiment in *GraceLand* also illuminates aspects of Cliff's representation of bodies impacted by toxicity. Derrida describes the specter in terms of "a paradoxical incorporation, the becoming-body, a certain phenomenal and carnal form of the spirit. It becomes, rather, some 'thing' that remains difficult to name: neither soul nor body, and both one and the other."[26] The specter traverses binary categories which gives it an elusive quality, resisting the fixity of labels and reflecting processes of becoming and border crossing similar to those instigated by toxic exposure. While Derrida invites attention to spectral experiences of embodiment, Elizabeth Freeman identifies some limits in his discussion, noting his focus on "a visual and occasionally aural economy" and a neglect of other aspects of bodily experience.[27] Putting Derrida's theorization of spectrality into conversation with Alaimo's theorization of transcorporeality thus expands the potential of both and creates a model particularly suited to analyzing the movement of toxins, substances that manifest an incorporeal corporeality as they become absorbed into bodies which cannot contain them in space or time; toxins travel across the physical boundaries of skin, the conceptual borders of the individual, and the temporal borders of generations, revealing the illusory nature of the binaries that undergird the construction of the bounded human.

In her novel, Cliff chronicles the corporeal effects of toxins, exploring how toxins become visible over time and through contact with spaces, including human and nonhuman bodies. Clare's lover, Bobby, attempts to repress his past, refusing to speak of it and imploring Clare to "bury" her curiosity. Eventually, Bobby admits that the festering wound he carries on his ankle is a consequence of his exposure to Agent Orange during his service in Vietnam; he exclaims, "Ever seen that movie *The Incredible Shrinking Man*? Where that dude gets covered by fine mist?... Think of that. It entered me."[28] While Bobby tries to withhold a narrative of his past, his body records its history of permeability through this wound that visually documents the transgression of borders between inside and outside, the penetration of Bobby's skin by a fine mist. The way his body records this history troubles Bobby's sense of identity, as he struggles to explain, "Think of that. It entered me," an expression that reflects the difficulty of conceptualizing the intra-action between body and environment and the threat it poses to familiar ideas of the bounded individual; this substance, "it" entered Bobby's body, and he still endeavors to separate "it" from "me" although his ruptured skin leaves him with an enduring reminder that his contact with the mist has irrevocably reconfigured his body. The language of penetration is echoed later in the novel in the descriptions of the impacts of bauxite mining in Jamaica, "people for miles around are covered by a fine dust which invades them."[29] Fine mist and fine dust, material substances that are barely visible, enter bodies by traveling through the covering of skin, which seems to provide a stable, visible border that separates the individual human from human and nonhuman others. When evidence reveals the porosity of this border, it disrupts the formulation of bounded bodies that supports capitalist divisions between human and nonhuman others; toxicity forces exposed humans to become aware of aspects of their own spectrality, as they recognize the enduring presence of nonhuman others within their bodies.

As Alaimo notes, toxins travel across spatial borders, challenging ideas of the body as clearly bounded, but Cliff also emphasizes the temporal dimension of toxic circulations. In addition to accumulating their effects within bodies over time, they also erupt across generations, spanning temporal borders in ways that pose representational challenges. Christopher Hitchens powerfully addresses the difficulties of portraying the expansive circuits through which toxins travel in his article about the effects of Agent Orange; Hitchens observes: "Some of the victims of Agent Orange haven't even been born yet, and if that reflection doesn't shake you, then my words have been feeble and not even the photographs will do."[30] As he argues, making damage that extends across generations comprehensible is crucial for environmental health and environmental justice, yet the temporal dispersion of this damage makes it difficult to comprehend through stories or capture through the visual evidence of photography. As Alaimo notes, "Notwithstanding the significant environmental justice work accomplished through the savvy use of photography and video, many EJ problems cannot be visually discerned nor photographically documented."[31] While the photographs that Hitchens references provide powerful documentary evidence of the damage toxins inflict on specific bodies in the present, Cliff attempts to develop strategies that can manifest connections across bodies, times, and places in ways that offer readers a chance to comprehend long-term consequences and accept responsibilities beyond the living present because as Derrida argues, "no justice ... seems possible or thinkable without the principle of some responsibility beyond all living present, within that which disjoins the living present, before the ghosts of those who are not yet born or who are already dead."[32]

To allow for this more expansive sense of justice, Cliff follows toxins across borders between generations. Bobby's revelation of the story behind his wound is elicited by Clare's pregnancy, and he admonishes her: "It entered me. It doesn't end with me. So if what you think might be true turns out to be true, you better think abortion, honey. Unless you want a little Black baby with no eyes, no mouth, no nose, half a brain ... I don't think you need my nightmare made flesh, that's all."[33] Cliff activates the potentiality of pregnancy—itself a process that blurs borders of self and other, life and death, and visually manifests the passing of time—to highlight Bobby's insight: It doesn't end with me. The toxins extend beyond the boundaries of his body and his life span, as they pass to Clare and a potential child. Clare suffers a miscarriage, infection, and infertility that make her womb, like Bobby's wound, a haunted space that records a specific history of intra-actions across bodies and environments, extending consequences into future generations not through the nightmare child that Bobby imagines, but through an absence of children. While Clare negotiates her body's porosity in her own distinct way, the experience also allows her and readers to consider the territory she shares with Bobby and with the land, who similarly confront the material consequences of toxicity. The shared materiality of the experience gets obscured in critical discussions that focus on the symbolic nature of motherhood and Clare's connection with Mother Earth; more than a symbolic figuration through which Cliff "returns the power of the womb to women,"[34] shared experiences of permeability point to the role of gender constructions in enabling material violence against feminized bodies.

Considering permeability as an experience that is shared forces a reconsideration of interpretations of the novel focused on Clare's reconnection with a feminine landscape at the same time that it expands possibilities for understanding Cliff's challenge to binaries and borders. Considering *No Telephone* in conjunction with *Abeng*, in which Clare Savage also figures, Jennifer Smith has argued that "the novels' treatment of the processes of the female body suggests a more complicated view of feminist retrieval of maternal traditions than has been previously acknowledged."[35] The circulation of toxins indicates a need to pursue this discussion further, beyond the processes of female bodies. Morton suggests that solidarity invites a process of rethinking what it means to have in common, and Cliff provides a variety of characters who share in common an experience of reckoning with the permeability of their bodies. In Western colonial discourse, permeability was figured in terms of female bodies. For instance, "As European men crossed the dangerous thresholds of their known worlds, they ritualistically feminized borders and boundaries" which supported a rhetoric of penetrating the landscape, allowing European men to preserve a sense of themselves as active in opposition to the passive, penetrated land/culture/woman.[36] This gendering of permeability does not reflect a biological difference in male and female bodies, though; it demonstrates ways that binaries operate to repress and project unwanted qualities onto the bodies of others. Cliff's interrogation of binaries and borders does not just reverse binary constructs to make devalued qualities and connections with the earth into a source of power for women; she reveals ways that binaries create a limiting understanding of the human that serves particular interests, oppressing certain humans and obscuring perception of shared experiences of corporeal vulnerability.

By narrating experiences of porous bodies, Cliff reveals that permeability is a human condition that becomes gendered through acts of refusal and projection, and she brings the repressed awareness of human porosity as well as the power dynamics that support this continuing repression to awareness. Bobby's body is penetrated and carries a wound that is described in vaginal terms—with lips that open to release a flow of fluids.[37] The imagery presents his black male body as wounded by penetration and as passing an inheritance of toxicity into the bodies of Clare and a new generation—the nightmare child. The language of being entered and invaded, being penetrated in unwanted ways, activates specters of sexual violence that further ally human and nonhuman experience. Colonial incursion has been discursively figured as a rape of the land, and Cliff's language that documents the continuing exploitation of the land for mineral wealth deploys similar imagery of violent penetration, as she describes "the bleeding landscape near Fern Gully, rusted, orange, where the ore had been scraped from the country."[38] The bleeding landscape evidences violent disruptions of the land's surface, while Harry/Harriet recounts suppressed histories of penetration of bodies that have been figured as less than human. Harry/Harriet recounts his rape by an officer that he describes in terms of being "pierce[d]," and he also observes that his experience was not an anomaly or an abstract symbol, but part of a pattern of violating the boundaries of bodies of disempowered people, "I only suffered what my mother suffered—no more, no less."[39] The toxins that force Bobby's past to erupt through the surface of his skin activate specters of his past that then resonate with other specters; the polyphony of specters allows Cliff to link disparate scales and experiences and confront ways that these different experiences of permeability are historically specific, but also enabled by a shared logic that operates to disavow porous bodies as less than human. Further, by crafting this spectral rupture of the silence surrounding permeability, Cliff demonstrates that the novel, which has participated in circulating the image of the bounded individual as that which is properly human, can be adapted to advance alternative understandings of the human and of human solidarity with the nonhuman.

In Cliff's novel, the shared experience of vulnerable borders and the repetition of language of penetration across present and past, human and nonhuman bodies affirms that people who have been denied full humanity are well aware of the porosity of bodies and the lack of human control over what penetrates their skin, a crucially important point to bring back into conversation with new materialist and posthumanist attention to permeability. For instance, further elaborating her theorization of transcorporeality in her book *Exposed: Environmental Politics and Pleasures in Posthuman Times*, Stacy Alaimo develops the concept of exposure as a political and ethical position. Alaimo argues that toxic exposure can offer "an invitation to intersubjectivity or trans-subjectivity, and ... a posthumanist or counter-humanist sense of the self as opening out unto the larger material world and being penetrated by all sorts of substances and material agencies that may or may not be captured."[40] From this point, she argues that "an ethics and politics of exposure may be undertaken," informed by "the intuitive sense or the philosophical conviction that the impermeable Western human subject is no longer tenable."[41] Her model offers helpful attention to ways that accepting the permeable human body destabilizes notions of human borders that separate and elevate mind over body and human over nature, and she does acknowledge the difference between those affected by disasters and those choosing exposure as an activist position.

However, adding attention to postcolonial contexts in which sovereignty over bodily surfaces has been denied to many human and nonhuman bodies, Cliff's novel invites further qualifications. Alaimo's desire to position experiences of environmental vulnerabilities as a starting point for ethics and activism leads her to claim, "The exposed subject is always already penetrated by substances and forces that can never be properly accounted for—ethics and politics must proceed from there."[42] Claiming that bodies are penetrated by substances that cannot be accounted for, on one hand, makes sense as a refusal of the humanist pretension to total knowledge that separates the knowing subject from the object of knowledge and that accounts for the realities of bodies as microbiomes that are also engaged in constant transcorporeal encounters, but in another sense, such claims might downplay the need to account for substances that have penetrated bodies as part of colonial and neocolonial violence. From the colonial concealment of the penetration of slave bodies and foreign lands to neocolonial erasures of toxic infiltrations of human and nonhuman bodies, a variety of beings are subject to violences that have been overlooked in mainstream historical accounts, and addressing these silences and erasures, as Cliff does with her novel, is vital to demanding social and environmental justice. Displaying a similar interest in refiguring the human, Morton claims, "Worlds are perforated and permeable, which is why we can share them."[43] In order to share our perforated worlds, we need to confront ways that conceptual borders and binaries have been deployed to perpetuate inequality and excuse certain human bodies from a shared position of vulnerability. Cliff develops a narrative structure that encourages this confrontation.

Conjuring: Touching Temporal and Spatial Borders

The ghosts that circulate through Cliff's text offer an alternative structure for the novel that places various temporal and geographical scales into contact, and the structure of conjuring reflects another way that Cliff bends the form of the novel away from isolated individuals and journeys that unfold in orderly sequence. In *The Great Derangement,* Ghosh identifies "the irony of the 'realist' novel: the very gestures with which it conjures up reality are actually a concealment of the real," and he concludes that new literary forms and new reading practices will emerge to incorporate the improbable events and the nonhuman forces that are excluded from the realist novel despite their vital roles in shaping contemporary reality.[44] Nonlinear temporal rhythms are crucial parts of many realities, and again, the experiences of postcolonial writers can be instructive in thinking through ways that artists have negotiated with pressures of literary realism that contradict lived experiences of reality. Glissant contends, "Western realism is not a 'flat' or shallow technique but becomes so when it is uncritically adopted by our writers,"[45] and he points to ways that conventions of realism reflect a particular understanding of and relation to time and space that is not universal. He urges postcolonial writers to adapt inherited forms, to explore connection with land and environment as structuring experiences of and depictions of reality. He proposes that the regularity of seasons structures works of Western literature, while the unvarying seasons of the Caribbean demand "a new economy of the expressive forms…. Our quest for the dimension of time will therefore be neither harmonious nor linear. Its advance will be marked by a polyphony of dramatic shocks."[46] Cliff's *No Telephone to Heaven* conjures specters and uses them to create a polyphonic structure for her novel that supports her attunement to collectivity. Published in 1987, this innovative novel precedes Ghosh's prediction that new literary forms will emerge to incorporate the improbable and the nonhuman by several decades, emerging during an era that also saw other novels such as Toni Morrison's *Beloved* deploy haunting as a structuring device to confront social injustices; this was also the time of a spectral turn in literary criticism and theory that explored ways that ghosts manifest past human violence. Recognizing Cliff's historical location in relation to spectral thinking does not prevent exploring her work in terms of contemporary formulations of environmental specters. Rather, it suggests that environmental concerns already inhabit other forms of spectrality; it is a matter of attuning our critical lenses to recognize these ecological specters that linger within literary texts, offering us alternative ways to conceive of human relationships with nonhuman and nonliving others and reminding us of the deep links between social and environmental justice.

Conjuring, bringing to presence spirits of those who are absent or dead, serves as a narrative device that connects distant spaces, times, and bodies; it reconfigures ideas about consequences and responsibility by making scales of connection comprehensible and claims about finality laughable. For instance, in Cliff's novel, we learn of Clare's relationship with Bobby through conjuring. Bobby disappeared from Clare's life while they were in Europe, and as Clare rides through the Cockpit Country of Jamaica in an open-backed truck, the narrator introduces Bobby with a cautionary tone: "Should Clare think of Bobby now at this remove of space and time, should she ponder him at all, their life together, as she moved away from Accompong into high ruinate, she might conjure him as she had conjured him before."[47] The passage locates Clare in time and space at the same moment that it disrupts any such divisions: she is present in the truck in the Jamaican forest, but Clare can also bring Bobby to this time and space; she has done so before and the narration hints that such movements are destabilizing and potentially dangerous. While Derrida and those who have been inspired by his work on haunting often concentrate on haunting as temporally transgressive, Esther Peeren reminds us that haunting disrupts space as well as time, and in literary manifestations, haunting creates "particular spatio-temporal constellations or chronotopes that enable particular stories to be told, stories that are never just any stories, but inevitably specific in terms of gender, race, sexuality, class, and so on."[48] Thinking about haunting in this way as creating distinctive configurations of time and space that enable specific stories to be told, it becomes important to approach the conjuring of Bobby as a historically specific haunting, a return of specific unsettled pasts to specific contemporary spaces. Conjuring allows temporally and geographically specific stories about Jamaica to be told, but also allows Cliff to materialize connections that range across thousands of years and thousands of miles, so that the local manifestations of military industrial capitalism are witnessed, but also contextualized in terms of larger patterns that need to be confronted to allow for meaningful social and environmental justice.

What, then, is significant about the time and space that Clare occupies when she conjures Bobby? The Cockpit Country that she is moving through is a haunted space for Clare, but is also the site of extra-textual hauntings. Because of the landscape features, hills, and the "cockpits" that were formed by water working its way through limestone, Maroons, escaped slaves, used this area to establish free communities and to fight against the British in the seventeenth and eighteenth centuries. Within the novel, Clare rides through this country with a group that is arming itself for rebellion and defining itself in the lineage of Nanny, a leader of the Maroons.[49] In her earlier novel, *Abeng*, Cliff invokes this history in greater detail as she describes how Nanny made a settlement in this "place of seemingly purposeless crevasses—created when the island sank during the Pliocene Period and the limestone layers dissolved in places—the dissolution stopping where the limestone met with indissoluble rock. Swallow-holes. Places to hide. Difficult to reach. Not barren but deep and magnificent indentations populated by bush and growth and wild orchids."[50] Cliff includes geological time scales that have shaped the land, and connects these landscape features that exceed and confound British designs to Nanny's resistance against the English troops, as the cockpits provide hiding places and obstacles for humans at the same time that they create an environment in which nonhuman life can thrive.

Currently, the cultural and material history of Cockpit Country is being conjured by environmentalist groups as part of a battle to legally define the borders of Cockpit Country in order to block permits for bauxite mining on this land. Glissant argues that destruction of the land is also destruction of history because the land serves as a repository of histories that have not been recorded elsewhere. Environmentalists are following this line of thinking and mobilizing the area's cultural heritage alongside its biodiversity to support arguments that bauxite mining should be banned in this area; they contend that decisions about the use of this land have a responsibility to those not currently present: the land should remain off limits to mining out of respect to both those who inhabited the land in the past and those who rely on the land as future habitat.[51] Bauxite mining was established in Jamaica in the 1950s, and as the battle over land use continues in the 2010s, impacts of mining practices circulate across human and nonhuman matter. Open-pit or open-cast mining techniques are used to extract bauxite from the earth; the bauxite is exported or processed in local plants that refine it into alumina. Residents who live near refining plants have complained about the dust and acidic rain and dew which have caused respiratory problems, destroyed property, and killed crops.[52] Impacts also extend across time; despite requirements that land be restored to its previous appearance after mining operations are complete, residents also report that filling in the holes and replacing the topsoil do not return the land to its former levels of productivity as agricultural land or restore it to suitable habitat for local flora and fauna.[53] Within the novel, Cliff chronicles such impacts, "the rivers run red...and the underground aquifers are colored from the waste of the bauxite mines and the aluminum refineries...the waste leaches into the land,"[54] while beyond the pages of the novel, local groups continue to work to demand justice for residents affected by the operations that already exist and to prevent mining activities from expanding into Cockpit Country.

When Clare conjures Bobby, she brings him into this contested space that joins histories of colonial and neocolonial exploitation and resistance to the present moment, and bringing Bobby into this space serves as a way to tell a specific story that links local and planetary scales of damage. Derrida explores multiple competing meanings of conjuring, indicating that it can describe conspiring with a ghost, summoning a ghost, or expelling a ghost.[55] Clare conjures Bobby in the second sense of bringing him to presence in her current space, while she wrestles with the other aspects of conjuring that mean conspiring with ghosts to keep their secrets or disavowing or chasing spirits away. Hershini Bhana Young theorizes the tensions in these aspects of conjuration in relation to the spectrality of slavery, contending that dealing with the ghosts of slavery requires moving "away from attempts to 'let go of the dead,' toward a critical social practice of inheriting the past....we are faced with the absolute necessity of recognizing and speaking to the ghosts that haunt all hegemony....for it is in our promise to converse with the specter that history as a universal narrative is disrupted."[56] Clare's conjuring of Bobby works in this tradition of bringing ghosts into contact with new times and spaces to create destabilizing effects in the present in ways that allow for confrontation, a claiming of the past and responsibility to it and for it rather than a letting go or a disclaiming. Her conjuring brings historical and contemporary contests over Cockpit Country into awareness, and then places the distant landscapes of Jamaica's forests and Vietnam's forests into intimate proximity. The link between these landscapes allows larger patterns of military industrial practice and ideology to emerge and make claims on the present; rather than conspiring to certify the death of the past, this conjuring registers expansive, ongoing impacts that demand redress.

The Vietnamese landscape that the novel invokes is a landscape scarred by the effects of Agent Orange, a chemical formulated in the United States and used to defoliate the landscape during the Vietnam conflict. Historian Edwin Martini reports:

> From 1961 to 1971 the United States and its South Vietnamese allies sprayed nearly seventy-three million liters (over nineteen million gallons) of chemical agents over two and a half million acres of southern and central Vietnam to defoliate the landscape and limit the access of the National Liberation Front (NLF, commonly known in the United States as the Viet Cong) to local food supplies.[57]

In his study, *The Invention of Ecocide: Agent Orange, Vietnam, and the Scientists Who Changed the Way We Think about the Environment*, David Zierler explains the creation and application of Agent Orange, a mixture of 2,4-d (2,4-dichlorophenoxya-cetic acid) and 2,4,5-t (2,4,5-trichlorophenoxyacetic acid), synthetic chemical compounds classified as selective auxins of the phenoxyacetic herbicide family, and he claims it defoliated nearly 5 million acres. The variance in details—Martini's figure of 2.5 million acres versus Zierler's 5 million—testifies to larger issues surrounding historical narratives of Agent Orange. In addition to lack of statistical agreement, Martini identifies a tendency to minimize consideration of the chemical agent in larger discussions of the Vietnamese conflict or to take polarizing stances, justifying military accounts or seeking to speak for victims, without adequately attending to historical documentation.[58] He further notes that as historical inquiry has slowly proceeded:

> Questions about the effects of Agent Orange on human and environmental health have, with the realization of its global nature, become more profound and more complicated over time ... From New Zealand to Canada, from Missouri to Korea, veterans and local citizens, including those born decades after the end of the Vietnam War, continue to grapple with the mysteries and frustrations and the very uneven resolution of the legacies of Agent Orange.[59]

While many questions about the damage inflicted by Agent Orange remain unresolved, studies such as those by Zierler and Martini draw attention to the ways that consequences extend across the globe and across generations, with

Zierler also calling attention to the need to investigate not only the massive scale of consequences, but also the ways that the logic that enabled such damage extends across seemingly distinct issues, as he cites the example of Martin Luther King, Jr. who in 1967 "posited his 'Declaration of Independence from the War in Vietnam' as a philosophical proposition that racism at home and the war in Indochina were each illegal enterprises that could not be challenged as discrete entities."[60] Cliff's novel further illuminates a shared logic of exploitation of the nonhuman and those not deemed fully human, the tactics of erasing the consequences from historical accounts, and the consequences of imposing resolutions that ignore lasting effects that reemerge across generations. Putting these landscapes into contact through conjuring allows Cliff to manifest connections between material conditions and the logics that have both created and concealed them, suggesting that movement across geographical, temporal, and conceptual borders is necessary to fully grasp and comprehensively challenge the hegemony of military industrial capitalism. Cliff uses the device of conjuring to allow for this movement and to break the novel away from confined temporal and geographical scales that collaborate in enforcing invisibility.

Conjuring introduces a particular way of knowing that differs from narratives that use the physical travels of characters to span spatial scales or deploy analepsis to create nonlinear temporal trajectories, although Cliff includes these kinds of movement as well. Conjuring allows Cliff to put multiple times and places into direct contact, so that instead of a sequence of presents that maintain epistemologies of imperial vision and ideologies of linear progress, she narrates places and times that intersect and overlap and stories that move in multiple directions, cultivating affective associations that rupture the prescribed line of progress. Returning to Peeren's reminder that haunting disrupts space as well as time, ghostly traces point to a disruption of the successive linking of presents that separate time as well as space, allowing for new configurations that reflect polyphony and multi-directional movement and that facilitate thinking across local and global scales by registering how times as spaces can be simultaneously present. For instance, Clare's conjuring of Bobby brings him to presence in Cockpit Country, but also serves to return her to the time that she spent with Bobby as they traveled together across Europe. Even when Clare and Bobby occupy the same time and space, Cliff points to the ways that times and spaces intersect and overlap, allowing multiple times and places to be co-present:

> He cast the terrain for her. She couldn't picture it. A country with burns across its surface. Not like a desert, no, not at all, he said, a thick green landscape stripped by the chemical held in the striped drum, which he had worn in a tank

strapped to his back, so he told her. She couldn't envision it, not clearly, but she did remember the bleeding landscape near Fern Gully, rusted, orange, where the ore had been scraped from the country. Emerging from the dark of the green cave, arched by primeval growth, emerging from the brake to find machines at work stripping bauxite from the country.[61]

While they are together in Europe, Bobby attempts to verbally conjure the landscape of Vietnam for Clare, who repeatedly calls attention to ways that Bobby's efforts to convey his experiences fall short: "she couldn't picture it," "she couldn't envision it." His words fail to make his experience tangible for her, but calling on her own experience helps to bridge the gap: she recalls an experience from her own past that puts the forests of Vietnam stripped by Agent Orange into contact with the forests of Jamaica mined for bauxite. The process is reversed later when Clare returns to the forests that her mother loved in Jamaica and "the recent past invaded, and she wondered how efficiently the chemical in the striped drum could strip her mother's landscape."[62] These scenes dramatize the limits of what words and pictures can do to help humans conceptualize the far-reaching impacts of toxins, but they also reinforce that toxins work in the mode of haunting, reemerging to blur distinctions between absence and presence, past and present, and moving across borders of nations and bodies to make impacts tangible. Further, they suggest what the novel as a form of conjuring can do, putting distant times and places into contact and demonstrating how moving across the borders of time and place and page might allow readers to put their own experiences into contact with distant worlds; like Clare, we can use memory and imagination to place characters' experiences alongside our own in ways that make them meaningful and comprehensible. In this way, Cliff cultivates an aesthetics of conjuring that resembles Glissant's aesthetics of rupture, where fragmentation and eruptions allow her to create a rhythm for the novel that illustrates multidirectional movement across local and global spatial scales and biological and geological temporal scales. This structure allows her to combat the limits of the realist novel that Ghosh identifies as collaborating in the concealment of contemporary reality.

This structure also reflects an epistemological alternative. Avery Gordon proposes that haunting acts as an alternative to "cold knowledge"; instead "haunting draws us affectively, sometimes against our will and always a bit magically into the structure of feeling of a reality we come to experience, not as cold knowledge, but as a transformative recognition."[63] Cliff's narration exemplifies the workings of this way of knowing for Clare; beyond the cold knowledge that a chemical that Bobby refuses to name directly as Agent Orange is the reason his wound will not heal, Clare's own haunting by the Jamaican landscape draws her into an affective encounter that moves between her past and her present, between Bobby's embodied experiences and her own. It also challenges readers to confront connections between these seemingly distant landscapes and distant practices of spraying Agent Orange and mining for bauxite. Contrary to standard historical accounts that provide a clear beginning and end date for the colonization of Jamaica or the Vietnam War, Cliff illustrates that the effects of these encounters continue to accrue in human, animal, and plant bodies, and she encourages us to see these events that are typically kept geographically and historically divided as manifestations of a similar logic of human domination over land and peoples. Conjuring makes these effects felt, not as a melancholy wallowing in the past or an attempt to exorcise it, but as Gordon suggests as a "transformative recognition," a way to make present justice possible and different futures imaginable.

Spectral Legacies, Queer Futures

By narrating haunted human skin—wounds and wombs—in concert with poisoned and mined landscapes, Cliff displays how epistemologies of haunting can help to imagine solidarity based on common ground such as sharing permeable bodies. However, she also explores the potential for humans to choose to care about others even in the absence of common ground. Cliff offers an imagining of collectivity that reaches beyond borders of nation, species, or generation and reconfigures concepts of inheritance in ways that support a radical concept of environmental justice. Derrida proposes in *Specters of Marx* that "inheritance is never a given, it is always a task."[64] In another essay, he extends his thinking about the critical engagement required from those who inherit:

> One can recognize an authentic inheritor in him who conserves and reproduces, but also in him who respects the logic of the legacy to the point of turning it back on occasion against those who claim to be its holders, to the point of showing up against the usurpers the very thing that, in the inheritance, has never yet been seen.[65]

Clare does not simply accept her biological inheritance as determinant of her future as her father hopes, and she does not accept her educational inheritance as given; she engages in the task of recovering suppressed histories and offering a new generation of Jamaicans a different way to contact the past and imagine the future. Similarly, through comments such as the one quoted in the epigraph for this chapter, Cliff suggest that she understands her work as a writer as a critical engagement with her heritage that involves turning her inheritance of the novel form back on those who claim to be its holders, making it reveal aspects that have not been seen, making it speak experiences of collectivity that have been repressed.

In her fiction, Cliff investigates possibilities for forging legacies and lineages beyond the heterosexual nuclear family. In her 1984 novel, *Abeng*, which narrates an extended history of the Savage family, Clare's father conveys expectations for her future: that she will choose a light-skinned husband and produce light-skinned children, for "she had a duty to try to turn the green eyes blue, once and for all—and make the skin, now gold, become pale and subject to visible sunburn."[66] In her father's vision, her future is tied to physical reproduction and the cultural reproduction of racial ideals that demand "the preservation of whiteness and the obliteration of darkness."[67] In this novel, Clare hints at a realization of a missed potential for other kinds of futures and other kinds of families, suggesting that her mother, Kitty, had had a dream of opening a school and teaching children lessons about "Black poetry and Jamaican landscape," that are abandoned when she marries Clare's father, a move that generates social approval because "a good-looking girl like Kitty was better off married anyway."[68] The narrator speculates on this lost opportunity, noting "Kitty should have been the daughter of Inez and Mma Alli, and Nanny too—and had she known of the existence of these women, she might have shared her knowledge."[69] In *Abeng*, Cliff gestures toward ways that the traditional resolution of the female plot forecloses possibilities for an alternative legacy beyond institutions of marriage and family.

In *No Telephone*, Cliff pursues the possibilities for different kinds of kinship and different endings for novels. Clare remains haunted by her lost fertility which makes her incapable of living the life her father had plotted for her, but she also learns to listen to and learn from ghosts. On her return to Jamaica, she becomes the teacher of native history that her mother had dreamed of being. She learns and teaches a history that she has gathered through traditional archival research, but also through listening to "the conch knife excavated at the Arawak site in White Marl ... the shards of hand-thrown pots ... the petroglyphs hidden in the bush .... the stories about Nanny" and "the flock of white birds [that] fly out at sunset from Nanny-town ... duppies, the old people say."[70] Her listener questions, "Duppies?" and Clare clarifies, "Ghosts; the spirits of the Maroons."[71] Moving beyond her earlier colonial education, Clare returns to Jamaica and recovers suppressed histories and local knowledge, and she finds this history contained not only or even primarily in books, but in objects, spirits, and animals. While conjuring Bobby is one manifestation of Clare's relationship with ghosts, she also develops an understanding of history that includes the wisdom of ghosts, and she works to share this history with children, a future generation although not her biological progeny.

The legacy that Clare is forging is one that she chooses in active resistance to the expectations that she inherits. In *Strange Natures*, Nicole Seymour productively highlights points of intersection and alliance between queer and ecological theory, and I propose infusing ghosts into these seams. Seymour proposes that joining queer and ecological thinking can spark new imaginings of the future:

> With a queer ecological perspective attuned to social justice, we can learn to care about the future of the planet in a way that is perhaps more radical than any we have seen previously: acting in the interests of nameless, faceless individuals to which one has no biological, familial or economic ties whatsoever. This kind of action operates without any reward, without any guarantee of success and without any proof that future inhabitants of this planet might be similar to the individual acting in the present.[72]

Encouraging an even more radical commitment than Morton's exhortation to rethink what it means to have in common, Seymour articulates an ethics of care for those with whom we may share nothing in common. Significantly, it is not just radical thought, but radical action that Seymour is describing: she doesn't just envision a change in stories or feelings about family; she establishes a continuum between learning, feeling, and acting. Specters can facilitate this process, helping to build connections to others that are not bound to us by biological ties and allowing distant and diverse others to make demands on us. In fact, the ending of Cliff's novel dramatizes Seymour's idea of choosing to act in the interests of nameless, faceless others without any guarantee of success, and reading the ending returns me to where I began, with a challenge to the focus on the bounded individual.

At the end of the novel, Clare commits herself to action with the rebel group, and she presumably dies when the group's planned attack on a movie set ends in an ambush. However, the novel does not end with human death; it continues as human language shifts into sounds, sounds that among other possibilities evoke tortured slave bodies and bird calls as day breaks anew, reinforcing links between human and nonhuman, and joining past, present, and future. Discussing the closing scene, Cliff has suggested that the depiction of Clare's death blends violence—she is "burned into the landscape of Jamaica by gunfire"—with harmony—she is "enveloped in the deep green of the hills and the delicate intricacy of birdsong"[73]—pointing to the ambivalence of the ending that is an annihilation of Clare's physical body, but a reunion with the land that has been her connection to her mother and grandmother. Critics who read the novel as a quest for individual identity and wholeness tend to create a romanticized interpretation of a return that completes Clare's quest and confirms her identification with the land/mother. Other critics seek to complicate this interpretation, objecting to the romantic idea of Clare being "enveloped in the deep green of the hills and the delicate intricacy of birdsong" which leads one scholar to question: "How will her dead eyes perceive the lush green, her dead ears hear the birdsong?"[74] and another to conclude that the "lack of a future in the text" delivers a critique of formulations of identity that rely on connecting blood and land.[75]

These interpretations of the ending of the novel reflect the assumptions from which the analyses begin: that Clare is the individual protagonist of the novel, thus the resolution must coincide with the end of her individual journey. However, reorienting the focus to the collective and attending to the movement of ghosts throughout the tale allows for a different approach to the novel's closing passages. Clare had learned and begun to teach others how to listen to specters; the ending of the novel suggests a shift in form through which she becomes a specter and the living world goes on. So it is not a matter of her eyes seeing the landscape or her ears hearing the birds; the world continues without the living presence of Clare. However, that does not mean there is no future. If we accept her lesson, we recognize forms of community beyond biological kinship, and we register that she is still able to teach and inspire action despite her change in form, which does not remove her from this community. Like the unnamed remains that enrich the soil at her grandmother's farm, Clare becomes a part of the land and its story, contributing to the continued life of a range of beings that may or may not resemble her.

Rather than indicating a sterile future or a loss of control of Jamaica's story to the Hollywood film crew, Clare's transformation through death reinforces the subordination of the individual human to a larger, multispecies story recorded by the land. Peeren argues, "the spectral view of history no longer relies on the presence of living witnesses to communicate… In terms of an ethics of history, this would force all of us to acknowledge and take responsibility for the times and spaces of our shared pasts and their influence on the present and the possible futures of our societies."[76] Through Clare, Cliff offers a spectral view of history which demands forms of social and environmental justice that accept responsibility to others, including others not yet or no longer living, others with whom we share things in common as well as others who are faceless and unknowable. Clare has learned from her experiences with hauntings that the separation into neat categories of past, present, and future is futile and that justice demands a way of thinking that accounts for effects that radiate over time. Morton contends that we remain afflicted by ways that we think social problems,[77] and Cliff's narrative that reconceptualizes the human in terms of permeability and collectivity provides a powerful opportunity to reconsider the ethical terms and scales on which we think justice. Cliff's work with the form of the novel reveals how borders of gender and species, family and nation, life and death conceal the wide-ranging impacts of capitalist organizations of human relationships at the same time that it conjures ghosts that can help us to think the future in terms of radical solidarity.

Part Two

Materializing Environmental Knowledges

3

Haunted Histories, Animate Futures: Recovering Noongar Knowledge through Kim Scott's *That Deadman Dance*

That was my concern, researching a novel: not what was, but what might have been, and even what might yet be ...

Kim Scott, "A Noongar Voice" (ellipsis in original)

To be haunted in the name of a will to heal is to allow the ghost to help you imagine what was lost that never even existed ... to long for the insight of that moment in which we recognise, as in Benjamin's profane illumination, that it could have been and can be otherwise.

Avery Gordon, Ghostly Matters: Haunting and the Sociological Imagination

Kim Scott's author biography announces that he is "proud to be one among those who call themselves Noongar,"[1] communicating his identity "as a descendant of those who first created human society"[2] in southwest Australia. However, Scott explains that he grew up knowing little of the language and culture that constituted his heritage: "There was no traditional upbringing of stories around the campfire, no earnest transmission of cultural values."[3] Instead, he found his Noongar ancestry surrounded by silences that he has sought to remedy, in part through his conversations with Hazel Brown, a Noongar Elder with vast knowledge of Noongar language, stories, and genealogies. In the collaborative work he produced with Hazel Brown, *Kayang and Me* (2005), Scott reflects on the role of writing in coming to terms with his cultural inheritance: "With Aunty Hazel I stood on the sandy shore of my Indigenous heritage, and sensed something substantial and sustaining waiting for me to grasp, and yet the only means I had to do so was this laying out of words upon a page."[4] Scott's language characterizes his writing as a response to a personal haunting: he senses something substantial, he feels its presence at the edge of his awareness, waiting for him in a way that he distinguishes from his previous research in archives that only allowed him access to "fossilized phrases."[5] Scott acknowledges his desire to take hold of the past by giving it a material shape, by transforming incorporeal substance into words on paper, but he also recognizes that writing itself remains a haunted medium that leaves unexpressed remainders. Scott confronts this aspect of writing as he translates Hazel Brown's oral stories into written form in *Kayang and Me*, and he also uses his fiction to imaginatively probe the limits and possibilities of the written word, for instance, as a central character of the novel *That Deadman Dance*, Bobby Wabalanginy, remarks that "some sounds had a shape on the page too... The alphabet might be tracks, trails and traces of what we said."[6] While Scott does not directly categorize his writing process as spectral, he does consciously reflect on the intersections among the kinds of literary work that he undertakes ranging from community language recovery projects to novels in English, and I propose that each site of Scott's work manifests hauntings that Scott engages in order to bring repressed Noongar language and stories into contact with audiences so that this knowledge can participate in shaping alternative futures.

Scott's literary publications, including the novels *True Country* (1993) and *Benang* (1999) and his collaborative recovery work with Hazel Brown, *Kayang and Me*, demonstrate his consistent engagement with Indigenous histories and languages. This chapter concentrates on his third novel, *That Deadman Dance* (2010),[7] in which Scott explores his heritage by imaginatively reconstructing a pivotal moment in Noongar history: the early encounter between Australia's Noongar people, British settlers, and whaling crews from various other nations. As Scott discusses the composing process for this novel, a vocabulary of haunting emerges again in relation to writing: "That's what language can do. The idea of one being linguistically displaced and dispossessed, even in one's own country; and then language comes back and one makes oneself an instrument for it and for the spirit of place."[8] In this instance, Scott describes language as a kind of revenant, returning to those who have been dispossessed of their heritage, and he identifies himself as a conduit; his storytelling becomes an instrument through which ghosts return language and histories to local communities and hail wider audiences beyond, all while revealing power dynamics of settler-colonialism that consigned Noongar language and culture to a position on the margins of Western discourse in the first place.

A model of haunting that builds from the work of sociologist Avery Gordon helps to elucidate Scott's formulation of his writing as a process of listening to the voices of others. Gordon extends the foundational work of Sigmund Freud on the uncanny and the work of Jacques Derrida in hauntology, as she builds her own conception of how haunting characterizes the contemporary world and its marginalized populations and discredited knowledges. Gordon defines haunting as "an animated state in which a repressed or unresolved social violence is making itself known,"[9] describing not only a movement across boundaries of past and present, but also an imperative to reconsider associations of vision with presence and knowledge. As Radway clarifies, the model of haunting that Gordon develops constitutes an alternative way of knowing "that is more a listening than a seeing, a practice of being attuned to the echoes and murmurs of that which has been lost but which is still present among us."[10] This theory conceptualizes the endurance of people and knowledge that have been denied mainstream visibility, and while it registers that erasure as a form of social violence, it suggests a recourse other than a return to visibility. Instead, Gordon's formulation encourages attention to ways that presence can announce itself beyond vision, surfacing through an epistemology of listening in which the knower cultivates receptivity to traces and refuses the reduction of knowledge to visual evidence.

Listening serves to bring suppressed knowledge to presence so that it can inform the actions of those who inherit it. However, the goal of conversing with ghosts differs among theorists of spectrality. For instance, Abraham and Torok develop a psychoanalytic approach to transgenerational haunting that focuses on secrets inherited from ancestors. In their framework, the secret is unspeakable because it is associated with shame or prohibitions, and the goal of speaking to the phantom becomes naming the secret to create closure and put the phantom to rest.[11] In the psychological model, individuals seek to resolve their haunting through narration that makes the past knowable and prevents its return as traumatic memory, whereas in Gordon's sociological model, haunting is conceptualized as a collective phenomenon, and the goal of speaking with ghosts is not to quiet them, but to learn to live alongside them, allowing unspeakable traces to remain to help imagine alternatives to current conditions. In accordance with Derrida's imperative to learn to live with ghosts in the interests of multigenerational justice, Gordon argues that haunting activates "a potent imagination of what has been done and what is to be done otherwise."[12] In the context of Australian literary texts, Crouch similarly notes the productive potential of maintaining "haunted anxieties" and allowing the "unsettling presence"[13] of ghosts to "structure an ongoing negotiation, a constant movement between possession and dispossession."[14] Such formulations of haunting encourage dwelling with ghosts rather than exorcising them, an approach that coincides with Scott's stated desire to use his novel to explore possibilities in the past encounter not in an effort to provide comforting resolution to past conflicts, but to activate resonances that invite critical thinking about dominant historical narratives and inspire innovative thinking about the future that refuses to be "trapped in the paradigm that is being set up for us."[15]

The framework provided by Gordon illuminates haunting as an alternative way of knowing that uses previously silenced voices to guide future action; however, this framework fails to adequately address the full range of voices that become audible as a result of the Noongar language and ontology that Scott shares. In addition to mobilizing voices of ancestral others, Scott's novel circulates the voices of nonhuman others: animals, wind, rain, land, and sea that are all interconnected with human kin in Noongar understandings of country. Gordon's figuration of ghosts as manifesting past violence and social erasure could be extended to include attention to the returns of nonhuman voices and repressed epistemologies that register these voices; such a framework would enable investigation into ways that these voices can inspire social justice that includes accountability to human and nonhuman others. This ecospectral approach would not diminish the violence done to human populations; rather, it would expand understandings of the scope of that violence by demanding awareness of how it also carries consequence for nonhumans. As Scott demonstrates how the voices of nonhuman others haunt historical discourses of first encounter and how the novel form can be adapted to facilitate their return, *That Deadman Dance* reveals the intellectual and affective work ecospectrality can perform. It facilitates recognition that the repression of nonhuman voices and the Noongar knowledge that values them was not an incidental impact of colonization, but a constitutive factor; settler inhabitance required a denial of the land's vitality in order to institute a regime of property and ownership, and the novel demands that readers acknowledge this violence and confront its ongoing impacts.

While multiple scholars foreground human cross-cultural exchange in their analysis of *That Deadman Dance*,[16] few include attention to the voices of nonhuman matter. Jane Gleeson-White begins to extend consideration to nonhuman subjects using an ecocritical framework; however, she argues that the novel "rewrite[s] Australia in the voice of the regional"[17] without fully addressing the movement of knowledge across temporal or spatial scales. Rosanne Kennedy's essay, "Orbits, Mobilities, Scales: Kim Scott's *That Deadman Dance* as Transcultural Remembrance," innovatively tackles movement across scales, observing that the novel incorporates varied temporal frames "from the 'social history' of the maritime frontier to the 'deep time' of the continent and the sea";[18] it also devotes sustained analysis to spatial scales through the instructive metaphor of orbits, which expresses how Indigenous rootedness in place coexists with Indigenous routes that include travel, cultural exchange, and return to community. In another essay that investigates how remembrance figures in the novel, Kennedy analyzes intersections between oppression of humans and nonhuman animals. While I share Kennedy's interest in Scott's narration of the nonhuman, my chapter attends to nonhuman matter more broadly, recognizing forces like rain and wind alongside humans and animals as members of the land community that constitutes country. Additionally, the lens of ecospectrality shifts the focus from practices of memorializing the past to the persistence of Noongar knowledge across temporal divides, despite efforts to repress it. Finally, by identifying the novel as a site of haunting, the ecospectral approach enhances attention to interactions between Noongar knowledge and Western narrative forms, concentrating on ways Scott adapts the novel to house repressed voices and activate haunting as an affective way of knowing that challenges readers to imagine futures that include accountability to the nonhuman.

The (in)ability of readers, particularly readers from outside the Noongar community, to grasp Noongar knowledge has drawn the attention of scholars. In an influential and controversial study, *The Postcolonial Eye: White Australian Desire and the Visual Field of Race*, Alison Ravenscroft cautions that there might be some aspects of Indigenous texts that non-indigenous readers cannot see and that instead of imposing meaning to quell anxieties about uncertainty, readers should accept the limits of their knowledge. Kate Rigby clarifies that the existence of gaps does not require refusing the invitation offered by Indigenous writers who choose to write in English.[19] Building on this conversation, I suggest that a framework of haunting encourages the invitation to be accepted with Ravenscroft's qualifications in mind; non-Indigenous readers can accept the chance to be "welcomed strangers,"[20] remaining aware that the access that a story offers is not complete, that knowledge is partial and situated, and cultural exchange does not erase those limits; rather some silences, gaps, and inexpressible differences might remain, and readers should allow those gaps to remain and do the work of haunting. As Ravenscroft illustrates in "The Strangeness of the Dance," an essay about contemporary first contact novels, many non-Indigenous writers strive to fill historical and epistemological gaps with the result of confirming familiar Western narrative expectations and closing off the potential to imagine different trajectories. Distinguishing Scott's novel from other first contact novels by Grenville, Wilson, and Clendinnen, she claims:

> Scott is not telling the same old story, populated with men and women who are remarkably recognisable to white readers as a version of ourselves, or familiar from our fantasies of our others. His writing calls his white readers to suspend our belief in our own knowledge of the smell, shape and sound of the world; he calls readers like myself into stories that are unbelievable (to me), impossible, implausible, even as they are "true story" for his Indigenous protagonists.[21]

Without using spectral terminology, Ravenscroft is describing a haunting in which Scott's novel forces white readers to occupy an uncanny space, a space that is familiar and yet impossibly different. I seek to draw greater attention to ways that narrative strategies affirm or challenge "our belief in our own knowledge of the smell, shape and sound of the world," and ways that different ways of knowing carry material consequences; specifically, I investigate how conventions of the novel confirm capitalist conceptions of a world of inert matter, and how Scott reconfigures the novel to return and share repressed knowledge of an animate world with the conviction that the circulation of this knowledge can shape futures in which humans respect the needs of nonhuman others. Overall, the framework of haunting connects the recirculation of repressed knowledge within the Noongar community and the dislocation that nonindigenous readers might experience by reading Scott's novel without neglecting ways the encounters differ based on positioning; connecting different experiences of haunting provides an effective way of conceptualizing multiple scales of connection and consequences as ghosts put temporally and geographically distant people and places into direct contact.

Circles of Movement, Scales of Haunting

Scott insists on the primacy of the local community, so it seems appropriate to begin tracing his engagement with ghosts by turning to that community and his language recovery work.[22] Scott founded the Wirlomin Noongar Language and Stories Project to reconnect historical archives, community elders, and descendants in order to return stories to local communities. This work operates in the mode of haunting as it confronts the past and the ways that Noongar became an endangered ancestral language not as a neutral result of change over time, but as a result of settler-colonialism which devalued Indigenous languages and knowledges while valorizing English. Scott stresses that language recovery is about returning knowledge and respect that was buried through imperialism, and he asserts that restoring language and stories can provide contemporary communities with access to precolonial narratives that inspire trust, creativity, and commitment to community in ways that dominant narratives of colonial oppression cannot. In "From Drill to Dance," Scott explains:

> The consolidation of language and story in home communities in ways that strengthen and create opportunities for community members to profitably share revitalized, ancestral knowledge with increasingly wider, concentric circles of people can be an important part of community development, and importantly, build something other than drawing upon the experience of oppression.[23]

Scott uses the image of widening circles to convey his vision that stories move through expanding circuits as they travel through community meetings, oral performance, illustrated texts, and audio and video recordings; as the circles slowly spread, repressed knowledge returns to active presence in the life of the community (and beyond). Scott's description of the movement of stories emphasizes community involvement in recalling and negotiating with the past, as members debate pronunciations and meanings, a process that also distinguishes this language recovery work from essentializing efforts to return to a pure, precolonial past of Indigenous harmony, a stereotype that Scott critiques. Rather, the Wirlomin Noongar Language and Stories Project illustrates how putting ghosts of the past into conversation with contemporary residents can empower communities to imagine futures that grow from knowledge and confidence in their heritage.

Scott offers the model of expanding circles to conceptualize his sharing of Indigenous knowledge through novels in English as an extension of his language work. Novels expand the circle to include audiences that are not part of the Noongar community, but the circle keeps the Noongar community at the center of awareness, as Scott affirms that language recovery

> merely as a source of "insight" for literature in English or indeed of perspectives unknown to wider society is of very limited value unless it also contributes in some way to the revival and continued survival of the language itself and—most especially—the well-being of the community descended from its speakers.[24]

Scott expresses his version of "the 'postcolonial angst' of those who, displaced linguistically, if not geographically, write in the colonizer's tongue, for an audience of which their own people are a tiny minority,"[25] acknowledging his fraught position in relation to the genre of the novel. Scott uses the novel to pose questions about "what might yet be,"[26] and he does not shy away from the challenge: What are the consequences of using the novel form to articulate these questions? Scott's reflections about the precarious position of his novel's central character Bobby Wabalanginy, who is a performer, storyteller, and conveyor of Noongar culture, provide insight about his own position as a postcolonial novelist. Scott acknowledges that his novel comments on "the dangers of commodification versus the great power of sharing your heritage, and helping people through sharing that heritage,"[27] which also reflects on Scott's position of narrating Noongar culture through the novel, a form of storytelling that, as Edward Said has argued, developed not only in historical proximity to Western imperialism, but also in ideological accord with it by deploying formal features such as regulatory plot structures and patterns of narrative authority that reinforce imperial ideologies.[28] Postcolonial writers such as Ngugi wa Thiongo have highlighted the colonial legacy of the novel and its continuing impact on Indigenous languages and cultures, while scholarship such as Graham Huggan's *The Postcolonial Exotic* encourages attention to the ways that publishing companies and metropolitan audiences impose expectations and commodify postcolonial writing and writers.[29] Scott clearly recognizes this range of dangers that accompany the choice to compose a novel in English, but instead of disclaiming the novel as a colonial artifact, he validates his own position of strength to be able to write a novel that places Noongar people and culture at the narrative center.[30] As he adapts a colonially inherited form and remakes it through interaction with Noongar knowledge, Scott's process as novelist echoes that of his character Bobby Wabalanginy, who adapts a British military drill and transforms it through his own performance.

Narrating the Repression of Noongar Knowledge

Instead of narrating a return of knowledge to characters in a contemporary setting, Scott transports readers to the scene of the repression of Noongar knowledge. Setting the novel in the past, Scott recreates a world where Noongar is a vital, living language that holds a position of power, rather than presenting readers with a contemporary scene of loss or absence. He crafts a nonlinear novel that moves readers back and forth across the years 1826–44 so that they become attuned to ways that the repression of Noongar knowledge constitutes an aspect of settler-colonial violence that is less recognizable as violence because it unfolds unevenly over time, similar to the dynamics that Rob Nixon describes as "slow violence" in the context of environmental damage.[31] Rather than a military battle over land that occurs on specific dates, the repression of knowledge proceeds in various increments and at multiple levels from individual interactions to organized policy, and because of its accretive nature, its elements may pass unmarked as forms of violence. By opening his novel with Bobby Wabalanginy writing the Noongar word "Kaya" on a slate, Scott commences his narrative with cultural exchange already underway.[32] The sections that follow move readers back and forth in time so that they witness Dr. Cross's openness to human difference as he recognizes Menak as "a very different man, of course, but a man for all that,"[33] and he builds a friendship with Wunyeran so close that he asks to be buried in the same grave, illustrating potential for sharing and mutual respect as each adopts ideas and practices of the other. However, moments of potential are interspersed with failures and rejections such as the settler Skelly expressing disdain for the "savages...with their parrots and jabber and nakedness,"[34] using animal association as a way to degrade the Noongar, discredit their language, and deny their humanity. Readers encounter the new governor instituting legal regulations that require Western dress and English-language communication in the growing town, and eventually the dis-interment of Cross from the grave he shares with Wunyeran to enforce a clear dividing line between Noongar and settler, erasing Wunyeran from the town's origin story and discursively constructing the settlement over the bones of Dr. Cross "1781–1833, Surgeon, Pioneer and Land Owner, 1826–1833, King George Town, Western Australia."[35] The novel sequences readers' encounter with the past, and the nonlinear structure complicates a typical narrative of unidirectional colonial progress or Indigenous decline, allowing readers to inhabit moments of sharing along with moments of degradation and to comprehend changes to relationships over time. This strategy prevents any oversimplified demonization of settlers or victimization of Noongar, who appear as complex and varied characters with a range of perspectives and experiences. It offers readers the kind of opportunity Gordon theorizes to recognize repression as violence, but also to imagine how it could have been and might yet be otherwise.

The Novel as the Haunted House of Matter

The novel transports readers to the past to make the dynamics of repression tangible, and it allows readers to experience the return of repressed knowledge in the present. Incorporating Noongar language and ontology into a novel in English performs the kind of haunting that Gordon describes as alerting readers "that what's been concealed is very much alive and present."[36] The novel conjures expressions that reflect affinities between human and nonhuman matter, returning this knowledge to the local community and sharing this way of understanding materiality with global readers. For instance, the narrator includes the Noongar term "mitjal" which he defines as "a rain like tears."[37] The Noongar word conveys a sensitivity to diverse types of rain, and rather than choosing an English term such as "drizzle" or "downpour," Scott translates the term using a comparison to tears, suggesting that the name for the type of rain expresses more than a measure of the rain's intensity. It carries the Noongar conceptualization of qualities that water and humans share. However, Scott simultaneously characterizes water in terms that extend beyond human likeness, suggesting that the water deserves respect for its own traits, not only for the ways that it resembles the human. The narrator records: "Deeper in the night the wind lifted and rain began to drum the earth. It fell and fell and fell; it gathered in the hearts of trees, in the forks of branches and cups of leaves, in clefts and cavities of rock and small indentations in the earth. Fell, overflowed, and began to move together again."[38] This passage exhibits a grammar and vocabulary of agency that provides an alternative to capitalist constructions of inert matter; the rain and wind are subjects and they are paired with active verbs: they lift and drum, fall and gather for their own reasons, without reference to human agents or intentions. The movement of the water generates effects, shaping the landscape and leaving a record of its past.

This description is communicated through human writing that cannot escape a human perspective or give direct access to water's voice, yet the language conveys an ontological orientation to a dynamic world in which various forms of matter share communicative abilities and agency, understood as an ability to create effects. It reveals how language can transmit a way of understanding human immersion in relationships with a living land community and how language can encourage attention to and respect for the voices and stories of nonhuman matter, for instance registering the water etching paths into the land as a story without attempting to fill all the gaps or claim total knowledge of that story. In *That Deadman Dance*, one of the Noongar characters, Wunyeran, realizes that he is seeing the land around him in new ways and asking new questions, which he attributes to the influence of language acquisition: "The questions you ask, learning a new way of speech. How it drives your thinking."[39] Wunyeran's experience demonstrates how languages can convey "a way of life, a way of being, of navigating the world."[40]

Language's ability to shape an understanding of the world impacts characters within the novel, but also holds out an opportunity for contemporary readers.

By incorporating Noongar vocabulary into his novel, Scott transmits aspects of the Noongar way of life, which sparks an opportunity for readers to ask new questions and see new connections. Scott reflects on how language is imbricated in ways of perceiving and acting in the world:

> That's of interest to me—looking at language and what concepts come out of it. I'm just touching on and suggesting that there is something really deep and conceptual in these Noongar terms... Bily (or bilya in some dialects) is river and it's also navel or umbilical cord. So there's a lot more complexity in these concepts of connection and inter-relationship, than there is in the world-wide use of a term like 'mother earth'.... Sometimes a group of hills will be called a word that also means 'backs'. So there's the human form and other life forms latent in the landscape.[41]

Tracing the resonances of specific Noongar words, Scott describes how language conveys a way of relating to the land and a way of conceptualizing commonality and reciprocity between "the human form and other life forms" that could foster meaningful connections and a sense of responsibility to nonhuman others. David Abram develops a related argument, proposing that human language is indebted to other animate voices and that rather than being a quality that separates the human from the nonhuman, language "inscribes us more fully in [the animate landscape's] chattering, whispering, soundful depths."[42] Scott demonstrates how Noongar language and ontology engage an animate world without strict boundaries between human and nonhuman matter, encouraging awareness of human participation in a communicative world rather than figuring language as a feature that distances humans from a mute, inert world.

Scott encourages readers to recognize a diversity of voices of water, wind, animal, and human, refusing to subordinate nonhuman matter to the human but also refusing to collapse difference. While he credits both water and humans with communicative abilities, he simultaneously preserves difference and acknowledges singularity. For example, he narrates different kinds of rain, including mitjal, but also including rain that spits and makes "sharp silver thorns."[43] Additionally, he distinguishes different kinds of impacts created by water. The narration "rain fell in great bodies, slamming the earth, then recovered, collected its many selves and flowed, chuckling, past flimsy houses"[44] identifies a particular, but collective body of water that chuckles at a particular group of humans: as it swirls around human construction projects and carries away a footbridge, the water laughs at the vanity displayed by some of the settlers who lack attentiveness to the water's agency and who define the ability to alter the landscape as a mark of their superior humanity. With these depictions,

Scott revises the novel's familiar focus on individual human characters and its relegation of nonhuman matter to the role of inert background, showing how human habitation depends on sensitivity to and relationship with nonhuman matter and recording the consequences of ignoring these dependencies, as settler construction is destroyed by the force of the water.

Further, Scott complicates anthropomorphic habits of comparison and uses the qualities of water as a lens for reimagining the human: "The crowd became like water again, moving and collecting, and Dr. Cross as if following some tiny gully rolled away on his own."[45] The fluid identity of water—its ability to reshape itself and move between manifestations as individual droplets and the joined force of a stream—becomes a way of re-seeing human individuality and recognizing Dr. Cross's ability to blend with and diverge from his fellow settlers. Throughout the novel, Scott uses associations with the nonhuman to advance understandings of human participation in collectivities, describing community rituals that allowed "for moving together like grains of sand rolled by water, like the flowers blossoming from their armbands or hair"[46] and repeatedly referencing ways that Bobby "was not just one self": he is an amalgamation of versions of himself from baby Bobby to young man Bobby to Old Bobby and he is composed of "all of them," the current members of the community and the ancestors and future generations who he connects with by "look[ing] into future graves, and into some people's hearts and minds."[47] Diversifying the direction of anthropomorphic thinking by suggesting that qualities of nonhuman matter can provide illuminating comparisons for the human, Scott reinforces mutuality rather than hierarchy, and he challenges notions of human identity that repress awareness of human multiplicity and immersion in processes that extend beyond the individual. Crafting such narration, Scott gives readers an opportunity to learn to perceive a plurality of human and nonhuman voices and to pick out individual voices as parts of a larger chorus, figuring individuals as always simultaneously parts of larger communities.

Scott also documents consequences of failing to listen. The failures that he notes coincide with other accounts of Australia's ecological history and illustrate how orientation to matter influences sensory perception, and in turn, materially shapes the land in ways that continue to exert impacts. Within the novel, the narrator reports that "sometimes Wooral addressed the bush as if he were walking through a crowd of diverse personalities, his tone variously playful, scolding, reverential, affectionate"[48] which causes his settler companions to reflect, "It was most confusing. Did he see something else?"[49] The narration implies that Wooral does indeed see something else, and his knowledge goes beyond vision: he listens to an animate land that he also engages through conversation. Beyond the novel, as Val Plumwood and William J. Lines separately discuss, early settlers were deaf to the sounds of unfamiliar birds, which led them to assume that Australia was lacking in bird life and to import "real" birds from home. Lines provides examples from colonial diaries that describe the "silence and tranquility," the "stillness" of the empty land.[50] Plumwood uses this example to demonstrate how a Eurocentric mentality could influence settler's perception of the land, causing them to understand it as empty and deficient, and to act accordingly to shape it to their European ideals.[51] Scott forces readers to consider how colonizing processes operated in parallel as he presents settlers who are deaf to the communication of both human and nonhuman inhabitants, and he demonstrates the results of this deafness: a denial of their status as inhabitants that provides a justification for colonial occupation, as the settlers fence off lands and displace Indigenous peoples with the challenge, "to what use do they put this ownership as against what we have achieved in so short a time?"[52] While Noongar language transmits conceptions of animate land, the settler construction of ownership denies the vitality and interdependency of the land community, participating in a dispossession of Indigenous inhabitants that continues to haunt modern Australia.

Scott chooses the space of the novel to recover the conflict between Noongar and settler understandings of nonhuman matter, confronting audiences with a haunting that might provide a foundation for a radical reexamination of relationships among Indigenous Australians, nonindigenous Australians, and the nonhuman others on which their habitation depends, while it also challenges expectations about how a novel can figure Australia as haunted territory. Unlike his most recent novel *Taboo* (2017) and other more conventional ghost stories in which a geographic location becomes the site for resurfacing past violence in the lives of characters, in *That Deadman Dance*, the novel serves as the site for returning repressed knowledge to readers, so that instead of being absolved of the colonial past through the resolution of the plot, readers become haunted by their newly attained knowledge. This approach differs, for instance, from Tim Winton's spectral narration in *Cloudstreet*; examining that novel, Crouch and Griffiths each invoke a model of haunting, and they concur that Winton's use of the haunted house to figure the haunted nation runs the risk of resolving settler anxiety to allow continued inhabitance in ways that reaffirm settler-colonial ideologies. Read against what Griffiths articulates as the failure of *Cloudstreet*, "the recognition of dispossession as exculpation from a more radical political addressing of, and to, settler-colonial history and Indigenous possession,"⁵³ *That Deadman Dance* complicates the haunted house trope. Scott reveals the novel itself as haunted space, exposing how novelistic conventions have been complicit in silencing the voices of nonhuman matter and relegating the continuing impacts of settler colonial violence to a past that is severed from the present and the future. At the same time, he reshapes the novel so that it becomes a space where repressed knowledge can return to presence. Noongar language and ontology reemerge within this space, unsettling settler-colonial notions of home and possession by highlighting the agency of the nonhuman and the dependence of human habitation on nonhuman members of the land community. Through this ecospectral encounter, Scott not only reckons with the complexities of narrating home in postcolonial contexts; he expands notions of home as an exclusively human space, the "intimate shelter" and "private comfort" that notions of the uncanny and the haunted house typically take as their starting point.⁵⁴ Encouraging readers to reconceive rather than reconcile the violence of the repression of Noongar knowledge, Scott activates the potential to imagine alternative models of inhabitance that reflect intimate connection to and responsibility for land as kin.

This Is Not the End: Resonances Rather than Resolution

Scott puts ghosts into motion, and unlike novelists who seek to impose resolution by exorcising ghosts, Scott strives to create an ending for the novel that allows ghosts to remain to help design the future. Returning to distinctions between trauma and haunting illuminates Scott's narrative tactics. Cathy Carruth clarifies that traumatic memories return "insistent and unchanged" because they have never "been fully integrated into understanding" or into "a completed story of the past" and as a result, "trauma thus requires integration, both for the sake of testimony and the sake of cure."⁵⁵ Contrary to trauma theory's focus on integration, Gordon's theory of spectrality seeks to disrupt existing paradigms; instead of closing the door on the past and confining the specter within existing domains of knowledge, she urges thought to follow the specter across constructions of past and future so that haunting enables alternative possibilities; in her words "haunting, unlike trauma is distinctive for producing a something-to-be-done."⁵⁶ In the case of the novel, narrating repressed Noongar knowledge does not serve to complete the story of the past; it illuminates a something-to-be-done. Anne Brewster invites Scott to discuss the novel's ending, which she admits to reading "as tragic, as filled with despair."⁵⁷ Scott returns repeatedly to this point, attempting to elucidate his hopes for creating an ending, and a novel, that neither conforms to the traditional historical script of defeat and victimization nor simply inverts that trajectory by supplying an upbeat closure. Instead, he acknowledges a desire to "set up all sorts of resonances to do with possibility and loss" and to challenge readers to take up these echoes in a way that makes "the end, the last page ... not the end. There are possibilities still."⁵⁸

Following Scott's encouragement to embrace the possibilities, the novel can be read not as an effort to resolve the past, but as an invitation to venture forward in the company of ghosts. The closing of the novel recounts settlers turning their faces away from Bobby's performance through which he is trying to communicate his understanding of land and his conviction that "you need to be inside the sound and spirit of it to live here properly."⁵⁹ With this closing, Scott implores readers to imagine and mourn what could have been if settlers had cultivated a practice of listening and had accepted the message Bobby offered through his performance. However, this scene is not the end in multiple senses. Although it appears as the final image, the novel refuses strict chronology and an older version of Bobby appears throughout the novel, continuing to tell stories to Noongar friends and to tourists. Scott indicates that Old Bobby's appearance as a storyteller throughout the nonlinear novel holds out important hope for the possibility of counter-narrative.⁶⁰ For example, Old Bobby continues to recount the story of the friendship of Dr. Cross and Wunyeran, refusing to let Wunyeran be erased and imagining a day when he will be memorialized alongside Dr. Cross,⁶¹ prompting readers to join him in questioning the ending of the traditional historical narrative and listening for the traces of repressed knowledge that complicate the very idea of the end.

Scott's approach to endings figures significantly in his adaptation of the novel form, and Edward Said's insights about the imperial implications of the form of the novel help to underscore the profound challenge that Scott delivers. Said devotes sustained attention to the form of the novel, arguing that the plot structure of the Western realist novel serves to reinforce a social, spatial, and moral order; in his words:

> [Characters] are permitted adventures in which their experiences reveal to them the limits of what they can aspire to, where they can go, what they can become. Novels therefore end either with the death of a hero or heroine ... who by virtue of overflowing energy does not fit into the orderly scheme of things, or with the protagonists' accession to stability (usually in the form of marriage or confirmed identity).⁶²

Said clarifies the vital role of the novel's ending, "as the conclusions of the novel confirm and highlight an underlying hierarchy of family, property, nation."[63] The endings of novels, then, serve to reinforce a European social order that solidifies connections between capitalist notions of family and private property by incorporating characters into the existing order or demanding a character's death as the consequence of challenging the order. In either case, order is maintained by enforcing a clear resolution. Scott's refusal to supply a fixed end point, whether one of destruction or redemption, fundamentally challenges this regulatory structure of the novel and the social hierarchy it stabilizes. It also reveals how as part of supporting a dominant capitalist social, spatial, and moral order, endings reinforce conceptions of matter. For example, by figuring death as a final end point, the traditional realist novels that Said describes confirm a separation of human life from processes of decay and renewal that the human body continues to participate in after and through death.

Instead of accepting generic expectations for resolution or accepting death as an end, Scott substitutes an emphasis on movement and resonance that corresponds to an epistemology of haunting that encourages attention to circulations across categories and beyond the individual human life span. In fact, Scott skillfully uses graves to display how competing constructions of matter support different thinking about ends. Describing the grave that Dr. Cross digs for his friend, Wunyeran, Bobby reflects that "Wunyeran's body, buried in not quite a foetal position, must have begun to dissolve into the earth along with the ochre and leaves and ash"[64] and he later speculates that "the damp earth...held Wuyneran, his bones."[65] Such depictions reveal an understanding of how matter endures despite shifts in form. Just as Bobby is able to conceptualize the coexistence of multiple forms of himself in life, from young Bobby to Old Bobby, Bobby comprehends Wunyeran as friend, but also as body and as bones, identifying a continuity between identities that is shared with shifting nonhuman forms of the ochre, leaves, and ash that also dissolve into the earth, taking on new manifestations that bear the traces of former embodiments. In addition to shared qualities of language and agency, Scott identifies death and decay as commonalities that span human and nonhuman matter. The narrator locates processes of decomposition in relation to larger cycles and evolutionary time scales through which wind and water shape the land over millennia, noting that the torrent that carried away building materials also would have "no trouble at all then, taking bones to the ocean. Always been this way. Bones from riverbanks washed down toward the sea."[66] In this figuration, human bones and animal bones are carried across land and water, circulating after death in ways that reshape and nourish the land. This understanding of the dynamics between life and death is juxtaposed with the framework of fixity deployed by the settlers, who seek to assign a final meaning to Dr. Cross, severing his remains from Wunyeran and from cycles of decay and regeneration in order to create a foundation for the nation. Instead of a narrative that accounts for the shifting forms that composed Cross in life and the processes of decomposition that return him to the land, Cross's new grave demonstrates capitalist presumptions to mastery over matter, attempting to arrest processes of change and designate Cross's proper place with the physical construction of a railing that encloses his grave and the discursive construction inscribed on the headstone that proclaims him as a landowner and founder of King George Town. The fenced grave physically marks off space as a final resting place for Cross, insisting on his separation from Wunyeran and from nonhuman matter and imposing a narrative of nation building that reduces the complexity of the character readers have met through Scott's novel. The grave, then, reveals more than an orientation to death; it demonstrates how the idea of the end coincides with the social hierarchy of family, property, and nation that Said highlights, and it also illuminates how all of these rely upon denying larger movements of matter in which death supports life over vast temporal and spatial scales.

Through the grave, Scott uncovers how fixity and individuality characterize a capitalist orientation to matter, land, and stories. The structure of the story that the town tells about Cross gestures to the dominant historical narrative and its effort to impose a single, fixed story that justifies colonial appropriation of land; it corresponds to an effort to keep Cross's bones in place and use them to claim individual ownership over the land, repressing awareness of ways that his life is intertwined with other human and nonhuman lives that came before and will come after and that would complicate the idea that the land can belong to a single individual. At the close of this chapter that tells of the separation of Dr. Cross from Wunyeran and the careless discarding of Wunyeran's bones, the narrator asks:

> Did all those bones reach the sea and join a path of whalebones across the ocean floor? Or years later become part of the foundations of the town hall and its clock with ticking faces looking north, south, east and west, and right at the very steeple top, that very great weight: a nation's fluttering flag? But forget it. That's long after this little chapter of a single plot and very few characters, this simple story of a Bobby and his few friends.[67]

Matter and its understanding are figured as key to the support of the nation's fluttering flag: Scott suggests that as this settlement is built over the bones of

Cross, the modern nation of Australia is built by asserting an understanding of matter that enables the separation of Australian from Noongar, human from nonhuman, and the instrumental treatment or erasure of the discarded remainder. He uses ironic meta-fictional commentary to deliver his challenge: while this is a story of a Noongar man and his friends, it is far from a simple story. Bobby's individual story cannot be so easily separated from larger stories of the nation and the ecosystem, showing that biographical time frames are implicated in other temporal scales: the mythic time of the nation, the evolutionary time of the rain shaping the landscape and the whales that the settlers are hunting out of existence, these too are part of Bobby's simple story.

Scott's not-so-simple story confronts readers with awareness of the imbrication of narrative strategies in imperial domination, as it highlights how nature came to be represented as inert as a result of colonial domination of Noongar culture, and it challenges readers with not-so-simple questions about how the novel and the nation have been built on the repression of matter's agency and vitality in order to support a scripting of human progress and development. Scott's adaptation of the form of the novel allows him to reveal the contest between competing understandings of matter and demonstrate how the novel can be shaped to help readers resist resolutions and listen for resonances that allow them to recognize connections that radiate across time, space, and species. Scott's references to the shared grave, the separation of Cross from Wunyeran, and Bobby's imagination of a day when the two will be memorialized together again surface throughout the novel, dislocating the authority to impose a single, fixed meaning and revising the plot structure of the novel so that death circulates through life rather than marking an end. Instead of conforming the temporal scale of the novel to the biological limits of a human life, Scott ends his novel with a story being offered to a new audience, prioritizing movement and transformation and showing how the form of the novel can be reshaped to carry notions of animate matter and convey time scales beyond the individual human life span.

Scott's strategies highlight connections that demand the attention of literary critics, asking critics to become attuned to changes in form and consider how formal innovations reflect and encourage different ways of understanding the world. Amitav Ghosh suggests that scale is a defining feature of the novel; while epics can wander "widely and freely over vast expanses of time and space," novels "conjure up worlds that become real precisely because of their finitude and distinctiveness. Within the mansion of serious fiction, no one will speak of how the continents were created; nor will they refer to the passage of thousands of years: connections and events on this scale appear not just unlikely but also absurd within the delimited horizon of the novel."[68] Ghosh posits that novels make places narratable through "a series of successive exclusions"[69] that narrow time and place to the exclusion of "those inconceivably large forces,"[70] and he distinguishes "serious" novels from works of science fiction that do engage expansive scales and forces. However, he seems to neglect the potential in works of "serious" fiction such as Scott's, and his own novels such as *The Hungry Tide* for that matter, that locate narratives in distinct places, but also reference the evolutionary time scales and massive forces of change that shaped the landscapes in which present-day action unfolds. Ghosh does not narrate how the continents were created, but he vividly evokes the deep time that produced the features of the Sunderbans. Scott presents recognizable temporal and spatial markers in the style of a conventional realist novel, but he also refers to the passage of thousands of years and repositions the human in relationship to the spatial and temporal scales of evolutionary forces of wind and water. Granted, he does not take readers to the narrative present of times that span thousands of years, but he refuses to isolate the present by narrating forces that shaped it and the effects it will continue to inflict over thousands of years; instead of a series of exclusions, Scott gestures throughout his novel to distant past and future times in ways that move the novel away from the fixity and finitude that Ghosh finds characteristic of the novel. While Ghosh concludes his discussion of stories by suggesting that new narrative forms will emerge that will require new strategies of reading, I am suggesting that these forms are already emerging and that novels such as Scott's (and Ghosh's) demonstrate ways that the novel can remain relevant to the representational and ethical challenges presented by current environmental crises.

The Future Beckons: Dwelling with Ghosts

Instead of leaving readers with an ending that neatly compartmentalizes the past and absolves us of the need to act, that makes recognition of past dispossession "the end," Scott's novel delivers a challenge: If we can feel the tragic failure of the past in the present, can that serve as a starting point and an inspiration to act in our world to make it otherwise? Scott's imperative to follow resonances rather than seek resolution suggests that there are many possible directions, and it would be a mistake to insist on a single path. For now, I will take the opportunity to trace one possible direction: the way the novel resonates with discourses of land that are imbricated in movements for social and environmental justice. Scott grants the importance of "land, giving back land" that has been a central focus in healing relationships between Indigenous and nonindigenous Australians,[71] but he also implies that models of social justice that stop at the return of land miss an opportunity for a more radical engagement with the past and overlook the advantages of a more comprehensive reevaluation of conceptions of land as property. In other words, current practice operates in the mode of trauma, incorporating Noongar knowledge into existing epistemologies and listening to the voices of ghosts in an effort to resolve the violent past. The 1992 Mabo decision and 1993 Native Title Act provide the legal framework for the return of land; while Indigenous knowledge does influence legal decisions—for example, a justice in a recent mining case cited Yindjibarndi custom of requiring strangers to request permission of elders to enter and engage in activity on land as a determining factor in his decision[72]—the legal framework preserves paradigms of property. On the other hand, the ecospectral approach that Scott develops transforms the terrain of the novel, and in doing so, reveals ways that haunting could impact other discourses; national legal frameworks could be reshaped to reflect Noongar understandings of country and imagine modes of inhabitance that respect human dependencies on and responsibilities to nonhuman matter.

At the same time that legal frameworks continue to rely on capitalist conceptions of inert matter, international academic discourses such as ecocriticism, posthumanism, and new materialisms are developing radical engagements with nonhuman matter. From Jane Bennett's political theory to Val Plumwood's environmental philosophy to Serenella Iovino and Serpil Oppermann's literary critical approach, scholars have been forging new frameworks for conceptualizing the vitality and agency of nonhuman matter.[73] One of the distinguishing features of this body of scholarship is the emphasis it places on how the material and the discursive, matter and stories, mutually shape one another. Contesting dominant capitalist conceptions of passive, inert matter, these scholars urge awareness of ways that matter creates effects and unfolds its own narratives, but they also confer on human storytellers a privileged role in teaching other humans how to listen to the stories of matter. They stress that reanimating the world through a vocabulary and grammar that registers the creativity of matter is more than an aesthetic preoccupation; it is part of "a survival project in our present context" of environmental precarity.[74] Scott's work offers an valuable illustration of what might be gained by situating the project of rethinking matter in relation to the imperial past and the violent repression of Indigenous knowledges, allowing the discussions to register ways that, as Ghosh remarks, "this renewed awareness of the elements of agency and consciousness that humans share with other beings" must be contextualized in relation to the fact that "a great number of human beings had never lost this awareness in the first place."[75]

In the epigraph for this chapter, Scott explains his speculative approach in this novel; he asserts that the focus of his engagement with the past is not meant to record "what was, but what might have been, and even what might yet be."[76] He encourages future-directed vision and demonstrates how Indigenous Australian knowledge and language for representing the agency of nonhuman matter might nourish local communities and travel beyond them to help create models of social and environmental justice based on mutual caring. Deborah Bird Rose argues that Indigenous conceptions of country might support such an ethic: "Multispecies kin groups are the result of creation... Within these country-based multispecies families, there is a moral proposition that is not so much a rule as a statement of how life works: a country and its living beings take care of their own."[77] Scott's novel resonates with such discourses, sharing Noongar knowledge with readers beyond the local community and inviting those readers to become attuned to the nonhuman voices of country which could enable alternative modes of inhabitance. However, Scott's work and his model of expanding circles also carries the reminder that such discourses must be wary of reinscribing the centrality of Western languages and knowledges by presenting Indigenous knowledge as supplement or by appropriating knowledge in ways that erase Indigenous communities as keepers of stories. Scott's strategy of prioritizing possibilities rather than closure confirms his commitment to stories and knowledge as growing, living things and supports his conception of the writer as conduit that can reach across spatial and temporal divides; operating from this orientation, he relinquishes the authority to impose the end and beckons readers to join him in listening to recovered voices and working in concert with them to compose more equitable futures.

4

Mapping Modes of Inhabitance: Haunting, Homing, and the Cartographic Imagination in Henrietta Rose-Innes's *The Rock Alphabet*

I am interested in the interactions—physical and psychological—between human beings and the landscapes they inhabit.
    Henrietta Rose-Innes, Interview with Mildred K. Barya, *Pambazuka News*

Can we live with our maps differently? Could we inhabit our histories differently?
    Paul Carter, *Dark Writing: Geography, Performance, Design*

Maps document histories of human relationship with the land. They become a concern for environmental justice and a site of hauntings because of the roles they have played (and continue to play) in contests over ways of knowing and inhabiting the land. For instance, the colonial maps that became dominant in South Africa, as in other settler colonies, enforced one culturally specific way of seeing the land and used it to administer property and populations, submerging local ways of knowing and contributing to social and environmental inequalities that continue to exert effects. Effects include continuing racial and gender inequality in land ownership despite land reform policies enacted to fulfill a Constitutional promise that all South African citizens have equal access to land,[1] but they also include the destruction of forms of inhabitance beyond models of ownership and an ongoing failure to recognize other forms of mapping as knowledge. For example, Lindsay Frederick Braun describes cartographic histories that construct a genealogy in which "Africa has no maps or geographical awareness until Europeans arrive."[2] This narrative positions mapping as a European innovation by establishing restrictive conditions for what counts as a map: "By demanding that only a direct analogue of the European map can be considered as evidence of sophisticated geographies among Africans, that knowledge is given a solely European origin in contrast to the distinct and usually retrograde knowledge of Africans."[3] Thus, the repression of knowledge that enabled colonial maps to take on the status of objective truth continues through historical narratives that fail to register other ways of knowing, including ways of relating to land through different models of vision, nonvisual epistemologies, and different strategies of representation. Such power contests between ways of knowing form the root of environmental conflicts, as Leah Temper, Daniela del Bene, and Joan Martinez-Alier note in relation to their own work with maps: "EJ struggles are often about one version of 'knowing nature' that is imposed, while other forms of knowledge are discounted or erased."[4]

In contrast to cartographic histories that perpetuate the marginalization of non-Western mapping techniques, critical cartography scholars have vigorously challenged the positioning of European maps as instruments of objective truth.[5] In addition to investigating how European mapping techniques advance a particular model of vision that distances the human from the landscape, scholars have generated productive angles for reconsidering the relationship between humans and maps, devising reading strategies attuned to alternate histories, erasures, and transformative possibilities. For instance, Paul Carter elaborates a challenge:

> Maps dispossess others but they also—at least as conventionally read—disable those whose interests they supposedly serve. They disempower us to remember, for example. They wipe out journeys. Their all-seeing panoptic is curiously, and terrifyingly, blind to the history of journeys whose residue is a texture, a ground pattern that identifies the qualitative adventure of a place rather than delineating its quantitative dimensions.... Can we live with our maps differently? Could we inhabit our histories differently?[6]

Carter's reflections encourage an approach to maps as more than navigational or administrative aids. His qualification that points to conventional reading practices and his questions "can we live with our maps differently?" and "could we inhabit our histories differently?" imply that maps do not have to detach space from the dynamics of time and interaction. Maps are capable of relaying stories of human inhabitance; however, we need to adjust our reading practices and our ideas about space and time to access these stories.

Attending to the temporal as well as the spatial aspects of cartographic knowledge, Carter's questions accord with geographers like Doreen Massey who implore scholars "to question that habit of thinking of space as surface" and instead think of it as a "meeting-up of histories."[7] Shifting attention to reading practices, Carter's thinking also coincides with the project of critical cartography scholars such as Denis Wood, John Pickles, and Denis Cosgrove who emphasize ways that maps depend on human interpretation, which opens possibilities for unconventional reading strategies and engagement with traces left by signs. Encouraging analysis of what maps preserve as well as what they omit,[8] these scholars extend reading practices beyond the documents themselves to include attention to ways that certain representations of space have been excluded from histories of mapping and denied recognition as forms of cartographic knowledge. They also illuminate the ground that maps share with narrative, highlighting ways that cartography, rather than producing an objective picture of the world, relies on acts of imagination and interpretation that emerge from situated perspectives. Putting the work of critical cartography scholars in contact with the work of environmental justice scholars helps to illuminate consequences of learning to live with maps differently; attentive to the haunting remainders of repressed stories, we could reconnect with ways of imagining human inhabitance that would challenge imperial models in which humans oversee and classify an inert land.

In her second novel, *The Rock Alphabet* (2004),[9] Henrietta Rose-Innes traverses similar intellectual terrain as she builds a fictional world that allows her to investigate possibilities for learning to live with maps differently. She creates characters who exemplify different ways of relating to maps, and she interrogates the consequences of different signifying and reading practices, associating totalizing, classificatory practices with stagnancy, isolation, and extinction and imaginative practices with playfulness, community, and survival. Rose-Innes uses the characters of Bernard and Beatrice Faro to confront an imperial, classificatory approach to reading maps and archiving knowledge that leads to a sterile relation with the land and the past, and she emphasizes the consequences of this strategy by placing the story of the Faros next to the journeys of Ivy and Jean, inheritors of the Faro legacy though not biological progeny. In their own ways, both Ivy and Jean develop dynamic, lived relationships with maps as part of their experience of inhabiting the land of the Cederberg and relating to it as home. In the sections that follow, I investigate how Rose-Innes grounds her thinking about cartographies in relation to a specific South African landscape, and I argue that she creates a spectral form for her novel that allows repressed knowledge to return to interrogate dominant constructions of land as property and to unsettle constructions of home that rest on ownership. Focusing on the current generation as heir to multiple epistemologies, Rose-Innes confronts readers with the responsibility for retrieving discredited pasts and negotiating conflicting legacies in order to enable environmental justice that challenges paradigms of ownership and property and advances understandings of human inhabitance as a process of participating in multigenerational, multispecies communities.

Locating the Cederberg

First, a short detour to contextualize Rose-Innes's choice to place her characters in the Cederberg Mountains and in conversation with the rock art found there. From her first novel, *Shark's Egg* (2000), to her most recent, *Green Lion* (2016), Rose-Innes's novels present the landscapes surrounding Cape Town, South Africa. In *The Rock Alphabet*, Rose-Innes travels between the city and the Cederberg, and her choice to foreground the urban and its fringes reflects an understanding of environment that differs from the pristine wilderness often celebrated in Western nature writing. In his work *Different Shades of Green*, Byron Caminero-Santangelo explores how African texts force reevaluations of definitions of environmental literature, and while he does not include Rose-Innes's fiction in his discussion, her work contributes to the emerging canon of South African environmental literature that he describes.[10] Her novel encourages attention to ways that environmental awareness emerges from human interaction with specific landscapes, and it demonstrates how space takes on meaning for humans through complex networks of histories, epistemologies, and discourses through which humans make sense of interactions with their coinhabitants. The Cederberg Mountains do not appear in the novel as a wilderness separated from human life, but as a storied environment that conveys an extended history of physical and discursive interactions between humans and South African landscapes.

Specifically, Rose-Innes's choice to position her characters in relation to the rock art of the Cederberg activates specters that disrupt government-sanctioned histories of mapping and inhabitance. Outside the novel, the contemporary South African government supports National Geo-spatial Information (NGI), a division of the Department of Rural Development and Land Reform that is charged with organizing spatial data to "facilitate orderly development."[11] On their webpage, they have constructed a national cartographic history which quotes Mr. J.J. Bosman who in 1905 proclaimed maps as imperative to prevent disputes and litigation about farm borders and as "among the first requirements of civilized administration."¹² This narrative establishes maps as crucial to landownership and legal administration, and the NGI locates their current work in relation to this imperial history, suggesting that "although there are records of surveying and mapping activities from the time of Van Riebeeck, founder of the Cape Town colony, surveying on a scientific basis only got under way in the late 19th century."¹³ The NGI constructs a narrative to orient its projects in a temporal progression, gesturing back to diagrams and representations from South Africa's early settler history in the 1650s. While the narrative discounts the scientific quality of these early images, it nonetheless includes them as a part of the story. Precolonial mapping technologies and indigenous histories of inhabitance are entirely absent from this chronology, although the Cape Colony where Van Riebeeck established his colonial garden was in close physical proximity to rock art that dates back thousands of years. These paintings that record human encounters with the land and animals of the region are ignored and denied a place in a national narrative of spatial imagining.¹⁴ As Braun's discussion of cartographic history attests, the NGI's narrative reflects broader patterns of constructing a "positivist, triumphal narrative of Western scientific progress and technological achievement" that erases African participation in colonial mapmaking as well as denying African cartographic practices the status of knowledge, resulting in a narrative in which "African maps, and by extension claims on the territory, are somehow absent."¹⁵

Another deafening silence in the NGI's cartographic history that seems worth noting is the lack of attention to the role of maps in enabling apartheid and the continuing unequal racial distribution of land in South Africa, despite the fact that one of the charges of the Department of Rural Development and Land Reform is restitution of land rights and land reform. Carter establishes that maps are "instruments of discourse," and he quotes J.B. Harley's conclusion, "all knowledges—and hence—cartography is thoroughly enmeshed with the larger battles which constitute our world. Maps are not external to these struggles to alter power relations. The history of map use suggests that this may be so and that maps embody specific forms of power and authority."¹⁶ As instruments of power, maps enabled imperial acquisition of land at the same time that they allowed histories of expansion to disappear from memory, as they do in the NGI narrative. Historians and literary scholars such as A.J. Christopher and Rita Barnard record counter-narratives that document how colonial legacies of cartography influenced the conceptualization and construction of South African space and how apartheid operated as a geographical system of power that deployed control over space to enforce social and political control.¹⁷

Barnard analyzes a variety of apartheid era spaces such as the black township that "amounted, in short, to a mechanism of control... It seemed designed to increase a sense of alienation and to prevent the individual from achieving any kind of cognitive map."[18] While the design of spaces prevented township residents from mapping their inhabitance, road maps at this time "did more than assist the traveler to get from one town to the next. They also worked to create a predominantly 'white man's country' by ensuring that white history, culture, and identity dominated the map. To achieve this, mapmakers used cartographic sleight of hand to make black Africa disappear from the map."[19] The work of these scholars vividly illustrates ways that maps reflect situated ways of knowing that participate in larger political, economic, and ideological battles over land in South Africa. By deciding to set her novel in the Cederberg, Rose-Innes responds to these contested histories of inhabitance and interpretation, bringing the rock paintings into contact with other histories of mapping. She engages with the Cederberg as a space that has been and continues to be constructed through interacting discourses, including scientific and legalistic discourses that position land as property to be controlled and developed, imaginative discourses that record traces of journeys and experiences, and touristic discourses that struggle to reconcile these ways of knowing for contemporary consumers, torn between contradictory goals of facilitating novel and exotic journeys and offering comforting illusions of control and mastery. Incorporating elements of all of these discourses that hold different consequences for how to relate to the land, Rose-Innes foregrounds the vital role of narratives in shaping understanding and contesting the land's future.

Novel Mappings: Narrating Home as Relationship

Rose-Innes proclaims her interest in physical and psychological interactions between humans and the landscapes they inhabit,[20] and she adapts the conventions of the novel to convey an understanding of the dynamics of these relationships. Her novel follows the intersecting lives of Bernard Faro, an archaeologist who becomes lost in the mountains of the Cederberg, his devoted daughter Beatrice, the young boys that Beatrice discovers in the mountains, Jean and Flin, and a young woman named Ivy who works at the Faro Institute, the repository for Bernard's archaeological collection. As she records the ways that these individuals relate to varied landscapes including the mountain and the Faro Institute, Rose-Innes narrates homing as a relationship. Instead of structuring her novel in a linear sequence of temporal progress toward total knowledge and domestication of space or spatial progress toward a fixed place marked as home, Rose-Innes organizes her plot with a series of physical and spectral returns that communicate inhabitance as an ongoing process of negotiation with others. She adapts the conventions of the novel to convey this awareness of human relationship with the land as a mutually constructing process, refusing to confine the land to a background role as setting for human lives.

Rose-Innes uses her novel to help recover the temporal aspects of mapping as a journey, but she also develops a structure for her novel that advances an epistemological alternative to the homeward journey narrative. The form she creates does not neatly fit into alternative categories described by narrative theorists; for instance, it does not adhere to the unnatural narrative temporalities that Jan Alber identifies such as retrogressive time that reverses progressive time, polychronic narration that superimposes multiple times, or an eternal loop that cycles endlessly;[21] however, it does partake of aspects of each of these. The novel narrates physical and spectral returns that bring multiple temporalities into contact, but instead of operating in an endless loop, the returns allow Ivy and Jean to learn to live between life and death and to refigure inheritance, recognizing ghosts along with nonhuman others as present participants in a community. Rejecting progressive sequencing and any bildungsroman-style expectations of following a single character's journey to mature acceptance of his place within the social order, Rose-Innes has her dual protagonists return not only to physical spaces but to habits of mind, specifically to childhood play, which enables them to disrupt the fixity of categories represented by Bernard Faro and his archive. Their stories chronicle an uneven process of learning to read signs and accept the play of meanings that allows them to locate their lives in relation to the lives and deaths that enable their survival.

Working with the discursive tools of the novel, Rose-Innes reflects processes of learning to relate to the land on the microlevel of individual descriptions of space as well as at the macrolevel of plot structure. Narrative theorists' formulations of the tour and the map as different strategies for representing space offer a helpful framework for approaching this aspect of the novel. Marie-Laure Ryan, Kenneth Foote, and Maoz Azaryahu explain that the map represents space "as seen from a fixed, elevated point of view that affords the observer a totalizing, simultaneous perception of the relations between objects."[22] This strategy offers a view that makes positions between landscape features or objects perceptible, but it also eliminates the dynamics of time and ignores journeys, much the way Carter describes in relationship to cartography. On the other hand, the tour restores the dynamics of time, creating "a description of space from the point of view of a moving, embodied observer who visits locations in a temporal sequence."[23] Ryan, Foote, and Azaryahu offer these terms to distinguish representations of space, but they also acknowledge that "a much more immersive way to textualize space lies in a combination of the map and the tour strategies."[24] The short opening chapter to Rose-Innes's novel creates such a combination that characterizes her approach throughout the text. The novel is divided into sections by dates rather than titles, and this one bears the label 1982, setting the action during a time when apartheid policies and resistance had been shaping South Africa for decades. This temporal marker is followed by a view of a cave, and then an image of a human woman, "crashing through the bushes toward it,"[25] depicting the space in a way that exceeds what the woman, Beatrice, can see and instead making her an object of the reader's gaze. This opening description is map-like in providing a view from an elevated, external position, but as the scene progresses, readers look with, rather than at, Beatrice, sharing her viewing position as she peers into the cave to discover two young boys. Rose-Innes deploys the tour strategy to allow readers access to space that is not completely visible from the elevated position and to introduce elements of interaction with the landscape that are absent in a static map. By combining map and tour, Rose-Innes directs attention to different ways of knowing involved, a point that she further emphasizes by shifting viewing positions according to different focalization. These tactics allow her not only to register relationship to space as an ongoing process rather than a fixed accomplishment, but also to reinforce awareness that multiple possible views coexist.

This blending of strategies continues throughout the novel, as Rose-Innes repeatedly creates shifting positions that put multiple ways of relating to the land alongside one another. For instance, the next short section jumps to 2005, the decade following South Africa's first free elections and the creation of a new Constitution that affirms the right of access to land for all South Africans. This section begins with an excerpt from a tourist guide, invoking a discourse that constructs relationship with the mountain from a detached position that implies complete knowledge. The guidebook proclaims: "And so we come to the so-called 'Rock Alphabet'. Anyone familiar with the poised shapes of real Bushman art would know at once that this is something else. The crude symbols are of unquestionably recent origin."[26] Rose-Innes vividly captures the ways that tourist discourse constructs expertise to interpret ancient (and contemporary) rock art, presuming to speak for the figures and claiming a totalizing knowledge. This excerpt gestures once again beyond the novel, this time to tourism companies that thrive on presenting the same kind of knowledge; for instance, the Cederberg Tourism web page entices visitors to the Cederberg with promises of access to a comfortable encounter with the past: "The Cederberg mountains are filled with silent stories of Bushman rock art...Their legacy litters the Cedarberg [sic], along well-known trails that need no guide to find the way."[27] Both passages position knowledge of the mountain as easily attained, and both imply a generic, disembodied knower. This discourse of detached consumption links contemporary touristic mapping and imperial mapping, which Carter describes when he writes, "the collective endeavor of the white settler has been the production of a recognizable country."[28] In both settler mapping and touristic mapping, the threat of the unfamiliar is tamed by imposing familiar features and narratives on the land that subordinate it for human visual consumption. Including the tourist guide allows Rose-Innes to play with circulations of meaning that extend beyond the stated years of 1982 and 2005; the tourist discourse shows a resurfacing of familiar features of imperialist discourse that spoke with authority in an effort to package and proclaim mastery over the land, and it also reaches back thousands of years to register the presence of inhabitants who made a physical impression on the land that is now being marketed and spoken for, made into a haunting remainder that is "silent" in tourist discourse but manifests traces of an alternative story of inhabitance. The verbal and visual discourses produced by tourism and imperialism, Rose-Innes thus reveals, configure space and transmit interpretive practices in ways that continue to influence what visitors see and how they understand the Cederberg.

After the excerpt from the tourist guide provides a generic, detached view, the chapter then shifts to focalize spatial relationships through the situated perspective of Ivy who looks out of a window at a family of American tourists. The tourists are captivated by their map, which occupies their attention to the exclusion of the living land, leaving the mountain "behind them, ignored."[29] While the tourism company web page naturalizes knowledge of the mountain—anyone would know how to interpret the signs and follow the paths—Ivy experiences confusion and dissonance, wondering how the tourists could fail to see the dazzling mountain behind them and remarking on the difference in what they see despite the fact that they occupy the same physical space that she does. As the chapter continues, Jean arrives and the focalization shifts so that the reader moves through the space of the mountain house along with him. His movement goes beyond the physical space of the house to visit memories of his childhood, reminding us that locating the self in relationship to space involves the coexistence of multiple temporalities as well as multiple discourses. In these two short framing chapters, Rose-Innes uses a combination of narrative maps and tours of space, shifting focalization, and intersecting discourses to highlight ways that the same mountain appears differently or even disappears depending on how humans construct the view.

The novel then shifts to 1996 for the majority of the story. This section contains twenty-seven chapters that alternately follow Ivy and Jean, until their paths connect, but the chapters do not remain confined to 1996; they travel to the childhoods of both characters through flashbacks, revealing how the adult characters continue to remain haunted by missing brothers and multiple legacies of inhabitance, and reinforcing ways that haunting combines spatial and temporal displacement. Finally, the novel concludes with a short section labeled 2005 that depicts the adult Ivy and Jean learning to reconnect life and death with the result that both characters come to consider themselves at home. Rose-Innes, thus, creates a macrolevel organizational structure for the novel that resists the idea of journey as movement toward a preestablished spatial destination. Instead, the characters' and readers' movement across times, spaces, and perspectives creates a journey in the sense of a process of learning how to live in relationship with the land. The notation of years positions this process in parallel to the shifting legal construction of land ownership in South Africa, but also as an alternative to it.

The emphasis on spectral circulations rather than linear progress is also conveyed by the symbolic meanings invested in space. The opening chapters leave readers with a sense of the physical features of the land; however, the space of the cave also initiates the story through the force of its symbolic meaning as a space that combines life and death, present and past, human and nonhuman. The opening chapter locates the children in between—they appear to be lingering between life and death as Beatrice encounters them in the liminal space of a mountain cave. Bernard Faro's notebooks also appear in this between time/space of the cave that mixes qualities of womb and crypt: "In the shadows, the little one lay still, eyes wide, unbreathing, cupped in a moulded nest of grey matter. Paper. Notebook paper, pencil sketches on torn pages. The woman leaned forward again, squinting in the dimness, and reached her hands to gather him up."[30] In this evocative passage, Beatrice serves as a midwife to a new birth for this child, pulling him out of the dark space of the cave, out of his embodied relation with the land and the maps that he could not read in any conventional sense, but that were serving as a nest that kept him alive. Removing the children from the cave and inserting them into her way of living (in a house, speaking English, navigating by orthographic maps and written notes) births them into the Faro family, but also ushers the children across a threshold that represents a break with their previous way of living and knowing.

Instead of using biological birth as a temporal origin, Rose-Innes introduces Jean through his emplotment into Western narrative, a strategy that gestures to the history of South Africa and the ghosting of indigenous presence that allows histories to begin with European settlement, languages, and traditions. In this way, Rose-Innes opens her novel by placing us in complex intersections of generational time, which as Deborah Bird Rose contends "clearly involves both death and birth, using the term 'birth' loosely to designate any coming-into-being," and it "evokes the temporal pattern of sequence; it is accomplished through the transmission of wisdom, memory, and traditions from generation to generation."[31] Rose-Innes, however, complicates this sense of inheritance and sequence by interrogating the claims of biological and cultural inheritances. Bernard's papers temporarily shelter the boys, and Beatrice adopts the children so that Jean becomes the legal heir to the Faro estate, but this giving of life and inheritance simultaneously represents a death, a severing of Jean's relationship with another inheritance: his biological parents and his embodied and cultural knowledge of the land.

While this parental heritage remains inaccessible to Jean, parts of it remain alive through his brother, Flin, which allows Rose-Innes to further adjust patterns of inheritance to include contemporaneous associations. During a flashback to Jean's childhood with Beatrice Faro, Jean reflects on his family tree and suggests: "It would be very simple. Just two names, connected by a small horizontal dash. Brother-brother. No up, no down. No one before, and none after, and no one else alongside."[32] Here, Rose-Innes gestures to conceptions of fraternal inheritance that move across the same generation, and this placing of brothers alongside one another reflects a larger organizing principle for her novel. Instead of tracing linear patterns of inheritance that unfold in chronological or reverse chronological order, Rose-Innes places multiple inheritances and their consequences alongside of and in interaction with one another; part of Jean's process of learning to live with maps involves learning to see the others that exist alongside him, beyond his brother. This conceptualization of inheritance not only structures time, but also space; as Massey explains, some conceptions of spatial history such as the palimpsest invoke images of layers that imply succession and thus deny the coevalness of different ways of knowing, while "the full recognition of contemporaneity implies a spatiality which is a multiplicity of stories-so-far."[33] Rose-Innes's spectral format enables an understanding of spatiality as stories-so-far, as she reveals the multiple different stories that unfold alongside one another.

The significance of this narrative structuring that emphasizes spaces, times, and discourses placed alongside one another in relationship can be further elucidated by bringing attention to specters, the presences alongside Jean that he feels and sometimes fears and cannot fully recognize. Derrida opens *Specters of Marx* by reflecting on the question of learning to live. Derrida muses, "If it—learning to live—remains to be done, it can happen only between life and death. Neither in life nor in death *alone*... And this being-with specters would also be, not only, but also a *politics* of memory, of inheritance, and of generations."[34] Living happens between life and death, and in the classical realist novel, the meaning of between life and death is linear and sequential: birth serves as the point of origin, and death as the end, with life happening between these plot points. Derrida cultivates a different sense of between life and death, using between to indicate interaction and a deconstruction of temporal sequencing predicated on thinking life and death as opposites that allow time to be structured into a line. For Derrida, the between is populated by specters; Deborah Bird Rose does not address specters, but she does develop her own conception of the relationality between life and death and the resulting politics of generations, and she articulates the consequences of this formulation in distinctly ecological terms. Rose draws on the work of James Hatley to argue that "that condition of being-birthed, of always coming after death, means that in generational time one's orientation toward the future is both toward death and toward others,"[35] and she emphasizes both the sequential nature of generational time and the synchronous processes of life support that reach across species: "All living things owe their lives not only to their forbears but also to all the other others that have nourished them again and again."[36] Complex temporalities connect life and death beyond a linear, biological sequence of inheritance, and Rose contends that writing can serve as "an act of witness" that can help contemporary audiences apprehend what she terms "embodied knots of multispecies time" in which "each individual is both itself in the present, and the history of its forbears and mutualists."[37] Rose's thinking helps to illuminate the ecological and ethical consequences of reconfiguring the novel to reflect a process of interaction between humans and the land. If a sequential structuring of the novel reinforces an understanding of inheritance as strictly linear, limiting thinking about directionality and consequences, Rose-Innes's narration of returns, overlaps, and contemporaneity pluralizes inheritance and facilitates accountability to the others that compose knots of multispecies time.

Legacies of Classification

The structure of the novel allows Rose-Innes to place multiple legacies of mapping into conversation and to position characters and readers in relation to these different legacies. The history of the map as imperial artifact is incorporated, but also modulated through Bernard. Bernard's quest to find the truth of the rock paintings, to collect and categorize artifacts, and to preserve the past in his institute represents one approach to interpretation; in Derrida's terms, this approach "seeks to decipher, dreams of deciphering a truth or an origin which escapes play and the order of the sign."[38] Bernard's desire for a fixed and stable meaning, a timeless truth, is pursued through an epistemology of classification and preservation that forms one inheritance that is passed to all of the other characters in the novel. Rose-Innes positions this transgenerational inheritance by marginalizing his life so that he appears through the traces he has left in the wake of his disappearance and death. Her formal strategies comment on expectations about absence and presence, life and death, as he surfaces in the novel first through a description in a tourist guide book, then through the artifacts he has left behind in his institute, and eventually through his skeletal remains that Ivy finds in the mountains. Instead of chronicling the actions he took during his life and presenting a present tense, present-day encounter with Bernard, Rose-Innes records ways that Bernard impacts others through and despite death, incorporating his life into larger processes of interpretation that radiate across generations. She presents Bernard's mapping practices through a process of reading his traces rather than offering direct access to his records, enacting the proposition that we can learn to live with maps and histories differently by cultivating different strategies of interpretation. Thus, while Bernard brings mapping practices focused on arresting time into the novel, Rose-Innes uses her own set of narrative practices to deny his practices the status of objective truth, repositioning them within her own narrative of mapping as a process.

Rose-Innes continues to decenter classificatory epistemologies by revealing the different effects that Bernard's legacy has on Beatrice and on Jean and Ivy. Beatrice clings narrowly to her father's legacy, and it blinds her to other possibilities for relating to the landscape. Seeking the body of her father, Beatrice instead finds his words, his notebooks. However, these documents fail to communicate across his absence; the written words do not operate in the mode of a haunting that speaks to her. She finds herself incapable of reading the language of her father, yet she blindly persists in the methods that she inherits from him. Rather than opening herself to the alternative knowledge that the boys possess, she demeans their knowledge as primitive, writing over their past and attempting to incorporate them into her system of signs. Beatrice cannot access the past of the boys; Jean is too young to remember, and Flin refuses to speak of the past, leaving their earlier years and the story of how they came to be alone in the cave with Bernard's papers a mystery. Beatrice responds to the uncertain origins of the boys by attempting to reassert her authority, naming the children after noted European anthropologists, substituting European origins and signs for their unknown past—the younger child is dubbed Jean after Jean Champollion who deciphered hieroglyphics and the older Flin after William Flinders Petrie, a methodological pioneer who influenced excavation, dating, and cataloging procedures for artifacts. Further, she has her assistant Mattie attempt to teach the boys to speak and write in English, a process which Jean accepts, but which Flin strenuously rejects: "He despised writing, hated it with a black hatred. It was a secret code Jean used to join the world, a code Flin did not want to know."[39] Flin does not want to be incorporated into this world of signs, and he fights to maintain his own knowledge: "Flin knew other things. About plants and animals, about direction,"[40] and he feels the imposition of English language as a threat to that knowledge, an alienation from the world to which his knowledge roots him.

Beatrice is positioned to inherit knowledge from multiple sources, from her father and from the children. However, she closes herself off to the possibility to inherit from the boys, and Rose-Innes links the tension between ways of knowing to forms of language. Writing such as her father's notebooks is supposed to carry the advantage of transmitting meaning across distances and beyond the human biological life span, acting to preserve memory across generations, but it also carries limits of distancing the human from direct contact with the world. In his works *The Spell of the Sensuous* and *Becoming Animal*, David Abram suggests that oral language and pictorial writing drew humans back to connection with the surrounding landscape whose sounds and forms they echoed, and he identifies the spread of alphabetic literacy as a cause of contemporary human disconnection from the nonhuman world. Abram contends that written texts dull our perception of human language as participating in a wider network of communications, and they present us with a voice that "seems to speak from an unchanging dimension apparently impervious to the growth and decay of bodily life. The alphabet, in other words, opens a new zone within human experience, a linguistic dimension that seems wholly unaffected by the flux of time."[41] Abram's description of the impacts of alphabetic literacy resonates with Deborah Bird Rose's concern about the separation of the processes of life and death. The alphabet allows humans to evade biological limits imposed by distances of space and time, but the result is a system that impacts how humans understand themselves in relation to death and to the nonhuman world. Humans become blind and deaf to the nonhuman others who sustain their life, so the knowledge that they pass across generations is a knowledge of human separation from the animate land. Rose-Innes links alphabetic language and classificatory epistemology in shaping Beatrice's orientation to the land, and she conveys the damaging consequences Abram describes through Beatrice's death. She disappears and dies in the mountains, equipped with the authority of the written word, but lacking living knowledge—the ability to read Flin's map that is imprinted directly on the land—that would allow her to survive.

Like writing allows for the preservation of meaning beyond the human life span, the archive allows for a preservation of the past that spans generations, but similarly processes of preserving and interpreting impose other limitations and consequences. In *Archive Fever*, Derrida considers the creation of archives and proposes, "It is thus, in the *domiciliation*, in this house arrest, that archives take place. The dwelling, this place where they dwell permanently marks this institutional passage from the private to the public."[42] Archiving involves a transition of private memory stored in the body to a public, external display of the past, but Derrida's language also emphasizes the consequences of curating the past, of arresting the dynamics of time to put them on display in a physical space, of making the past a permanent display stored in a specific, present place. He reinforces connections between memory and physical, architectural space, but he points to the double nature of this housing: "It also *shelters* itself from this memory which it shelters: which comes down to saying also that it forgets it."[43] He elaborates this statement in "Archive Fever in South Africa," explaining that storing memory externally creates the feeling that the past is remembered, it is safe, which frees individuals to forget, "forget it to go on, to survive."[44] As part of the project *Refiguring the Archive* that investigates how archives in South Africa are being repositioned, Achille Mbembe further interrogates the relationships between remembering and forgetting, emphasizing the process of archiving as a disconnection of life and death, as the materials to be archived are "remov[ed] from time and from life" and "assigned to a place and a sepulcher."[45] The gathering together of signs to create the archive aims to preserve memory, but as a single, cohesive narrative that must exclude any elements that would disrupt that narrative; thus, the authority to compose the archive, to decide on the single narrative that becomes a public, collective inheritance holds political consequences and unleashes ghosts. The archive serves as a prosthetic for carrying memory beyond biological human limits, but as Derrida and Mbembe begin to uncover, the life that the archive extends to the signs of the past transforms death, giving the illusion that the past remains accessible while a specific authoritative interpretation of the past is substituted for heterogeneous voices and interactions.

Rose-Innes delves into these dynamics of preservation through the physical space of the Faro Institute which associates Bernard's archival epistemologies with stagnation and death. As the time shifts to 1996, the next generation is being trained to accept the isolation imposed by classificatory practice. Ivy is a young woman who inherits a position tending the Faro collection from her great-aunt Mattie, the woman who raised her when she was orphaned. Ivy describes the dulling effect of working with the artifacts:

> Frequently, she felt herself to be a piece of equipment, some kind of tube or compressor, with the jumbled stacks of old specimens piling up against her on the one side, while on the other she produced a thin grey stream of annotations. Sometimes, unconsciously, she would narrow her eyes and squeeze her mouth in imitation of a nozzle, and make a humming sound as she filed at her desk. *Stone thing. Bone thing. Bone bone stone stone bone.* She worked sloppily, her cataloging becoming scrappier and more perfunctory.[46]

Rather than speaking to her about the past, the artifacts and the process of cataloging them seem to take Ivy out of awareness of time and embodiment, turning her into a machine that unconsciously produces writing and sounds that have no audience, that speak to no one. In fact, the "thin grey stream of annotations" that result from her labor are described to echo industrial waste, suggesting that her efforts produce useless, artificial by-products. Such descriptions associate the Faro family and their legacy with science, industry, and empire, at the same time as the language characterizes such knowledge as sterile and lifeless production. Ivy mindlessly catalogs boxes full of animal fossils, rocks, and human skulls, only to return them to the darkness of storage, leaving any potential knowledge or productive inhabitation of the past literally boxed off. Cataloging, naming, and classifying attach words—human interpretations— to the artifacts of the past, but they fail to animate the stories or communicate experiences to any living audience. Death is detached from life, disembodied, made into an object of knowledge, and as such it becomes useless for learning how to live. This process demonstrates the logic that Rose has named double death: "The notion of double death contrasts with the ecological and evolutionary contexts in which death is immanent in and necessary to life. Double death breaks up the partnership between life and death."[47] Death becomes a private asset to be managed and cataloged, and inheritance is managed by a lawyer who comes to inventory the collection of artifacts to ascertain their monetary value. This depiction of the space of the archive and its impacts on Ivy reinforces the judgement that interpretive strategies that seek to gain total knowledge by arresting the play of meaning have a debilitating effect; the archive spatially manifests the deadening consequences of walling human life and human history off from interactions with the other generations and species that sustain them.

Reshaping Inheritance: Play, Imagination, and Cartographies

Rose-Innes demonstrates how one orientation toward mapping and interpretation leads to double death, but she also locates this as one among various possibilities. Jean, Beatrice's adopted child and legal heir, and Ivy, Mattie's niece and heir to her position working for the Faro family, illustrate a different possibility: they develop a transformative relation with maps by exploring the multiple legacies they inherit. Both children are trained in the Faro's cartographic epistemologies, but both are also heir to alternatives that operate in a mode of haunting. Jean is bequeathed the Faro family property including several houses and the archaeological collection. He inherits land as property, but he remains haunted by the voice of his brother, calling him back to an embodied and imaginative relation with the land, an alternative legacy that is also his to claim. When Jean returns to Cape Town from London in 1996 to deal with the estate, he also must reckon with the ghost of his brother. He admits, "Even in London, Flin had never stopped speaking to him. In his solitary room, Jean had listened to the sounds of the mountains, continents away, humming with their dry electricity, calling with Flin's soft, husky voice."[48] In contrast to Beatrice who cannot make the ghost of her father speak, Jean cannot make the ghost of his brother stop speaking to him. Instead of a past that is neatly contained in an archive, put to rest in a specific place, Flin becomes present to Jean in Cape Town as well as in London, his voice and the sounds of the mountains animating the past, allowing Jean to experience sensory contact despite temporal and spatial distance. For Jean, returning to Cape Town provides an opportunity to confront this haunting, yet his return is not presented as an effort to retreat to an idealized past. As Mishuana Goemen argues in relation to indigenous mappings, "Re-mapping is not just about regaining that which was lost and returning to an original and pure point in history, but instead understanding the processes that have defined our current spatialities."[49] Narrating Jean's negotiation with the specter of Flin, Rose-Innes emphasizes the need to confront the processes that have defined the current spatialities of South Africa, including the repression and the discrediting of non-Western strategies of mapping as well as the persistence of this knowledge and its availability as a contemporary resource.

This knowledge that refuses to stay buried forces Jean to reckon with alternative ways to navigate and locate himself in time and space. Jean reveals that he had previously planned to return to the Cederberg "cleanly, objectively, properly, with a map and a compass and city clothes and hiking boots," but that he crumples up the map and discards it, realizing that "this is not the mountain he needed to explore... If he ever went back to look for Flin, he would have to find him with his nose, his eyes, his ears, sniffing the wind, listening for voices. The old way."[50] Jean contrasts his relationship with the topographical map that leaves him "looking down into the paper world as if from a great height" with his talent for embodied navigation: "he had always had a gift for direction, like a homing pigeon."[51] While Jean acknowledges a call to follow the Faro legacy and approach the mountains with map, compass, and city clothes to mediate, he also recognizes the distance this overseeing approach imposes between him and the land. At the same time, he remains aware that he has the capacity to relate to the land differently, allowing the play between all of his senses to draw him into contact with the land and close that distance. Presenting his directional abilities through comparison to a homing pigeon, Rose-Innes also encourages contemplation of the variety of methods of navigating and imaging landscapes that are denied the status of maps. This comparison extends consideration beyond marginalized human cartographic knowledge to register nonhuman navigation, confronting Western science with the limits of its own knowledge, as homing pigeons have vexed scientists who have struggled to understand how homing pigeons map their routes.[52] It also expands understanding of the process of homing; recognizing animal imaging as part of a relationship with the land and part of the process of relating to a specific place as a home, Rose-Innes demonstrates how mapping and homing could be understood as processes that reinscribe the human within a nonhuman community that shares similar practices, instead of being constructed as abilities that isolate the human.

Accepting this other way of knowing and navigating involves recovering a capacity for play. Just as Flin maintains a presence in Jean's life through haunting, play operates across the novel in a mode of haunting. It constitutes an epistemological alternative to the fixity of classification as in Derrida's theorization of the play of meaning, but Rose-Innes plays with play by associating it with childhood games and acts of imagination. She uses flashbacks to document the presence of this way of knowing throughout the lives of Ivy and Jean and to show how it needs to be revalued in their adult lives. During their childhood, imaginative play enables Jean and Ivy to create and inhabit alternative spaces, particularly in relationship to houses where they do not feel at home. The house is typically a place of comfort and safety, which as Vidler argues, is why the haunted house is so unsettling. As he notes, "The house provided an especially favored site for uncanny disturbances: its apparent domesticity, its residue of family history and nostalgia, its role as the last and most intimate shelter of private comfort sharpened by contrast the terror of invasion by alien spirits."[53] Rose-Innes reorients this generic motif, suggesting that for these orphaned children houses fail to provide safe, comfortable, or nostalgic space; instead houses dispossess them and disrupt their abilities to feel at home. Alien spirits do not terrorize them, but guide them, as voices and visions accompany them through their playful negotiations with the uncomfortable space of the house.[54]

Flashbacks juxtapose the uneasy inhabitance of Jean and Ivy's present, their discomfort and drifting between temporary housing, with their reactions to the Faro house as children. Jean confesses that "it was the only geography for which he had no instinctive feeling."[55] He and his brother deal with this unfamiliar space through a form of cartographic play. The narrator reports, "They were inventive—they had to be, seeing as they both had preternaturally precise senses of place and direction... Their first impulse in a new environment was to find nooks and crannies, to map out the territory and the safe spots within it."[56] Flin and Jean map space through physical interactions that reconfigure meanings, turning nooks and crannies into sanctuaries in an otherwise threatening territory, a move that confounds any facile equation of the house with safety by revealing the work of mapping and imagining that is required to make it safe. They extend their mapping out into the community, playing "a game of trespassing. They would set out into the night, in a given direction, heading straight through gardens, over walls and fences. Of course, that was before electric fences and guard dogs."[57] These acts of mapping are conducted as childhood games, but they activate a play of meanings as well, disrupting the borders of private property and evoking sociopolitical spatialities of South Africa through references to gardens, walls, and electrified fences which return attention to the physical and imaginative constructions required to support the illusion of the home as a place of security. Ivy's use of imaginative play is slightly different. When Ivy visits the Faro house as a child, she is frightened and uses play to create an alternate world. She becomes enthralled with a patterned carpet, as she regularly does at her great-aunt's house "plung[ing] with great concentration into imaginary worlds, peopling the spaces between the curling lines and flourishes... already she could see the patterns transforming into streets, houses, mountain ranges, rivers."[58] Instead of using mapping to claim the physical space in which she finds herself, Ivy plays with the markings on the carpet, using these signs to transport herself to a different space, reflecting ways that imagination can participate in construction of space beyond visible surfaces.

These scenes that associate mapping with imagination and childhood games hint at the ways that mapping, including imperial representations, hinges on imagination and the play of meaning. Cartographic discourses often downplay reliance on play and imagination, discrediting them as immature in contrast to the scientific qualities of mapping that they seek to elevate. Rose-Innes directs attention to these dynamics, showing how constructing imagination and play as irrational epistemologies serves as a discursive weapon, and she combats this figuration with her own construction of play that chronicles its value to adult characters, offering it as a viable alternative that can help to formulate more equitable models of inhabitance. Describing how the adult Ivy and Jean reconnect with the power imagination held in their childhood, Rose-Innes identifies imagination as a resource, a survival tool for the contemporary world.

A capacity for imaginative play with space and with the meaning of signs enables Ivy and Jean to move outdoors, beyond the confines of the house and the archive, and read the signs of the Cederberg in ways not available to Bernard or Beatrice Faro. Even when standing directly in front of them, Beatrice was blind to signs that Flin marked on the rocks, but Ivy shares with Jean an ability to see these signs, and they initiate her into a new way of relating to the land. Ivy's access to the signs also suggests that this cartographic language is more than just Jean's biological inheritance because he was birthed in the mountains; it is a strategy of reading and living with maps available to those who embrace the opportunity. With this depiction, Rose-Innes insists on classificatory and imaginative epistemologies as coexisting ways of knowing and relating to the land, as stories-so-far that have shaped the current spaces of South Africa and that can be used to shape different futures. She does not posit an essentialist picture of a return to an idealized past. In fact, by concentrating on the play of meanings, she suggests that there is no past to access if that means a single stable narrative such as that constructed by the archive; instead, she explores how individual interactions with signs can activate a relationship with an animate landscape in the present that includes the presence of ghosts. Depicting this knowledge as co-present and available to those who accept it, Rose-Innes challenges the current generation to negotiate with multiple legacies to figure out how they can be used to benefit all. While positing this inheritance as open to all conveys an admirable ideal, it also prompts me to return to Kim Scott's caution about sharing recovered knowledge to make sure that descendants of the group who created the knowledge maintain central roles in disseminating and benefiting from this knowledge.[59] Any specific human community or culture connected with this way of knowing is notably absent in Rose-Innes's story, left as part of the unreachable past that Jean can no longer remember. While the novel actively critiques tourist guidebooks that attempt to speak for the rock art and kitsch culture that incorporates the signs with no sensitivity to their historical meanings, the choice to make the culture that Flin and Jean came from unknowable creates a gap that runs a different kind of risk of decontextualizing knowledge and disempowering culture.

Rose-Innes focuses instead on the transformative impact of embracing this knowledge for Ivy and Jean in the present. For Ivy, reading Flin's map alters her way of seeing and understanding inhabitance. She reveals that as she follows Flin's signs, she feels accompanied by his presence, which she describes not as a frightening or threatening haunting, but as "playful."[60] This new strategy of reading does not require a total rejection of other ways of knowing; while she is following the signs in the mountains, she finds Bernard Faro's compass, which she later returns to Jean as a reminder of that part of his heritage. However, becoming attuned to the play of signs changes Ivy's view of the land: where once she had seen dead landscape, she now sees life. As the adult Ivy returns to the house in the Cederberg, she claims that the house "looked like home,"[61] but this understanding of home does not require the land to be her sole possession. Instead, she realizes "she was not alone. A single black ant had approached... suddenly she sensed around her, netting and infiltrating the landscape, a great antbeing, sensitive to the unique vibration of sugar; a being of a million parts, with a little emissary in every nook and cranny."[62] In contrast to Beatrice who maintains her blindness, Ivy experiences a shift in ways of knowing that allows her to respect the otherness of the ants, crediting them with their own ways of mapping and inhabiting the land.

The ability of play to resituate the human in relation to nonhuman others is further demonstrated when Jean returns to the Cederberg. Jean similarly begins to register the nonhuman presences that he once found threatening as inhabitants with their own forms of communication: "the ground wriggled with figures and signs, under his feet the worms and the beetles, the stir of wings above him in the sky, the tic-tic of little claws."63 Whereas Abram describes how alphabetic literacy distances humans from the signifying practices of nonhumans, Rose-Innes demonstrates how openness to the play of signs allows Jean and Ivy to register the marks of other animals as forms of language. This awareness refigures their sense of home and community. Jean had proposed a family tree in which his only connection was to his brother, no one else alongside him, but as the novel closes, he and Ivy learn to live together in the Cederberg, alongside the worms and beetles and ants, and alongside the rock art that connects them to the stones and to generations of previous human and nonhuman inhabitants. Instead of trying to speak for the rock art, Jean touches it, allowing for a play of sensations and meanings that enables him to feel connection with the distant creator of the sign and reconnect with the youthful version of himself who accepted the value of play.64 This connection advances his re-valuing of writing and reading practices; it contrasts with Ivy's discovery of a photocopy of Jean's hand from his childhood, a black and white replica that gives Ivy the impression of "pressing up against a window, trying to get out."65 The photocopy presents an exact visual image of the hand, but the arrested form deprives it of life, freezes it in time, while Jean's interaction with the handprint left in the mountains connects him to histories of human inhabitance and to the traces that other animal and nonhuman forces leave on the landscape, markings from animal tracks to river beds that record journeys and encounters.66

The novel closes with an image of Ivy's dream garden, an imaginative space that she had retreated to as a survival mechanism while she worked at the Faro Institute. The space is now vividly colored in contrast to the black and white of the Institute, and Ivy walks hand in hand with her brother, a ghostly figure that reveals to her "the secret alphabet that lies beneath" the visible surfaces of skin and stone.67 In a review of the novel, Michiel Heyns observes, "Together, she and Jean come to terms with the rock alphabet, the inarticulate language of inanimate things and animals, not as a Flin-like rejection of human pattern, but as a timeless basis that 'lies beneath' the 'human things.'"68 The framework of multispecies play I have been building leads me to a slightly different interpretation, suggesting not that Ivy and Jean discover a timeless, universal truth—the origin of all meaning before signs—beneath the surface of the human, but they discover how signs work in a mode of play and haunting to connect humans to a timeframe that exceeds the biological human lifespan, to register the voices of nonhuman others, and to affirm dependencies of life and death. Rose-Innes's use of images like the garden and handprints that reappear over time with differences also conveys that processes of change do not remain internal to the characters; they also manifest themselves through representation itself. The imagery externalizes a change in ways that characters experience the nonhuman world, so that ways of understanding connections between life and death and positioning the human in relationships of dependency on nonhuman others become comprehensible and transmissible through acts of representation and reading. In this way, she confirms that the ability to relate to maps differently relies on strategies of reading and representation, and she opens possibilities that developing and validating imaginative cartographic practices might enable humans to expand understandings of inhabitance. Representations that emphasize human interdependencies might then shape actions, enabling decisions about land use that take into account past, present, and future, and human and nonhuman residents.

Building an ecocritical canon of South African literature, Caminero-Santangelo examines texts such as Paton's *Cry, The Beloved Country*, Head's *When Rain Clouds Gather*, and Mda's *The Heart of Redness*, considering how these writers craft stories of cosmopolitans distancing themselves from "corrupt colonial modernity" to "establish a natural home in a rural place," and he finds that these writers "reiterate or risk reiterating colonial representations of local African communities needing leadership of European or Europeanized experts with knowledge, skill and sensibility necessary for understanding and protecting the land."[69] Rose-Innes engages with some of the same complexities that Caminero-Santangelo explores, and *The Rock Alphabet* productively extends the discussion by repositioning European knowledge, not suggesting that it could or should be entirely dismissed—it constitutes a heritage that is inextricably part of the story and practice of living with the land—but denying it a privileged position as expert by locating it as one legacy among others and reporting its damaging impacts as much as its benefits. As a story crafted by a white South African writer who has wrestled with ways her family's process of making a home contributed to the violent displacement of others, the narrative also serves to validate her inhabitance; it accommodates Rose-Innes's process of relating to the land of South Africa as home and reflects her own situated and partial perspective.[70] At the same time, it refuses to silence the ghosts of past violence; reinserting histories of inhabitance and mapping that are erased by other contemporary narratives such as the NGI's national cartographic history, the novel insists that multiple stories of inhabitance and multiple histories of violence continue to be part of the legacy that current residents inherit. These ghosts are conjured in Rose-Innes's novel to demand attention to the repression of ways of knowing, navigating, and mapping the land, but other ghosts remain at the edges of the story; silences linger around the cultures that produced and continue to nourish alternative knowledges. Locating the novel's engagement with mapping in relationship to a sample of other contemporary projects might further illuminate the value of rethinking relationships with maps and reinforce the need to support cultural recognition and community participation as vital components of environmental justice.

Representing Environmental Justice

Distribution of land, access to resources, and exposure to environmental threats continue to be inflected by race, gender, and class inequalities that are legacies of South Africa's imperial and apartheid past. However, focusing only on the level of distribution leaves the systems and relationships that produce injustice unchallenged, shuffling risks around rather than seeking to eradicate their causes. As Greg Ruiters contends, environmental justice discourse and activism hold potential to advance more comprehensive challenges that address "the production and prevention of injustice."[71] Ruiters chronicles a contraction of understandings of justice in the context of South Africa:

> In pre-democratic South Africa, the concept of justice was expansive. But since the negotiated political settlement in 1994, which largely preserved apartheid private property relations, this concept has gradually been reined in ... Ideals of deep changes in property and social relations developed in the African National Congress's Freedom Charter and Congress of South African Trade Unions' Workers' Charter are receding.[72]

Legal regulations and enforcement provide one avenue for environmental justice, but Ruiters suggests that more comprehensive work for justice requires radical changes to existing paradigms. Instead of working within frameworks of private property and legal rights that have the effect of "detemporaliz[ing]" justice and creating fixed, abstract standards, justice needs to be understood as a process that unfolds and adapts over time as it draws on local knowledges, identities, and experiences and seeks ways to build solidarity across communities.[73] Representations—from narrations of mapping to community mapping projects—have a vital role to play in making the temporal and spatial scales of justice comprehensible; they are equipped to mobilize local knowledge and experience and facilitate solidarity across scales to support a "much more broad definition of justice which includes conceptions of, and demands for, recognition, participation, and capabilities for both individuals and communities."[74]

Mapping might seem like an abstract site of intervention, but environmental justice scholars are experimenting with ways to use maps in the service of environmental activism. For example, Temper, del Bene, and Martinez-Alier describe their work developing the Environmental Justice Atlas, an interactive digital mapping project that invites scholars, activists, and community members to share information by annotating a world map with information about environmental resource conflicts. Explaining the motivations for the project, these scholars identify a need to go beyond individual case studies of conflicts in order to discern broader patterns and relationships between incidents; at the same time, they remain attentive to the need to respect the particularities of local situations and facilitate communication, especially inviting participation of those living with the conflicts.[75] As a result, the design of the map allows viewers to zoom in to learn about conflicts in specific communities and zoom out to see larger patterns— different kinds of conflicts (fossil fuel conflicts, water conflicts, biodiversity and conservation conflicts) correspond to color-coded dots on a world map. The ability to shift between scales addresses concerns raised by environmental scholars about visual tactics that make bigger patterns comprehensible by sacrificing the visibility of local interactions.[76] The EJ Atlas vividly illustrates the potential to live with maps differently: to use maps to demand attention to injustice, to document resistance, and to support community collaboration, creating a virtual space where the principles of environmental justice are enacted.[77]

Examples drawn from the recent history of Cape Town also illustrate how learning to live with maps differently might contribute to goals of radical environmental justice. For instance, District Six is a neighborhood of Cape Town that has become a symbol for apartheid-era dispossession, as the non-white residents were forcibly removed and their homes were demolished in accord with apartheid regulations. As of April 2018, twenty years since land restitution claims were filed after the dismantling of apartheid, 80 percent or 969 claimants have been ignored in planning for the return of land to displaced inhabitants, which has motivated some of the claimants to take legal action against the minister for Rural Development and Land Reform.[78] Running parallel to the legal action, the District Six Museum has played an influential role in preserving the memories of former inhabitants and facilitating the imagination of reinhabitance. Avoiding limitations of archives identified by scholars such as Derrida and Mbembe, this museum seeks to interact with the community and present a diversity of voices and experiences, rather than consolidating a homogenizing history. The museum's web page describes how it has cultivated "narrative and route development" as its central practice, telling the stories of human inhabitance and interactions with the land through guided walks, home visits, and presentations by local residents.[79] The museum, thus, makes exploring ways to live with maps differently part of its daily practice. It also addresses the challenges of attempting to preserve a history of violence through absence as well as presence. For instance, the Museum offers a tour that "meanders through destroyed and existing sites situated around the Museum," and constructs exhibits around a "large painted map in the central space" which manifests the physical space of the neighborhood, but which also invites visitors to bring it to life by inscribing their histories of inhabiting spaces, including spaces which no longer exist.[80] The curators explain:

> The space is a living one, dedicated to working with memory: in remembering the events of forced removals, in considering the varied impacts of apartheid legislation on the lives of people and in choosing to focus on historical experience and subjectivity as ways of creating community and shaping society. We believe that the work of remembrance, within the context of the present, has a continuing significance for all South Africans.[81]

The museum upholds the vital role for narrating, mapping, and navigating routes as methods of fighting for "human rights, urban justice and the creation of a more just and inclusive civil society."[82] The museum validates a role for imagination and representation, countering the idea that the work of remembering the past and planning the future belongs to experts. As Ruiters and others argue, relying on legal action alone to shape the future of the land allows the regimes of capital and private property to remain unchallenged as creators of injustice; the cartographic play encouraged by the museum offers an alternative framework for building community, incorporating local knowledge, and respecting diverse voices to confront temporal and spatial aspects of injustice and to build solidarity to design other futures.

Cape Town's Water Usage Map, deployed during the city's water crisis in 2018, provides another glimpse into ways that South Africans are living with maps, maybe not so differently. Whereas the District Six map seeks to create a living experience that involves the community in remembering and creating space together, the Water Usage Map was engineered by the City of Cape Town so that residents could visualize their water consumption. The map provides an overview of the city, and users can zoom in to the level of street addresses to view water consumption; properties that are within the range of the water guidelines are marked with a green dot. The city altered its plan to mark water wasters with a red dot in an effort to highlight the positive; a spokesperson for the mayor reported, "This behaviour-modification tool attempts to acknowledge good savers and encourage those who have yet to join the efforts."[83] While the visual design of the project resembles the Environmental Justice Atlas, the description of the map as a "behavior modification tool" reveals a crucial difference. This terminology reflects the power dynamics involved in knowledge creation: the city deployed the map to exert social pressure, a move which sparked controversy about privacy, about the accuracy of the water readings, and the ethics and potential dangers of turning neighbors against one another in the service of water conservation. While this mapping project articulated expressly environmental goals—to turn the map green and save water—it appeared to many Cape Town residents as an effort at surveillance. It failed to activate a transformative relationship with space because it was a vision imposed on, rather than created by, residents.

As part of broader efforts to live with maps differently, *The Rock Alphabet* demonstrates how representations can contribute to environmental justice advocacy. In *The Rock Alphabet* as in her larger body of work that includes stories such as "Homing" and "Poison" and novels such as *Nineveh* and *Green Lion*, Rose-Innes consistently reinforces a conviction that representations are more than abstractions that detract from the material world; they structure human relationships with nonhuman others and that does not diminish those relationships. Instead, acknowledging the role of representation allows for greater critical scrutiny of the representations that humans create and encourages reckoning with their effects, empowering us to take responsibility for ways that our imaginations and discourses impact human and nonhuman lives, in fact, challenging us to meaningful activism that rejects representations that comfort us with illusions of human superiority or separation. Rose-Innes initiates a valuable inquiry into ways of living with maps and inhabiting histories differently by creating a structure for her novel that allows multiple inheritances to make claims on readers; placing her novel alongside other mapping projects invites continued engagement with the possibilities for developing practices of mapping and interpretation that support inclusive understandings justice, and it reinforces the need to pay attention to the roles of participation and cultural recognition as we continue the process of making homes alongside all of the others that sustain us.

5

Life in the Graveyard: Architectures of Survival and Extinction in Arundhati Roy's *The Ministry of Utmost Happiness*

When you look at the pace at which our planet is being destroyed, then you could conclude, perhaps metaphorically, that we are all living in a graveyard of sorts, from whence we must plan our survival.
　　　　　　　　　　　　　　　Arundhati Roy, Interview with Ziya Us Salam

Haunting is part of our social world, and understanding it is essential for grasping the nature of our society and for changing it.
　　Avery Gordon, *Ghostly Matters: Haunting and the Sociological Imagination*

In her second novel, *The Ministry of Utmost Happiness*, Arundhati Roy stretches the form of the novel to include a vast range of characters, times, and places in order to account for the diverse scales and interactions that create contemporary conditions of environmental and social injustice. However, the reception of her novel demonstrates a version of the dilemma that Amitav Ghosh describes when he argues that genres that try to engage these scales run the risk of being excluded from what he terms "the mansion of serious fiction."[1] By trying to adapt the form of the novel to account for the complexity of the world in which she lives, Roy risks having her work disclaimed as a novel. Indeed, reviewers have struggled with the form of her narrative, with some outright questioning its categorization as a novel and others finding fault with its temporal sequencing, its shifts in narrative perspective, and its lack of psychological depth. For instance, one critic wonders: "Is novel the right word, though? I hesitate. *The Ministry of Utmost Happiness* [is a] hulking, sprawling story,"[2] while another considers the work "a curious beast: baggy, bewilderingly overpopulated with characters, frequently achronological."[3] The word "unwieldy" appears quite frequently in reviews that reflect on Roy's efforts to bring so many characters and narrative threads together, while the harshest reflection on her effort to encompass everything concludes: "This is a pretentious impossibility," a claim that the reviewer supports by suggesting that empathy is limited and this kind of vastness is simply "intolerable to our human frames."[4]

Roy has created a work that doesn't fit comfortably within established categories, and that clearly deters some readers, but it also seems that disrupting expectations is what Roy sets out to do. In her nonfiction writing including *Capitalism: A Ghost Story* and *Field Notes on Democracy: Listening to Grasshoppers*, she affirms the need to facilitate long-term thinking and break through the divisions that expert discourses create to keep issues of gender, religion, and caste; consideration of the needs of humans, plants, and animals; and interventions in politics, economics, or art separated from one another. She implicates capitalism and corruptions of democracy in conspiring to keep consequences and interdependencies out of awareness and in facilitating violence against a range of human and nonhuman others, and she heralds the possibility that artistic interventions such as novels and poetry might help to bring contemporary humans back in contact with consequences and connections that span categories. Talking with writer Viet Than Nguyen, Roy recognizes the novel as a form that is suited to help bring these links to awareness, and she offers an important modification to his question about her portrayal of intersections. He observes:

> There is a way in the novel in which you are trying to connect all these different aspects of life and politics in India, not just humans, not just people of different castes and backgrounds, or different political beliefs but also humans and the dead, humans and animals, humans and the environment, all of that. It's part of what makes *The Ministry of Utmost Happiness* a really powerful novel, because there's huge ambition in there to connect all these different things.[5]

Roy replies:

> The truth is you don't have to connect them; they are connected. I think increasingly that's the way people are trained, whether its academics or journalists, to mark off their field ... like if you specialize in environment you are not supposed to know anything about caste or whatever it is. Whereas novels, the power of novels is that they *do* connect.[6]

Here, Roy establishes that she is using the form of the novel to try to bring existing connections back into discourses that have tried to bury these links, and part of what I am suggesting is that critical approaches to her novel have a part to play in this process. Literary scholars could replicate the focus on categorization and isolation that Roy is critiquing by denying her work recognition as a novel or remaining focused on finding it a proper label, or we could explore how she provides an opportunity to think across constructed borders.

Pablo Mukherjee notes a similar pattern in responses to Roy's first novel, *The God of Small Things*, published twenty years previously; he chronicles the problem of critics who want to separate her literary work from her activism, social concerns from issues of the environment, and any politics from analysis of literary form, and he encourages critics to follow Roy in refusing these divisions. He contends, "A proper critical response to Roy's art must combine aesthetic, political/historical, and environmental approaches in such a way that these categories appear in their real, mutually interpenetrated condition."[7] My inquiry attempts to follow this advice, moving across borders of aesthetics and politics and linking the social and environmental, realizing that such analysis also runs the risk of unwieldiness, but accepting that risk as a part of a necessary reckoning with scales that we cannot afford to write off as beyond human comprehension. Instead, we can accept Roy's invitation and attempt to walk through the world that she offers, considering how her formal strategies are both aesthetic and political interventions; they are efforts to reclaim territory, physical and imaginative, which her discussion of her craft in terms of architecture reinforces.

While Roy defends her work's categorization as a novel, she offers the insight:

> It is not a story with a beginning, middle and an end, as much as a map of a city or a building... Because to me a story is like the map of a city or a map of a building, structured: the way you tell it, the way you enter it, exit it... None of it is simple, straightforward, time and chronology is like building material.[8]

Roy's comments provide a way of approaching the structure of her story, a framework for investigating how she uses chronology as building material and how she configures particular spaces as ways in and out of characters' lives. This chapter explores how Roy constructs her novel with multiple hubs that connect human and nonhuman lives across space and time as a way of countering the repression of the interdependence of life and death that is perpetuated by linear sequencing and the limited understanding of ethical responsibility that flows from notions of singular origins. It investigates how Roy merges form and content to make the consequences of narratives part of the story; she illustrates how the narrative separation of life and death leads to limited conceptions of community and responsibility, and she experiments with ways that validating their connection could facilitate solidarity across generations and species to support inclusive, thriving communities.

Beginnings v. Origins: Forms for Narrating Community

In a review of the novel, Ziya Us Salam adopts Roy's language of architecture, noting "she quietly laid, brick by brick, the structure of *The Ministry of Utmost Happiness*, a work so unconventional that it renders all norms obsolete."[9] While I agree that Roy's work is unconventional, I challenge the idea that it renders norms obsolete. Instead, I suggest Roy directly engages with conventions and refigures them to reinforce her point that language and narratives need to be reclaimed in order to allow for social and environmental justice.[10] Examining the entrances that Roy fashions for her narrative with the assistance of narratological insights about what it means to begin illuminates significant ways that Roy creates a spectral structure for her novel that serves to interrogate norms of existing literary and political discourses. In the opening pages of her novel, Roy foregrounds a mix of biological and cultural factors involved in the rapid decline of vulture populations in India, and she anchors this meditation on death and extinction in the space of a graveyard; the graveyard then becomes a key device for narrating interactions across times and spaces throughout the novel. She sequences the novel as a series of exits and returns, a strategy that presents death as a form of connection that orders the novel in terms of spectral returns, rather than simply inverting progressive chronology to make death a beginning rather than an end.

While Roy uses the graveyard as an entrance to her story, she also suggests that this entrance is not the only way in. She pluralizes possibilities for beginning, demanding attention to what it means to begin and calling attention to the ideological impacts of using human biological markers of birth and death as naturalized conventions of beginning and ending. In his work *Beginnings*, Edward Said distinguishes beginnings from origins, suggesting that the former indicates a process: "beginning is basically an activity which ultimately implies return and repetition rather than simple linear accomplishment... beginning and beginning again are historical, whereas origins are divine."[11] Similarly, in his contribution to Brian Richardson's edited collection *Narrative Beginnings: Theories and Practices*, one of the few other studies focused on beginnings, Niels Buch Leander distinguishes between starts and origins as aspects of beginning, associating starts with capacities for choice and change and origins with efforts to attribute causality, to provide an explanation that is also a kind of a resolution.[12] This distinction coincides with Said's sense that beginnings describe an activity that can involve effects radiating in multiple directions as well as the possibilities for return and beginning again, indicating potential for ongoing motion and change rather than a clear-cut end. On the other hand, origins suggest a fixed spatiotemporal point from which all events proceed, and also imply an end, a conclusion or goal reached that imposes closure.

These understandings of beginnings bear on Roy's novel, which I suggest offers multiple beginnings in order to illuminate ways that narrative plotting of origins can affirm restrictive notions of community and collaborate in obscuring ongoing connections and responsibilities by enforcing a predetermined end-point. By positing life and death as points rather than processes and by reinscribing boundaries between groups that define whose lives and deaths matter, narrative constructions of origins can reinforce ideological divisions. Undertaking a feminist analysis of beginnings in her work *Opening Acts*, Catherine Romagnolo notes ways that concepts of origins have been used in "master narratives of marriage, motherhood, nationhood, race and citizenship," to "provide the scaffolding for restrictive notions of social identity."[13] Roy's work offers an opportunity to contribute to such conversations about the ideological impact of narrative beginnings and to expand attention to the ways that they have been used to restrict notions of identity in relationship to nonhuman others. In her novel, Roy not only reveals the complicity of narrative origins in exclusionary constructions of identity and community; she forges an alternative spectral form that can accommodate biological and social processes that extend beyond the individual human lifespan. My analysis explores what Romagnolo terms the "discursive beginning" and Richardson calls "the beginning of the sujet,"[14] the opening passages of the novel, alongside the other kinds of beginning that Romagnolo identifies as "conceptual beginnings" or thematic treatment of beginnings and origins and "secondary discursive beginnings," openings of new sections of the text, arguing that Roy thematically and formally engages with beginnings as a way of confronting contemporary realities of interconnection.

For example, Roy's novel opens in the graveyard, but it also begins again about a hundred pages later with the discovery of a child in Jantar Mantar. Roy explains her understanding of this part of the book as another kind of beginning, in the sense that it sets events into motion:

> Though it's not the start of the book, the nerve center is this place in Delhi called Jantar Mantar, where all the ragged and beautiful resistance movements, all the dreamers and idlers and nutjobs and protesters, you know, gather... And from there, you know, the nerves of the novel spread out, because all of it is brought together in that place.[15]

Rather than limiting her storyworld with a single point of origin, Roy builds her novel around nerve centers, which resemble both the functioning of a biological body and the navigation of a human constructed city. In both cases, effects move through networks that extend in multiple directions at the same time. This configuration highlights movement and interaction, ways in and out of space and in and out of contact, as opposed to a linear organizing of bodies and spaces that relies on separation. The appearance within this space of a baby whose biological origins are unknown allows Roy to engage with expectations about origins, family, and belonging, setting these questions into motion and revisiting them throughout the novel.

Novelistic representations of origins, in both formal structure and content of novels, provide opportunities to confirm or challenge ideological constructions of birth and identity, which as Romagnolo highlights, have been used to reinforce restrictive notions of belonging. Exploring how literary texts construct origins, Said identifies a pattern of filiation in classical realist novels, explaining:

> The primordial discovery of a novel is that of self... In a novel such as *Tom Jones*, for example, the foundling is discovered immediately after birth, only to be rediscovered—and this is the function of the narrative—through a series of adventures that clarify the circumstances of that birth: he is given paternity.[16]

Biological birth is given meaning through a narrative that establishes paternity, the identity of the child in relation to the father. This process confirms the child as legal heir to property and cultural heir charged with maintaining traditions. Roy is not alone in expressing concerns that such constructions of origins can fuel dangerously exclusive senses of community. Development scholar Greg Ruiters points to ways that origins constitute an environmental justice concern when he writes, "justice and solidarity need to be synthesized if blind communitarianism with all its essentializing notions of identity and exclusions is to be avoided."[17] In the context of India, Roy has analyzed ways that nationalist discourse mobilizes ideas of origins and purity to generate support for "development," pointing out a rise of Hindu communalism and a tendency to target groups that don't share those origins. She also suggests that religious identity and notions of origins are being deployed in struggles that are more directly about political power and access to "mineral-rich lands that corporations have their eyes on and governments want vacated."[18] Examining the history of communal violence in Gujarat, Ashgar Ali Engineer makes a similar argument, contending: "It is not our case that religion played no role; it did. But this role was not fundamental... The real issue was share and control of political power."[19] Roy uses the space afforded by the novel and the capacity that it holds for connection to juxtapose different understandings of origins and reveal how the aesthetic and the political are implicated in one another.

The beginning instigated by the child found in Jantar Mantar allows Roy to interrogate the construction of origins in political discourse. She introduces new life in a space where activists are voicing their demands and imagining new futures, and she problematizes assumptions about where children and birth fit into visions of the future and narratives of justice. The scene of this infant's discovery occurs about a quarter of the way into the book, and it pointedly raises questions about the relationship between symbolic and biological motherhood as it shifts attention from paternal inheritance to the figure of the mother. The protestors that fill Jantar Mantar are mobilizing images of motherhood for various causes from the old man fasting "against a backdrop of a portrait of Mother India" that has the effect of "electrif[ying] Hindu chauvinists" and reviving "their controversial old war cry, *Vande Mataram*! Salute the Mother!"[20] The same square contains "The Association of Mothers of the Disappeared, whose sons had gone missing, in their thousands, in the war for freedom in Kashmir."[21] These women are not only deploying images of motherhood; they are using their own identity as mothers to give authority to their political demands. Despite the differences between groups, the ways that a focus on motherhood reinforces a limited notion of kinship become clear when a living baby appears: "The Mothers of the Disappeared did not know what to do with a baby that had Appeared. Especially not a *black* one/*Kruhun kaal*/Especially not a black *girl/Krhuhun kaal hish.*"[22] This child is a distinct individual, marked by race and gender, conveying the idea that these markers influence what kinds of future the child might have and what kinds of responsibility the crowd might accept for this life. While a generic mother is mobilized as a symbol for justice, a motherless child uncovers the boundaries of care. By the time the argument about what to do with the baby subsides, the child has disappeared, providing a thread to the next part of Roy's narrative that involves a shift in place and in central characters, as we leave Anjum, who has been the central character to this point, and instead follow the current life and past connections of Tilo, the woman who has taken the baby and who later returns to join Anjum as part of the cemetery community.

The found child serves as a connective device for the narrative and also reinforces thematic concerns about kinship, as the child forces attention beyond the metaphorical mother mobilized in political discourse to call attention to links between reproductive and social justice that shape material conditions of living. Michelle Murphy powerfully demonstrates how issues of reproduction are inextricably connected to other issues of justice:

> Reproductive justice politics stretches beyond babies, birth and bodies and out into struggles of survival that are not just personal survival, but struggles over what more-than-life relations might persist into the future for collectivities. It also asks what relations should be dismantled, refused, shunned? This extensive sense of reproductive relations thus includes policing and military violence, reserves and borders, heterosexuality and family, property and labor, land and water, and questions of redistribution of resources and life chances.[23]

It is this extensive scope of connections that Roy is attempting to make comprehensible through the spectral structure of her novel that uses apparitions as a way to disrupt the equation of biological birth with origins. By placing a raced, gendered infant body into a politically shaped material space, Roy demands consideration of how the child's life and death are tied to issues of military violence, family constructions, and access to resources, and the narrative that unfolds around the child brings all of these social elements into play. In *Seizing the Means of Reproduction*, Murphy contends, "Reproduction is not so much a 'thing' as an overdetermined and distributed process that divergently brings individual lives, kinship, laboratories, race, nations, biotechnology, time and affects into confluence."[24] The individual life of the baby, then, is relocated as a point of connection to other lives and systems, testifying to the dependencies that bring it into being, sustain it or oppress it, and otherwise ripple out from it.

Deploying a foundling as part of her narrative constitutes one way that Roy puts herself in relation to existing literary traditions and modifies those traditions. In her novel, the trajectory of the found child does not follow "a series of adventures that clarify the circumstances of that birth" as Said suggests of the classical realist novel. Instead, the child's story unfolds through a process of spectral returns that multiply her parents rather than identify a single origin. Derrida notes that specters work in the mode of repetition: "One cannot control its comings and goings because it *begins by coming back*."[25] Late in the novel, when the biological origins of the child found in Jantar Mantar are revealed, this story is added to her history; it does not override her other connections but registers a coming back of her biological mother who is then welcomed as another member of the community through a funeral ceremony. Discussing the gendered nature of beginnings, Susan Winnett notes that narrative patterns can impose separations between generations, as traditionally the mother is made to disappear at the start of the daughter's story; the death of the mother confers authority on the daughter to start her own story. In her essay "Maculate Reconceptions," Winnett analyzes texts that reconfigure this pattern, refusing to kill off the mother and instead illuminating the need to be able to look to both the past and the future in order to reconceive the mother–daughter story as one of relationship rather than succession.[26] Roy contributes to this reworking of narrative patterns, as the death of one mother marks not an end, but a return of part of the daughter's story; death does not preclude the biological mother from participating in the narrative of the daughter's life, yet at the same time the biological relationship does not negate the role of other mothers.

Instead of "clarify[ing] the circumstances of that birth" by restricting identity to biological inheritance, Roy uses the return of this mother's story to illustrate the idea that mothering involves reciprocal processes of becoming that span generations as well as biological and social interactions. As the residents of the graveyard listen to the story of the mother, each

> recognized, in their own separate ways, something of themselves and their own stories, their own Indo-Pak, in the story of the unknown, faraway woman who was no longer alive. It made them close ranks around Miss Jebeen the Second like a formation of trees, or adult elephants—an impenetrable fortress in which she, unlike her biological mother, would grow up protected and loved.[27]

The narrative of the biological mother is added to the network of connections that surround Miss Jebeen the Second, whose name memorializes the history of Tilo, the woman who took Miss Jebeen the Second from Jantar Mantar when she was a baby. The first Miss Jebeen was the biological daughter of Musa, a man that Tilo loved, and her name also brings the lives and the deaths of Musa's family in Kashmir into the community of the graveyard in Delhi. Contrary to exceptionalist narratives that use birth to signify origins that mark belonging to a specific group, this story celebrates the funeral of the mother as a kind of beginning that extends connections across difference. The residents are able to welcome an unknown, deceased woman into their family, and the connection moves not only across life and death, but also across species, as human solidarity is figured in relation to trees and elephants as other givers of love who come together to offer support. "Thus ended the funeral of Miss Jebeen the Second's first, second, or third mother, depending on your perspective,"[28] and that multiplicity and diversity in perspective is allowed to let be; the plurality of mothers is celebrated rather than disclaimed in order to impose a single point of origin that legitimates an exclusionary sense of belonging, and the child's name is adapted to Miss Udaya Jebeen, blending aspects of her heritage to reflect a continually growing sense of self. With her revision of the foundling narrative, Roy reveals how its traditional version collaborates in advancing an understanding of belonging that excludes nonbiological family members, as well as the nonliving and the nonhuman; she simultaneously shows how the found child narrative might be refigured with an ecospectral twist to support a more inclusive sense of community that I have been talking about throughout this study by drawing on Timothy Morton's formulation of solidarity, a form of community that extends across differences without requiring the dissolution of difference.[29]

Spatial and Spectral Building Blocks: Investigating Models of Community

In Roy's novel readers are confronted with multiple stories of individuals who are incorporated into communities in different ways, diversifying the novelistic plot of progress toward a confirmed identity rooted in paternity. Instead of a narrative that pursues a confirmation of individual identity, the multiple threads of Roy's novel echo one another as they intersect, introducing difference and creating juxtapositions that invite critical thinking about different models of community. While Miss Udaya Jebeen's story rewrites expectations about foundling narratives, she is not the only foundling in the novel. Earlier in the novel, Anjum finds a young girl, Zainab, at a mosque and takes this child home to her community of Hijras, where the child is raised by "more mothers (and, in a manner of speaking, fathers) than any child could hope for)."[30] In addition to incorporating the appearance of a child without known origins as a repeating pattern, Roy also displaces birth as a singular event; she narrates birth as multiple and not limited to biological becomings. In her novel, the entrance of infants into the world happens alongside Aftab's rebirth as Anjum, Dayachand's transformation to Saddam, the arrival of a dog who had been a nameless test subject, but becomes Biroo, a cherished member of a multispecies community that also includes goats, a horse, birds, and other dogs as well as the ghosts of humans, and vultures, and sparrows. These acts of remaking the self and re-placing self in relation to community confound ideas of singular origins that determine a life's trajectory or restrict membership in a group, showing how ideas of kinship can flourish beyond biological reproduction, and indeed implicating limited notions of family as contributing to violence and extinctions.

Following all of these beginnings exceeds the scope of this chapter, but focusing on the multiple beginnings in the life of Anjum can provide insight into how Roy uses entrances and exits from physical spaces to illustrate the role of narrative strategies in constructing cultural understandings of the relationship between an individual and a group. The novel opens with Anjum inhabiting the graveyard, and the following chapter returns to the scene of her biological birth as Aftab, disrupting chronological sequencing that moves in a line from birth to death and refusing the idea that a single beginning can determine the succession of events that follows. Introducing Anjum as an adult inhabiting the graveyard positions that mode of inhabitance as a touchstone, a point of contact and comparison with other spaces and models of belonging. As Anjum moves between a biological family home and a self-composed human community in the Khwabgah and the multigenerational, multispecies community of the graveyard, Roy interrogates different narratives of belonging and models of community and reveals how birth and death operate in terms of constituting membership in these communities.

After presenting the adult Anjum, the narrative begins again with her birth as Aftab, an intersex baby whose mother struggles to come to terms with a child who confounds her expectations about categories. Biology provides Aftab's membership in this family community, but the failure of his body to meet social expectations puts his membership at risk. Roy presents Aftab's parents' attempts to craft his body and identity to match cultural norms, depicting the family home as a space that demands conformity with established social categories as a condition of acceptance. While she uses space as a building block to place different times and perspectives into contact, Roy includes few details about the physical space of the family home, but elaborate details about the family tree: "Mulaqat Ali traced his family's lineage directly back to the Mongol Emperor Changez Khan through the emperor's second-born son, Chagatai"; he has a trunk full of documents to verify his claims and tells stories about the days when "his ancestors had ruled an empire."[31] Origins and an orientation to the past as a source of pride structure Mulaqat Ali's sense of identity.

The modern nuclear family home, according to feminist analyses of population discourses, has served as an emblem of safety and security. However, as these studies reveal, the home provides a space of protection for humans of certain races, classes, and genders, while excluding others and marking them as expendable. The home works in tandem with the wastelands that are disclaimed to maintain the illusion of the home as a safe space.[32] Roy illustrates and complicates this formulation by chronicling how the nuclear family becomes inhospitable to biological members who don't neatly fit into established social categories; the opposition between safe populations and expendable populations becomes muddied by acknowledging that biological kinship can fail to secure one's safety because biological kinship is also interpreted through cultural constructs. Mulaqat Ali's identity is deeply rooted in a sense of an exceptional ancestry, and in the present he seeks "a solution to what he saw as Aftab's affliction," through surgery and through "the cultural project of inculcating manliness in Aftab."[33] When he is fifteen, Aftab leaves home to move into the Khwabgah, a word that translates into House of Dreams, and his father never speaks to him again; the severing of this paternal tie is reported in epic and elliptical terms as "the misfortune that had befallen the dynasty of Changez Khan."[34] The Khwabgah houses a third-gender community, a collective of Hijras, and Aftab's movement is presented thus: "only a few hundred yards from where his family had lived for centuries, Aftab stepped through an ordinary doorway into another universe."[35] The genetic lineage of centuries provides one aspect of his inheritance, but it does not determine Aftab's present. He chooses to participate in constructing another kind of community where he can become Anjum, and the narration reinforces the idea that such alternatives exist as part of the real world. Aftab walks through an ordinary door, not a supernatural portal, underscoring that the choice to reject limiting models and embrace other kinds of kinship might require courage, but it does not require a breach with everyday reality.

The physical move from the family home to the Khwabgah marks a desire for other models of belonging. However, Roy also confronts ways that ideas about origins continue to influence understandings of belonging even in this community created around nonbiological kinship. In his analysis of beginnings, Said notes that changes in form reflect changes in ideology, and he suggests that a significant change in style and in thinking about self in relation to others is reflected in the shift from classical realist to modernist novels. Said contends, "Modernism was an aesthetic and ideological phenomenon that was a response to the crisis of what could be called *filiation*—linear, biologically grounded process, that which ties children to their parents—which produced the counter-crisis within modernism of affiliation, that is, those creeds, philosophies, and visions re-assembling the world in new non-familial ways."[36] Scholars have since attempted to complicate stark oppositions between realism and modernism, especially in relation to postcolonial writers who adopt strategies from multiple heritages; one such effort has led to the articulation of a concept of peripheral realisms that investigates "the world-system as partially, potentially describable in its concrete reality... via its local appearances or epiphenomenal effects."[37]

Nicholas Robinette pursues such possibilities in relationship to contemporary postcolonial novels, refusing a radical opposition between realism and modernism and positing that "a will to portray social totality and a capacity for literary experiment are ready allies in postcolonial literature."[38]

Roy's work fits with such thinking about forms that blend a desire to experiment in the interests of portraying social totality in the sense that these scholars derive from Lukacs, "with 'totality' defined not as something out there but as the demand to consider interrelations and interactions between disparate phenomena."[39] These models offer insight into Roy's strategies for representing the realities of contemporary India as she describes material conditions and interrogates how they are shaped by interactions between ideological models of belonging; she creates spaces within the novel that correspond to different models and experiences of belonging, but she does not present them as marking a linear progression with a model of filiation that belongs to one specific era that then becomes supplanted by a new model of affiliation. Instead, she engages the messy realities of interaction that include ways that aspects of filiation are retained in efforts to imagine other forms of belonging and ways that models of filiation and affiliation exist alongside one another. As she conducts this exploration, Roy shows how contemporary reality is not defined by a single version of belonging and how the novel form can accommodate interactions between different configurations of individuals and groups.

As she introduces readers to Anjum's new home, Roy attempts to reflect the diversity within this community, trying to avoid any simple stereotype of the Hijra:

> The world of the Khwabgah was just as complicated, if not more so, than the Duniya. The Hindus, Bulbul and Gudiya, had both been through the formal (extremely painful) religious castration ceremony in Bombay before they came to the Khwabgah. Bombay Silk and Heera would have liked to do the same, but they were Muslim and believed that Islam forbade them from altering their God-given gender, so they managed, somehow within those confines. Baby, like Razia, was a man who wanted to remain a man but be a woman in every other way. As for Ustad Kulsoom Bi, she said she disagreed with Bombay Silk and Heera's interpretation of Islam. She and Nimmo Gorakhpuri who belonged to different generations had had surgery.[40]

With this depiction, Roy represents an array of individuals who comprise the Hijra community and acknowledges gender's intersection with religion and generation; she reveals that this is not a homogenous community devoid of individual difference. At the same time, Roy scrutinizes ways that this community forms a sense of kinship around gender identity, investigating how this identity might also draw support from limiting ideas of social origins that reinforce other kinds of borders. For instance, the leader of the community is invested in curating a history of the community that insists on its distinctiveness and its endurance over time that echoes the nationalist discourses that Roy identifies as sources of dangerous division. Ustad Kulsoom Bi tells the group: "This house, this household, has an unbroken history that is as old as this broken city... Always remember, we are not just *any* Hijras from *any* place. We are the Hijras of Shahjahanabad... They're all gone now, those mighty emperors and their queens. But *we* are still here. Think about that and ask yourselves why that should be."[41] She reinforces a sense of communal identity and exceptionality that has allowed her group to survive while others have perished, revealing how recovering and documenting history validates the identity of this marginalized group, but at the cost of dividing it from other groups and figuring survival as a project of separation and competition rather than mutual thriving.

While Roy acknowledges the importance of recognizing the historical presence and endurance of marginalized groups in the face of overwhelming violence that includes silencing and erasure, she also seems to hint that practices of documenting this presence could participate in more radically refiguring the terms of belonging, rather than replicating the tactics of dominant discourses including those of national filiation. For example, Roy directly links the process of narrating the history of this community to other narratives of national history by having Ustad Kulsoom Bi confirm her lesson with a trip to the city's fort to listen to the official narrative which includes the "clearly audible, deep, distinct, rasping, coquettish giggle of a court eunuch" which the leader of the Khwabgah takes as evidence of a special provenance: "That is our ancestry, our history, our story. We were never commoners, you see, we were members of the staff of the Royal Palace."[42] This effort to identify origins and claim an inheritance will become refigured in the graveyard community that operates by pluralizing parentage and accepting those marginalized by mainstream society, but here Ustad Kulsoom Bi uses ancestry as evidence to support the claim that the Khwabgah deserves to survive while other groups have perished, a claim that she elaborates by identifying "principled living and iron discipline" as the key virtues of the Khwabgah, "its strength and the reason it had survived throughout the ages, while stronger, grander things had perished,"[43] a narrative that seems to suggest that they earned the right to survive while other did not merit continuance. While the Khwabgah community is formed around values of acceptance and consent, it simultaneously retains some of the divisive patterns of exceptionalist thinking. Devising a spectral structure that allows discourses to reverberate across communities and across time frames, Roy allows readers to consider the underlying role of narrative in constructing communities. She conveys the idea that narratives constitute both part of the problem and its solution: exclusionary models of filiation were not simply left behind as aesthetics and ideologies shifted; they continue to play roles in very direct and obvious ways as well as exerting more subtle influence and persisting through combination with other strategies. By orchestrating movement among multiple spaces and multiple forms of community, Roy highlights the continuing interaction between different models and the impacts that they have in shaping understandings of kinship that have consequences for conceptualizing survival and extinction.

The dangerous impacts of exclusive constructions of community are vividly illustrated when Anjum is assaulted by a mob in Gujarat. Anjum returns to the Khwabgah after experiencing an attack that mirrors the actual killing of Muslims that went on for several months in Gujarat in 2002;[44] her friend and travel companion is killed along with many others, and the only reason that she is not is because of superstitions attached to her Hijra identity, the fear by the attackers that they would incur bad luck if they harmed a Hijra. Anjum struggles with the idea that her individual life holds no value to the people who are willing to kill her friend, and it is only superstition that allows her life to be spared.

In her nonfiction writing about the killings in Gujarat, Roy insists on applying the term genocide, and she analyzes how such killings participate in nationalist plans for "Unity" and "Progress," goals that link a defense of Hindu identity to economic growth and prosperity. She illustrates how groups constructed as Other become acceptable targets for killing, as she documents how Babu Bajrangi, who she identifies as "one of the major lynchpins of the Gujarat genocide," claims: "We didn't spare a single Muslim shop, we set everything on fire, we set them on fire and killed them... hacked, burnt, set on fire... We believe in setting them on fire because these bastards don't want to be cremated, they're afraid of it."[45] This rhetoric makes no attempt to hide animosity, using the group identity of "Muslim" to mark both people and property, refusing any awareness of the value or distinctiveness of individual human lives, and certainly precluding any awareness of shared humanity. The justification for this violence traces back to limiting ideas of origins, and cultural differences are weaponized, using fire as a way to inflict death and prevent the practice of death rituals that serve as social markers of belonging in the Muslim community.

Ideas of superior origins and purity of group membership are implicated in genocidal killing, and Roy challenges readers to consider how this logic can be turned against a wide range of groups designated as Other. In her preface to the essays collected in *Field Notes*, she explains that as she compiled the essays for the book, she was horrified to see how some of her questions about the future had been answered in the time since the original publication. In the aftermath of the Gujarat killings, she had mused, "Can we expect an anniversary celebration next year? Or will there be someone else to hate by then? Alphabetically: Adivasis, Buddhists, Christians, Dalits, Parsis, Sikhs? Those who wear jeans or speak English or those who have thick lips or curly hair?"[46] Composing the preface in 2009, she recounts evidence of these groups becoming targets of violence. In this way, Roy illustrates that the problem extends beyond animosity to Muslims or any specific, single group. Mounting a related argument about the need for feminists to oppose all forms of oppression, including oppression against nonhuman animals, Susanne Kappeler argues that "compartmentalizing violence and oppressions according to their objects misleads us to focus on particular groups of the oppressed—(victim) identities that are created through that oppression. Instead, we need to look at the common factors of power."[47] She reaffirms the idea that if we accept categories created through oppression and leave each group to fight oppression on the terms of its own identity, we fail to confront the ways that patriarchal, capitalist, nationalist, and speciesist thinking intersect, and we fail to mount the overarching challenge necessary to disrupt these confluences of power. Kappeler contends that figurations of violence in terms of numbers is part of this pattern of thinking, with a focus on mass killings, mass rape, mass extinction preventing the full recognition of violence against any other as a problem:

> The very concept of "mass" is a signifier of speciesist thinking, which in the context of defining genocide becomes ethnicist or nationalist thinking, reflecting an international concern regarding the protection of ethnic species only: only once a people or ethnic community as a whole is seriously threatened in its numbers does it deserve our international protection—like a threatened animal species may incur our protection shortly before its extinction.[48]

Demanding attention to ways that discourses that seek to condemn violence can contribute to the erasure of the value of the individual, Kappeler raises additional questions about the consequences of understanding individuals in relationship to groups. In her fictional work, Roy uses the content and the form of her novel to experiment with different ways of representing relationships between individuals and community and challenge the erasure of distinctive individuals that make group identities both units of oppression and tools for conservation and protection, pointing the way to more radical revisions of community.

Kappeler observes that in dominant discourses of population, "Affirming the life of the collective entity means to affirm the instrumentalization of individuals as reproducers, sacrificing their lives and their right to life in the interest of the collective entity's survival."[49] Roy shows how such instrumentalization happens within constructions of family and nation in India in relationship to death as well as birth. For instance, in counterpoint with killing in the name of national purity, Roy depicts those who are willing to die for their community, as she narrates Musa's life in Kashmir, the paradise that has become a graveyard. Tilo reflects about Musa's sense of belonging that makes him willing to fight and die for Kashmir, "She had always loved that about him, the way that he belonged so completely to a people whom he loved and laughed at, complained about and swore at, but never separated himself from."[50] While this portrait offers her romanticized notion of his immersion in community because, as she admits, she has never felt such a connection, the novel also includes a starker look at the consequences of Musa's choices: "He knew that Kashmir had swallowed him and he was now part of its entrails... Thus began his life underground. A life that lasted precisely nine months—like a pregnancy. Except that in a manner of speaking at least, its consequence was the opposite of a pregnancy. It ended in a kind of death, instead of kind of life."[51] Musa's commitment emerges from his sense of connection to people and place, but results in his alienation, as he takes on a different name, avoids his family, and eventually loses his physical life in the struggle. He reflects directly on the costs of unifying in this way to fight for Kashmir: "we have to simplify ourselves, standardize ourselves, reduce ourselves... everyone has to think the same way, want the same thing... we have to do away with our complexities, our absurdities, our nuances."[52] Musa's fragmented thinking here leads him to conclude that this process of homogenization is necessary in order to fight for land and culture, but at the same time, it leads to annihilation of the individual who is sacrificed to this monolithic whole. By examining these varying contexts, Roy encourages a wide-ranging confrontation with the roles of birth and violent death in forging a sense of belonging and ways that individual identity is subsumed to a group, homogenizing individuals and making them expendable in contrast to models of solidarity that allow distinct individuals to connect across difference. As I turn to the space of the graveyard, I pursue the possibilities that Roy imagines

Rethinking Kinship from the Brink of Extinction

Roy contributes valuable insight to contemporary scholarly discussions of extinction and its cultural foundations by affirming that living deliberately along with death can create a sense of continuity and accountability between the human and the not yet or no longer living, while extinction is bound up with cultural and economic forces that ignore or seek to make less visible the interdependence of life and death. While the space of Jantar Mantar and the event of finding a child serve as the nerve center of the novel, the graveyard brings multiple temporalities and perspectives into contact and allows alternative stories of community and kinship to unfold. As a range of characters inhabit the space, the graveyard becomes "no longer a derelict place for the forgotten dead," but a space that "held open the doors between worlds (illegally, just a crack) so that the souls of the present and the departed could mingle, just like guests at the same party."[53] This line distills a key element of Roy's approach: instead of presenting the graveyard as a gothic space of horrors that disrupts the comforts of home by manifesting the violence of the past, Roy cultivates it as a home that welcomes guests human and nonhuman, living and no longer living. These guests share spaces of death and exclusion, but use them to communicate across borders of religion, caste, gender, and species. In this sense, the graveyard becomes a physical and conceptual space from which humans can plot not only survival, but a future of mutual flourishing. As Roy notes in the epigraph for this chapter, contemporary humans are all living in a graveyard of sorts, a metaphor that frames reckoning with interdependencies as a survival project and highlights how a continuing refusal to confront these links paves the path to extinction, which Roy carefully distinguishes from individual death.

While Roy acknowledges that the graveyard serves as an apt metaphor for our current state of environmental precarity and mass extinctions, she is also quick to point out that her depiction of graveyards does not constitute magical realism. Citizens of Delhi really do live in graveyards and life and death really are connected. The fact that this is not more widely recognized as reality does not make her work magically real; it demands attention to why these aspects of reality are denied, by whom, and for what purposes. Sociologist Avery Gordon proposes, "Haunting is part of our social world, and understanding it is essential for grasping the nature of our society and for changing it."⁵⁴ Gordon clarifies that hauntings are created by social violences that have not been recognized as such, so they resurface across time to demand attention. Roy engages with the realities of life in the graveyard as a way of bringing social violences to awareness, bringing ghosts to presence so that they can help living humans challenge injustices and transform society. As readers and critics, we can help these ghosts make demands on the present only if we don't dismiss her representations as magic, if we don't accept discourses that disconnect the lives and deaths of nonhumans and humans as definitive of reality.

So what is the reality of graveyards in India? And why would Roy use graveyards as ways in and out of her characters' lives? Beyond their symbolic resonance, they manifest conditions of living and dying and ways that these processes include a wide range of material and cultural practices. The graveyard serves as a point of entry to the novel, with the first line of the first chapter announcing, "She lived in the graveyard like a tree."⁵⁵ But before the novel opens with this human presence, Roy includes a short preface in which human presence appears only through the traces it has left on the nonhuman. The scene opens at a transitional time, "when the sun has gone but the light has not" and when animals are coming and going; the flying foxes are departing for the evening, while the crows are coming "home."⁵⁶ The description includes movement and sound and life, but it also registers absence and silence "left by the sparrows that have gone missing, and the old white-backed vultures, custodians of the dead for more than a hundred million years, that have been wiped out."⁵⁷ The passage marks the absence of these birds, despite other activity and other presence, and it uses language that suggests causation. The vultures have not simply died; they have been wiped out. They have been poisoned by diclofenac, a medication administered to relieve pain in aging cows or increase milk production.⁵⁸ When the vultures attempted to carry out the function of incorporating death back into life that they have been performing for centuries, they were poisoned. Roy uses a long sentence with a string of clauses to link steps in wiping out the vultures to ordinary citizens and daily behaviors that typically go unscrutinized: "As cattle turned into better dairy machines, as the city ate more ice cream, butterscotch-crunch, nutty-buddy, and chocolate-chip, as it drank more mango milkshake, vultures necks began to droop as though they were tired and simply couldn't stay awake."⁵⁹ While the steps in the process, especially the ice cream, may seem benign or even desirable, linking them together reveals suppressed connections and responsibilities, at the same time that it enacts a rhythm of accumulation in which one step gets left behind as we move to the next. In fact, the passage ends by registering the efficiency of capitalist discourses that conspire to maintain the invisibility of consequences that accrue over time: "Not many noticed the passage of the friendly old birds. There was so much else to look forward to."[60] Capitalist temporalities that promise future progress and prosperity direct vision away from immediate and past consequences, burying awareness of the vulture's absence or the consequences of this loss.

Roy directs attention back to this erasure to register ways that discourses that distract humans from consequences of loss constitute and perpetuate social violences that participate in processes of extinction. While the loss of vultures goes largely unnoticed, its absence exerts effects throughout the community. Thom Van Dooren studies connections among humans, vultures, and other animals in India in terms of biological and cultural functions. He explores how vultures serve a vital role ecologically, as they scavenge animal bodies more quickly and thoroughly than other predators, preventing the spread of disease, but he also includes attention to cultural issues that allowed vultures to thrive, such as "Hindu reverence for cattle" which positioned vultures as "a free and efficient means of carcass disposal for the millions of cows that they kept but did not eat,"[61] and religious associations ranging from the mythical Hindu vulture king, Jatayu, to the Parsee practice of "lay[ing] out their dead to be consumed by vultures in dakhmas (towers of silence)"[62] that made vultures vital parts of human stories and death rituals. Based on his attention to the imbrication of vultures in biological and cultural processes, van Dooren concludes:

> When vultures no longer inhabit the places and take up the relationships that they once did, the connectivities that make life possible in these places are unmade ... all those whose lives and well-being are entangled with vultures are drawn into a process of intensified suffering and death ... poorer nations, and, in particular, poorer communities within them are more readily exposed to harm.[63]

Thus, what seems like an isolated loss of a bird species circulates uneven impacts across human and nonhuman communities. By using the absence of vultures and the lack of attention their extinction has generated as a way in to the novel and in to the graveyard, Roy activates this range of associations and responsibilities that join beings across life and death. Looking at the network of consequences that lead to extinctions and that radiate out from extinctions, van Dooren argues that extinctions are "a far more diffuse and complex phenomenon" than the moment of death of a last individual; they involve "a prolonged and ongoing process of change and loss that occurs across multiple registers and in multiple forms."[64] Roy's novel opens, then, not only with entrance into the space of the graveyard, but with entrance into thinking about long-term processes of living and dying as part of the social totality that literature can attempt to describe.

This opening also specifically points to the role of capitalism in structuring temporalities and habits of vision that lead to extinctions. In his work on extinction, Ashley Dawson conceptualizes extinction as "the leading edge of contemporary capitalism's contradictions," suggesting capitalism's relentless expansion is responsible for the current rate of extinctions, while these extinctions also pose an underacknowledged threat to the growth of capitalism itself.[65] Similar to theories that contest the label Anthropocene and offer the concept of Capitalocene in its place, Dawson's formulation serves to place the blame for destruction on capitalism, a specific economic and social order, rather than figuring human nature as innately destructive. Such a move acknowledges the differential positioning of humans within capitalist systems, registering that not all humans contribute to destruction in the same ways or at the same rate, and it also enables the insight that as a human-constructed order rather than an inescapable aspect of human nature, the cause of the problem can be addressed.[66] Roy's linking of consequences and even the rhythm of her sentences communicate a similar interest in making the role of capitalism in contemporary extinctions comprehensible and in marking differences in deaths that lead back to life and those that lead to extinctions. Deborah Bird Rose offers the concept of "double death" to address this difference. She explains that in ecological and evolutionary contexts, life and death are interdependent processes in which the death of some bodies nourishes other species and other generations. However, in double death, this balance is disrupted. Rose contends that "contemporary man-made mass extinctions are an amplification of double death: the irreparable loss not only of the living but of the multiplicity of forms of life and of the capacity of evolutionary processes to regenerate life."[67] The opening description of the wiping out of vultures identifies capitalism as a cause of double death, a cause of the dissociations between processes of life and death, that Roy attempts to counter.

She proceeds to use the space of the graveyard to investigate the roles of capitalism and corruptions of democracy in fostering disconnections and limited notions of community and responsibility and to explore how choosing to dwell with ghosts might help to reconnect processes of life and death. The graveyard offers a specific configuration of time and space that reflects aspects of social and environmental injustices in contemporary India. For instance, the issue of allotting land for cemeteries is a controversial one in India's growing cities, where available land is shrinking and burial is figured alternately as an endangered right for those practicing minority religions (Muslims comprise approximately 13 percent of the population of Delhi while Christians constitute around 1 percent) or as a frivolous practice that should be ended to allow for other uses of the land.⁶⁸ Roy explains her understanding that "a cemetery or a graveyard in India is usually a Muslim graveyard. As you know, the Hindus don't bury their dead—they cremate their dead," and this difference in death rituals becomes implicated in larger social conflicts, as Roy continues, "Muslims have been pushed to the bottom of the economic and social chain, you know? They are now denied housing. They've been pushed out of the political arena. They are, you know, lynched on the streets—now openly, and so on. And so graveyards have become a kind of ghetto, you know, where people congregate."⁶⁹ Graveyards in the daily reality of Delhi are socially and politically contested ground.

Similarly, within the novel, Roy uses the graveyard to confront ways that populations that are excluded in life are also being excluded in death. She chronicles the experiences of bodies that are rejected for bathing and burial because of social judgments and narrates the construction of the Jannat Guest House that combines space for the living with services for these disclaimed dead. When we first meet the character of Saddam, he is introduced as a young man who works in the mortuaries because:

> The Hindu doctors who were required to conduct post-mortems thought of themselves as upper caste and would not touch dead bodies for fear of being polluted. The men who actually handled the cadavers and performed the post-mortems were employed as cleaners and belonged to a caste of sweepers and leatherworkers who used to be called Chamars... Saddam was the only Muslim among the cleaners who worked in the mortuary.⁷⁰

We later learn that Saddam has reinvented himself as a Muslim to suppress the trauma of his past in which he was "born into a family of Chamars... This is what our people did... when cows died, upper-caste farmers would call us to collect the carcasses—because they couldn't pollute themselves by touching them."⁷¹ During a routine trip to dispose of a dead cow, Saddam (who at that point in his life was Dayachand) and his father encounter a police officer who asks for triple the fee he is usually paid for each cow, and when they can't pay, he accuses Dayachand's father and his friends of killing the cow. When an angry crowd storms the police station, he allows the mob to take the men and beat them to death while Dayachand watches on the sidelines.⁷² Saddam's story draws powerful connections between social traditions that make working with death the responsibility of lower castes and corruptions of law and democracy that allow mobs to channel their rage onto social others through acts of physical violence. The incident surfaces as a flashback, adding context to his current presence in the graveyard and his willingness to care for the bodies of the rejected dead.

The events that brought Anjum to the graveyard are similarly experiences of traumatic violence, but they are revealed in a slightly more extended fashion. The narration returns readers to the scene of Anjum's birth and youth, but duration is manipulated so that readers dwell briefly with Anjum's mother as she passes through seven different reactions to her intersex baby and then speeds up as summaries fill in the early years of Aftab's life with a few specific scenes from various stages of his growth. Aftab's life until he turns fifteen and leaves home for the Khwabgah is compressed into just a few pages; life in the Khwabgah as Anjum is recounted in greater detail, with more specific scenes and dialogue that allow readers to inhabit key moments, but again, these moments are selected from over a span of years, ranging from a description of Anjum's eighteenth birthday party to the events that lead to Anjum leaving this home, "Anjum lived in the Khwabgah with her patched-together body and her partially realized dreams for more than thirty years. She was forty-six when she announced that she wanted to leave."[73]

In the graveyard, scenes unfold at a slower pace, creating a rhythm that allows Roy to affirm life and death as part of processes that implicate individuals in the lives of others across generations and species. Manipulating order and duration, Roy choreographs interactions among multiple models of belonging without evoking stages of development. While the narratives of the family home and the Khwabgah reveal restrictions in models of community that encourage Anjum to seek other options, the narrative of the graveyard also shows that models of filiation continue to play a part in this new imagining of kinship. Anjum has not disavowed connection with her biological family; she includes their ghosts, recognizing the presence of and recounting stories about her father and grandparents, her sister, and the midwife who delivered her. She literally constructs her home around this family, building rooms around their graves and telling their stories so that they become part of the community.[74] The difference is she uses these stories as opportunities to connect to rather than exclude others, interacting with multiple pasts rather than constructing a single lineage.

Relating to the ghosts of her family members and incorporating them into her life also allows her to deal with the specter of the violence that has driven her to the graveyard. While she is unable to speak about the violence that she experienced in Gujarat when she returns to the Khwabgah, the details emerge as haunting her when she first arrives at the graveyard. With language that echoes her arrival at the Khwabgah, Roy uses spatial movement to indicate a change in relationship between self and others: "Only a ten minute tempo ride from the Khwabgah, once again Anjum entered another world."[75] Her passage into another world allows the ghosts of the experience to visit, and Anjum undertakes a process of learning how to live with them:

> The saffron men sheathed their swords, laid down their tridents and returned meekly to their working lives, answering bells, obeying orders, beating their wives and biding their time until their next bloody outing... Only Zakir Mian, neatly folded, would not go away. But in time, instead of following her around, he moved in with her and became a constant but undemanding companion.[76]

The Hindu perpetrators of the attack, the saffron men, go back to their ordinary lives of violence, but her friend, Zakir Mian, does not need to leave her and be exorcised from her memory. With the time and space that the graveyard allows, he becomes one of Anjum's many companions. This interaction reveals a different way of living with the past than Anjum had experienced in the family home or in the Khwabgah, where the past was kept separate from the present and used as a source of pride to anchor a collective identity.[77]

Anjum's loss and alienation bring her to the graveyard, but her openness to living with ghosts allows her to use her position on the edges of society to create new forms of community that challenge exclusions imposed in the name of the democratic, capitalist Indian nation. She initially wants to forget the violence that she has experienced, to unknow it, but by learning to live with it, she allows it to create the possibility for solidarity that extends beyond biological family or even beyond the self-chosen family of the Khwabgah. This community reaches out to include the dead as well as the living, and animals as well as humans. Anjum builds a mode of "living with" that accommodates the specters of violence she has personally experienced, but her openness to otherness also leads her to accept those like Saddam who are living, but outcast, alongside the outcast dead, like Rubina, a prostitute who is refused funeral services because of the address listed on her death certificate, alongside the discarded nonhuman, such as Biroo, "a beagle who had either escaped from our outlived his purpose in a pharmaceutical testing lab."[78] The graveyard serves as a spatial and temporal hub for connecting the living and the dead and forging a community that literally comes to thrive as a garden and a funeral parlor, a paradise where processes of death and life nourish one another.

The multitude of characters and the movement between their stories can feel overwhelming at times. As the novel draws to a close, Roy continues shifting and blending temporal, spatial, and species scales, moving from "the one-thousand-year-old city" reflected in a puddle of Miss Udaya Jebeen's urine to the labor of Guih Kyom the dung beetle, waiting on his back "to save the world in case the heavens fell."[79] This movement illuminates the diverse scales of interdependencies that impact living and dying, memorializing the past and planning the future. As opposed to a narrative of survival that points to distinguished origins and justifies the exceptional status of one community that deserves access to land or resources, that deserves to thrive while remaining screened from the consequences that this thriving imposes on human and nonhuman others, Roy's narrative uses marginalized status to call attention to the damage done by capitalist and nationalist narratives and the exclusions that they foster. While her work associates restrictive notions of origins with dangerously limited notions of community, it also plots multiple beginnings to depict ways that choices about where we begin a story could recalibrate understandings of belonging and responsibility, allowing for thinking about futures that go beyond limited survival to imagine the flourishing of multigenerational, multispecies communities.

This unwieldly assembly ultimately leads back to Roy's activism and work for social and environmental justice. In *Capitalism*, Roy critiques ways that capitalist narratives reduce the concept of justice and ways that NGOs divide life into separate sets of issues all "hermetically sealed into their own silos,"[80] and she contends that resistance movements can help to imagine alternatives that reclaim ideals of justice and equality. Her fiction contributes to this project by rejecting the division of issues into neatly packaged categories and emphasizing that comprehensive justice requires devising methods of listening to the voices of a diverse array of others. Her novel attempts to create space for this range of voices and perspectives, but it also invites further critical thinking about how readers might react to strategies that transform familiar aspects of the novel in order to hold open the door for other voices and make multiple scales comprehensible.

Such thinking about forms of storytelling that support environmental justice can certainly benefit from including the insights of scholars who have turned attention to narrative beginnings, insights that might be adapted and enriched by thinking about consequences not only for understanding human identity, but also for understanding human relationships with the more than human world. Taking a cognitive approach to beginnings, Patrick Colm Hogan highlights beginnings as narrative *choices* that carry consequences for understanding cause and effect and assigning responsibility, particularly through the ways they condition the emotional and moral responses of readers. He argues that the human emotion system "leads us to think of causal sequences in terms of stories, not in terms of the complex, interacting systems of natural science.... The result of this is an inclination toward the projection of singular and absolute origins."[81] Hogan points out that stories with singular and absolute origins can obscure the complex causes of events in ways that have vital consequences for responding to those events, and he elaborates that because the emotion system predisposes humans to think in terms of stories, logical explanations that seek to offer more complex arguments about cause and effect tend to fail. His focus is on narratives of war, and he concludes his discussion by observing that "responses to war propaganda may be effective when they offer an alternative story but tend to be ineffective when they try to undermine the story form itself."[82] His work affirms the emphasis on stories found across much environmental scholarship, but it also offers more specific attention to forms and effects of narrative devices; ecocritics might productively extend such thinking to environmental narratives to explore how the strategies used to start stories of environmental injustice carry consequences for human understanding of causes and effects, how to assign responsibility, and what actions to take in response to current conditions. His work also illuminates Roy's sense that her nonfiction essays can offer logical reasons why capitalist narratives of development enforce dangerous divisions, but literary fiction can offer readers a different story that allows dependencies across generations and species to appear as part of contemporary reality. But it also opens additional questions: human emotion systems may condition us to want simple stories with clear-cut causes and effects that identify singular villains, but as Roy insists such stories are inadequate for effectively addressing the multiple, dispersed, and systemic causes and effects of environmental threats. Roy and the other artists in this study reconfigure genre conventions and stretch the novel to meet the challenges of representing the scales over which environmental threats unfold, refuting the idea that novels are not suited to address environmental challenges, but approaching Roy's strategies with Hogan's research in mind raises questions about the impact that these new forms might have on readers, questions that might be productively elucidated by continuing conversation with the field of cognitive narratology.

As the end of my study looms, I want to emphasize the potential for such continuing conversations. Throughout, I have been contending that specters serve as one specific narrative device that can help to make complex scales and ethical responsibilities tangible, while still immersing readers in stories that provide recognizable human characters and contexts. However, that is clearly not the end of the story. This chapter with its emphasis on beginnings underscores the value of attending to narrative choices about points of entry and exit that might productively illuminate scholarly endeavors as well. I offer the concept of ecospectrality and the readings of these select novels as one way to further open discussions about environmental justice, identifying spectrality as a way in that has potential to shift how we understand cause and effect and responsibility, and a way in that invites ongoing entries and exits that extend beyond the bounds of this study. By choosing Anglophone texts a starting point, I have tried to illustrate how the writers and experiences included in our critical discussions have profound consequences for thinking about environmental futures; for instance, formulations of the Anthropocene that rely on universal claims about the human continue to obscure histories of violent exploitation and repression as well as presents marked by vastly different material experiences and epistemological resources. Starting with the specters of Anglophone literature makes different ways of thinking about relationship and accountability, and thus different ways of thinking about justice, possible.

Conclusion: Plotting Just Futures in the Company of Ghosts

Ghosts reach out from the pages of Anglophone novels not only to demand attention to past violence, but also to guide thinking about equitable futures. *Ecospectrality* encourages greater attention to these ghosts, contending that the figure of the ghost and the variety of spectral narrative practices that writers cultivate provide powerful resources for representing the scales of contemporary environmental challenges, while they also facilitate understandings of distinctiveness and dependencies in ways that counter Anthropocene formulations that rely on a generic, bounded human. Throughout the study, I have been emphasizing that ecospectral texts deploy hauntings not in an effort to impose resolution on the past, but to reveal how the past can inform and motivate future action. As I bring the study to a close, I want to take a chance to reflect more directly on the kinds of futures that spectral narratives might help humans to plot.

While the ability of stories to help humans understand and respond to environmental inequalities has been widely recognized by scholars, environmental educators, and activists, thinkers also raise vital questions about the kinds of futures environmentalist stories can help us to imagine. For instance, Ursula Heise inquires:

> What affirmative visions of the future can the environmentalist movement offer, visions that are neither returns to an imagined pastoral past nor nightmares of future devastation meant to serve as "cautionary tales"? What new ways of conceptualizing the relationships between humans and nonhuman species might an environmentalist perspective rely on, beyond saving nature only as a resource for humans or, conversely, privileging nature to the point where human aspirations become secondary?[1]

Heise wonders how environmentalists might cultivate futures that avoid separations and simplifications that pit idealized pasts against apocalyptic futures. She encourages us to consider: what kinds of stories might motivate people to act to shape equitable futures and communities where humans and nonhumans can thrive together?

Questions about the kinds of futures we can imagine intersect with concerns about the narrative forms that might be capable of conveying these futures. Writers like Amitav Ghosh have expressed passionate commitment that fiction does have a vital role to play: "the great, irreplaceable potentiality of fiction is that it makes possible the imagining of possibilities... to think about the world only as it is amounts to a formula for collective suicide. We need, rather, to envision what it might be."[2] However, Ghosh remains dubious about the novel's ability to accommodate the scales of environmental conditions and raises concerns that the genres that have been most engaged in portraying environmental futures operate by separating that future from other time frames. He laments that climate fiction is

> made up of disaster stories set in the future, and that, to me, is exactly the rub. The future is but one aspect of the Anthropocene: this era also includes the recent past, and, most significantly, the present... The Anthropocene resists science fiction: it is precisely not an imagined "other" world apart from ours; nor is it located in another "time" or another "dimension."[3]

In response to these concerns about how to imagine environmentally just futures, *Ecospectrality* points to the potential of hauntings to transform the terrain of the novel and anchor visions of the future in relationship to the past and the present.

To help illustrate how the spectral innovations of Anglophone writers circulate environmentalist visions of the future, I would like to bring one more novel into my discussion. Alexis Wright's *The Swan Book* imagines a future shaped by climate change disaster, but it locates this destruction in relation to the colonization of Australia, the displacement of Indigenous people, and the discrediting of Indigenous conceptions of relationship with the land. Doing so, it suggests that contemporary stories of environmental annihilation are manifestations of the same capitalist logic of separation and domination that enabled British colonial conquest in centuries past, revealing how consequences resonate across past and present and indicating a need for radical transformation in conceptions and practices if we expect different results in the future. This strategy addresses Ghosh's concerns about representations that detach future from present and past, and it also shifts the terms of Heise's discussion of the future in several important ways. Wright's novel locates the violent repression of

Indigenous ways of knowing as part of the cause of contemporary environmental devastation, so that instead of offering "new" ways of conceptualizing human relationship with the nonhuman, it demands accountability for and shows the consequences of destruction of existing ways of knowing that could serve as resources. It takes away the possibility of imagining a return to an idyllic past, but allows awareness of continuity to emerge by putting a violent colonial past into contact with present and imagined future conditions of drought and devastation to create a vision of the future that is more than a nightmare cautionary tale: it is complex and contradictory, like the past and present from which it builds.

Wright's portrait of the future comments just as powerfully on the past and the present by showing how despite narratives that code time-spaces as idyllic or apocalyptic, hope and hopelessness coexist. After closing her tale with dismal images of dying swans, she adds an epilogue that leaves open the possibility that they might return to this place someday, facilitated by acts of love from other species, as the central human character Oblivia cares for and carries a surviving swan, Stranger. However, refiguring the relationship between humans and other species, the novel does not portray humans as exclusively responsible for saving other species; it imagines other animals as preserving and reconfiguring aspects of the human as well. The epilogue ventures a present in which myna birds "swear at the grass in throwback words of the traditional language for the country that was no longer spoken by any living human being on the Earth,"[4] as well as a future in which myna birds will also preserve the last scraps of the English language, and all that will be left is the denial, "Not true."[5] It moves across temporal scales with humans, nonhumans, and the ghost of the drought woman who "lived in the dry country for several thousands of years," and it mixes moments of despair in which Oblivia does not want the burden of carrying the swan and "t[ells] him straight in the eye to give up" with moments of recognition that to carry a swan "to this ground where its story once lived. Well! Talk about acts of love."[6] This ending credits humans and nonhumans with stories, language, connections to home, and abilities to adapt to changing conditions without elevating the preservation of specific individuals, cultures, or species. Such a move does not invert the binary and privilege nature by subordinating the human; rather, it imagines shared conditions that locate the human alongside other beings. Using the colonial history of Australia as an analog, the novel creates a future in which hope and love persist alongside acts of exploitation and violence. In this way, Wright offers a reformulation of the relationship of the human and the nonhuman that highlights shared vulnerabilities, so that human decisions do matter, but the human is displaced as the one species that can know and control a future that includes coexisting possibilities of choosing to love others across boundaries of species and generation and denying kinship and ignoring the call of the other. Wright's view of the future, then, is empowering because instead of offering a fantasy of salvation or an unavoidable apocalypse that removes the need for human action, it affirms that the future resembles the present in that it contains multiple potential outcomes that can be impacted by human choices, and it confronts readers with the consequences of those choices.

Refusing to detach imaginations of the future from pasts of material and epistemological violence, Wright and other Anglophone writers are positioned to transform understandings of contemporary environmental injustices. In *Culture and Imperialism*, Edward Said asks, "Are there ways we can reconceive the imperial experience in other than compartmentalized terms, so as to transform our understanding of both the past and the present and our attitude toward the future?"[7] Visiting the haunted worlds that Anglophone writers conjure provides one way to reconceive the imperial past and the environmentally fraught present in terms of connectivity so that we can understand the wounds and the wisdom of the past and their continuities with and contributions to the present. From this position of awareness, we can reshape actions in the present as well as visions of what the future can be. Encouraging thinking across established borders of time, space, and disciplines, Said uses the word "transform." In fact, "transformation" is a word that surfaces throughout my study: Abani asks us to imagine "the complete notion of the transformation of what is possible,"[8] Gordon suggests that ghosts have the potential to spark "transformative recognition,"[9] and Rose-Innes chronicles the ways that imagination leads to transformation in ways of seeing and knowing as she records Ivy's imaginative play: "She could see the patterns transforming into streets, houses, mountain ranges, rivers."[10] Transformation implies more than surface change; to build on Gordon's terms it indicates recognition as re-cognition, a willingness and ability to engage in different patterns of thinking.

The incorporeal corporeality of specters suits them to act as agents of transformation, altering modes of thought by attuning readers to movement across binary categories that have restricted understandings of overlap and interdependence. Specters, then, provide a way to tell different kinds of stories that might lead to different ways of understanding responsibility and acting to achieve environmental justice. As Ruiters notes, "Justice requires a global approach, proactive on all scales and infused with an understanding of how environmental problems are produced, rather than merely with their distribution."[11] This kind of justice depends on transformation: transformation of narrative forms to help humans comprehend multiple scales and dependencies and transformation of ethical and legal frameworks to address effects that cross borders of generations, nations, and species. Specters are uniquely positioned to support this kind of expansive re-cognition, to facilitate justice as including participation and cultural respect and to invite emotional connections that might inspire action.

As an alternative to the child and the nuclear family, the specter provides a figure that can guide inclusive imaginations of environmentally just futures. The child has been used in popular environmental campaigns to offer a concrete and personal way to evoke responsibility across generations. Environmentalist campaigns beseech audiences to think about the future Earth they want their children to inherit, and images of children amid scenes of destruction are mobilized to catalyze emotional reactions. The use of the child and the framework of biological inheritance to generate environmentalist concern have been critiqued from various angles including feminist and queer environmental theory that raise questions about the image's naturalization of heterosexual reproduction, but also about the reproduction of anthropocentrism, capitalism, and related inequalities. For instance, Seymour questions campaigns that have relied on sentimental rhetoric of the family that "suggests that concern for the future qua the planet can only emerge, or emerges most effectively, from white, heterosexual, familial reproductivity."[12] Instead of fearing for the future of the child and the future of the heteronormative, middle-class family, the specter allows us to imagine kinship and community across generational, geographic, and species borders.

Additionally, Anglophone writers who use the figure of the ghost and spectral narrative strategies to imagine alternative futures help to reorient debates about environmental futures that have revolved around popular Western imaginations of apocalypse. In an article titled, "Why Do We Fail When We Try to Tell the Story of Climate Change?" David Wallace-Wells suggests:

> On-screen, climate devastation is everywhere you look, and yet nowhere in focus, as though we are displacing our anxieties about global warming by restaging them in theaters of our own design and control—perhaps out of hope that the end of days remains "fantasy." We don't want to see climate horrors clearly, for the obvious reasons, and so the list of TV shows and movies that approach it in an off-kilter way is almost too easy to compile.[13]

Though *The Swan Book* is the only novel I have discussed that directly foregrounds climate change, all of the novels in this study depict contemporary environmental challenges without resorting to comforting illusions that humans are in control or that destruction is not part of existing reality. By connecting present threats to past conditions, these novels introduce an important perspective that is missing in many discussions dominated by attention to American texts and contexts. Claire Colebrook has previously made a similar observation: "To think of these 'end of the world' narratives as cautionary tales is to assume the position of ... those happy few for whom conditions of scarcity, violence, volatility and 'existential threat' are not part of day-to-day existence."[14] Focusing on Anglophone writers and texts facilitates a shift in perspective about what constitutes an environmental threat, what environmental justice means, and what forms environmental storytelling can take.

While I am arguing that expanding the texts under consideration can productively complicate conversations about environmental futures, I do not intend a handful of texts to speak for all non-Western experiences and perspectives nor do I wish to discount Anglo-American perspectives. In this study, I deliberately juxtapose novels that emerge from and reflect a range of distinct ecological and cultural conditions, but additional perspectives and intersections remain to be explored. Indeed, the comparative study of literary texts could serve as a critical counter-move to complicate Anthropocene formulations of the universal human as agent of environmental destruction. Studying novels in conversation allows for a shifting among scales that makes local particularities and global interdependencies comprehensible, and it contributes to the cultivation of solidarity. Building on Morton's definition that solidarity "allow[s] for others to exist in some strong sense, joining their ways of accessing things or at least appreciating them,"[15] I am suggesting that tracing themes and strategies across texts identifies common ground and allows for larger patterns to emerge that implicate global narratives and practices of capitalism. However, noting these shared traits does not collapse differences or ignore what is distinctive about each text's way of accessing and representing local realities. Further, bringing different strands of environmental thinking (from environmental justice scholars, feminist environmentalists, queer environmentalists, and animal studies scholars to new materialists, posthumanists, and econarratologists) together around the figure of the ghost allows for illuminations of blind spots as well as points of intersection that can spark additional scholarly inquiry, encourage innovative imaginings, and motivate action for futures contrary to those plotted by Western capitalism. It allows me to emphasize the point that environmental scholars and activists need to remain attuned to the wide variety of environmental, social, and narrative traditions, refusing to equate any single experience with universal reality. Finally, putting various critical lenses and narrative traditions into conversation focuses attention on dynamics between ways of knowing to prevent appropriating repressed knowledge as new environmental resources and to foreground accounting for the repression of alternatives to Western, capitalist constructions as part of the work of environmental justice.

Ghosts challenge readers to transform our ways of looking, ways of thinking, and ways of responding. They don't separate the future in order to absolve us of the need to act; instead they beckon us to take up the challenge that Gordon identifies: to acknowledge the violence and the pain and injustice of the past and to act to make it otherwise. The writers in this study show how the novel form can be adapted to serve this goal; novels can open doors to other experiences and knowledges, which returns me for a final time to the image of the open door. As I noted at the start, this study is offered in a spirit of opening doors to invite texts and writers into conversations about environmentally just futures; it has engaged with a wide range of scholars from different fields to open doors to intersections and to explore possible frameworks that could support the survival project of reorienting the human. It is committed to the proposition that stories and imagination matter, and it stresses the idea that the way we pursue environmentally oriented scholarship matters too: our methods can open doors to exchange and understanding or seal us off in our separate chambers. My plea is to keep opening doors.

Notes

Introduction

1. See Rob Nixon's *Slow Violence and the Environmentalism of the Poor* (Cambridge, MA: Harvard University Press, 2011), Timothy Morton's, *Hyperobjects: Philosophy and Ecology after the End of the World* (Minneapolis, MN: University of Minnesota Press, 2013), and Amitav Ghosh's *The Great Derangement: Climate Change and the Unthinkable* (Chicago, IL: University of Chicago Press, 2016). Nixon's theorization of slow violence and Morton's theorization of hyperobjects respond to the representational challenges posed by environmental threats, while Ghosh concentrates on the representational difficulties presented by scales of climate change. Simon Estok notes "agentic capacity as a scale that urgently needs attention" and argues that the "scale of ethical inclusion" needs to expand to address nonhuman animals ("Hollow Ecology and Anthropocene Scales of Measurement," *Mosaic* 51, no. 3 [2018]: 38–39). Exploring how affect moves across a range of scales, Tonya Davidson, Ondine Park, and Rob Shields contend in *Ecologies of Affect: Placing Nostalgia, Desire and Hope* that "scale is spatial, social, and political, encompassing scales of interactions, scales of meaning, and scales of engagement" ([Waterloo: Wilfrid Laurier University Press, 2011], 322). This collection of examples starts to demonstrate the range of ways that ecocritical scholarship confronts questions of scale.
2. Davidson, Park, and Shields, *Ecologies of Affect*, 322.
3. Astrida Neimanis, Cecilia Asberg, and Johan Hedren, "Four Problems, Four Directions for Environmental Humanities: A Critical Posthumanities for the Anthropocene," *Ethics and Environment* 20, no. 1 (2015): 74.
4. See, for instance, Lizabeth Paravisini-Gebert, "Colonial and Postcolonial Gothic: The Caribbean," in *The Cambridge Companion to Gothic Fiction*, ed. Jerrold E. Hogle (Cambridge: Cambridge University Press, 2002), 229–58.
5. In terms of ecogothic, Tom Hillard explains a foundational connection: "Because Gothic literature is so obsessed with fears of all types, the Gothic provides a useful lens for understanding the ways that many authors—regardless of when they are writing—represented fears and anxieties about the natural world" ("Deep into That Darkness Peering: An Essay on Gothic Nature," *ISLE: Interdisciplinary Studies in Literature and Environment* 16, no. 4 [2009]: 689). Hillard's 2009 essay responds to Simon Estok's original challenge in "Theorizing in a Space of Ambivalent

Openness: Ecocriticism and Ecophobia" that ecocritics "need to talk about how contempt for the natural world is a definable and recognizable discourse" (*Interdisciplinary Studies in Literature and Environment* 16, no. 2 [2009]: 204). Estok continues to develop his concept of ecophobia through subsequent work including the recent *The Ecophobia Hypothesis* (New York, NY: Routledge, 2018). Returning to the ecogothic, Andrew Smith and William Hughes edited the first book-length collection devoted to the topic, and they define their focus in similar terms of anxiety in the face of nature: "The Gothic seems to be the form which is well placed to capture these anxieties [about climate change and environmental damage] and provide a culturally significant point of contact between literary criticism, ecocritical theory and political process. While the origins of this ecoGothic can be traced back to Romanticism, the growth in environmental awareness has become a significant development" (*EcoGothic* [Manchester: Manchester University Press, 2013], 5). Their collection focuses on British, Canadian, and American ecogothic, with one concluding essay exploring the possibilities of a global ecogothic. A special issue of *Gothic Studies* devoted to the EcoGothic similarly focused on British, Irish, and Italian texts and contexts ("The EcoGothic in the Long Nineteenth Century," 16, no. 1 [May 2014]). The formulations that emerge from these Euro-American texts continue the pattern of highlighting aspects of fear and anxiety.

6   In some psychoanalytic approaches to haunting such as that developed by Nicolas Abraham and Maria Torok, the goal of confronting ghosts is to resolve the conflicts that they represent and prevent the return of the past. See *The Shell and the Kernel*, trans. Nicholas T. Rand (Chicago, IL: University of Chicago Press, 1994).

7   Critics who address issues of spectacle and visibility include Delice Williams in "Spectacular Subjects: Abjection, Agency, and Embodiment in Indra Sinha's *Animal's People*," *Interventions* 20, no. 4 (2018): 586–603; Andrew Mahlstedt in "Animal's Eyes: Spectacular Invisibility and the Terms of Recognition in Indra Sinha's Animal's People," *Mosaic* 46, no. 3 (2013): 59–74, and Nixon, *Slow Violence*.

8   Indra Sinha, *Animal's People* (New York, NY: Simon & Schuster, 2008), 274.

9   Ibid., 108.

10 Ibid., 139.

11 Anthony Carrigan, "'Justice Is on Our Side'? *Animal's People*, Generic Hybridity, and Eco-Crime," *The Journal of Commonwealth Literature* 47, no. 2 (2012): 166. Anthony Carrigan deftly addresses ways that Sinha uses references to a range of Western texts to invoke forms of agency and subjectivity and complicate the labeling of events in Khaufpur/Bhopal as tragedy. He does not pay as much attention to ways that Sinha incorporates a range of Indian aesthetic forms as he cultivates this generic hybridity, and despite his reference to the uncanny summoning of the *Oresteia*, haunting is not a major analytic framework in his analysis.

12 Sinha, *Animal's People*, 275.
13 Ibid., 49.
14 Ibid., 29.
15 Ghosh, *Great Derangement*, 32.
16 Timothy Morton, *Humankind: Solidarity with Nonhuman People* (London: Verso, 2017), 63.
17 Ibid., 54.
18 Ibid., 42.
19 In the context of Anglo-American ecocriticism, Lawrence Buell elaborates the concept of environmental imagination in his works *The Environmental Imagination: Thoreau, Nature Writing and the Formation of American Culture* (Cambridge, MA: Harvard University Press, 1995) and *The Future of Environmental Criticism: Environmental Crisis and Literary Imagination* (Oxford: Blackwell Publishing, 2005). The role of imagination has been given sustained attention by postcolonial ecocritics including in the trailblazing works by Cara Cilano and Elizabeth DeLoughrey "Against Authenticity: Global Knowledges and Postcolonial Ecocriticism" (*Interdisciplinary Studies in Literature and Environment* 14, no. 1 [2007]: 71–87) and Anthony Vital "Toward an African Ecocriticism: Postcolonialism, Ecology and Life and Times of Michael K" (*Research in African Literatures* 39, no. 1 [2008]: 87–106) that also analyze the mediating function of literature. In *Postcolonial Ecocriticism: Literature, Animals, Environment* (New York, NY: Routledge, 2010), Graham Huggan and Helen Tiffin build on theses formulations to discuss the mediating and advocacy roles of literary texts. In charting the territory of environmental humanities, scholars again reinforce the roles of narrative and imagination, see, for example, Elizabeth DeLoughrey, Jill Didur and Anthony Carrigan's introduction to *Global Ecologies and the Environmental Humanities* (New York, NY: Routledge, 2015).
20 Claire Colebrook, *Death of the Post Human: Essays on Extinction, Volume I* (London: Open Humanities Press, 2014), 10.
21 Maria del Pilar Blanco and Esther Peeren, "Introduction: Conceptualizing Spectralities," in *The Spectralities Reader: Ghosts and Haunting in Contemporary Cultural Theory*, ed. Maria del Pilar Blanco and Esther Peeren (London: Bloomsbury, 2013), 7.
22 Ibid., 2.
23 Elain Gan, Anna Tsing, Heather Swanson, and Nils Bubandt, "Introduction: Haunted Landscapes of the Anthropocene," in *Arts of Living on a Damaged Planet*, ed. Anna Tsing, Heather Swanson, Elaine Gan, and Nils Bubandt (Minneapolis, MN: University of Minnesota Press, 2017), G2.
24 Jacques Derrida, *Specters of Marx*, trans. Peggy Kamuf (New York, NY: Routledge, 1994), xviii.
25 Ibid., xvi.

26 Avery Gordon, *Ghostly Matters: Haunting and the Sociological Imagination* (Minneapolis, MN: University of Minnesota Press, 2008), vxvii.
27 Ibid., 57.
28 Donna J. Haraway, *Staying with the Trouble: Making Kin in the Chthulucene* (Durham, NC: Duke University Press, 2016), 4.
29 Ibid., 3.
30 Ibid., 12.
31 Rob Nixon, "Environmentalism and Postcolonialism," in *Postcolonial Studies and Beyond*, ed. Ania Loomba, Suvir Kaul, Matti Bunzl, Antoinette Burton, and Jed Esty (Durham, NC: Duke University Press, 2005), 235.
32 Frantz Fanon, *The Wretched of the Earth*, trans. Richard Philcox (New York, NY: Grove Press, 2005), 182–3.
33 Hershini Bhana Young, *Haunting Capital: Memory, Text and the Black Diasporic Body* (Hanover, NH: Dartmouth College Press, 2005), 32.
34 Ibid., 31.
35 Ibid., 41.
36 Byron Caminero-Santangelo, *Different Shades of Green: African Literature, Environmental Justice, and Political Ecology* (Charlottesville, VA: University of Virginia Press, 2014), 15.
37 Ibid.
38 Gordon Walker, *Environmental Justice: Concepts, Evidence and Politics* (New York, NY: Routledge, 2012), 34–7.
39 David Scholsberg, *Defining Environmental Justice: Theories, Movements, and Nature* (New York, NY: Oxford University Press, 2009), 79.
40 Ibid.
41 Young, *Haunting Capital*, 31.
42 DeLoughrey, Didur, and Carrigan, eds., *Global Ecologies*, 2.
43 See Nancy Easterlin, *A Biocultural Approach to Literary Theory and Interpretation* (Baltimore, MD: Johns Hopkins University Press, 2012).
44 Dana Phillips, *The Truth of Ecology: Nature, Culture, and Literature in America* (New York, NY: Oxford University Press, 2003).
45 Ursula Heise, "Afterword: Postcolonial Ecocriticism and the Question of Literature," in *Postcolonial Green: Environmental Politics and World Narratives*, ed. Bonnie Roos, Alex Hunt, and John Tallmadge (Charlottesville, VA: University of Virginia Press, 2010), 258.
46 Erin James, *The Storyworld Accord: Econarratology and Postcolonial Narratives* (Lincoln, NE: University of Nebraska Press, 2015), 13.
47 Edward Said, *Culture and Imperialism* (New York, NY: Vintage, 1994), 71.
48 Ngugi wa Thiongo develops these arguments in studies including *Decolonizing the Mind: The Politics of Language in African Literature* (Portsmouth: Heinemann, 2011) and *Something Torn and New: An African Renaissance* (New York, NY: Civitas

Books, 2009), while Edouard Glissant elaborates his observations in works including *Poetics of Relation* (trans. Betsy Wing [Ann Arbor, MI: University of Michigan Press, 1997]) and the essays collected in *Caribbean Discourse: Selected Essays* (trans. J. Michael Dash [Charlottesville, VA: University of Virginia Press, 1999]).

49 For examples of ecocritical scholarship attuned to questions of form see James's *Storyworld* and the essays collected in DeLoughrey, Didur, and Carrigan, eds., *Global Ecologies*.

50 DeLoughrey, Didur, and Carrigan, eds., *Global Ecologies*, 5.

51 For examples of reevaluations of realism in relation to postcolonial writing see Jed Esty and Colleen Lye, "Peripheral Realisms Now," *Modern Language Quarterly* 73, no. 3 (2012): 269–88; Nicholas Robinette, *Realism, Form and the Postcolonial Novel* (New York, NY: Palgrave, 2014).

52 Jed Esty, "Realism Wars," *Novel* 49, no. 2 (2016): 316–42.

53 Warwick Research Collective, *Combined and Uneven Development: Towards a New Theory of World-Literature* (Liverpool: Liverpool University Press, 2015), 66.

54 For efforts to resituate and reclaim realism within literary studies see *A Concise Companion to Realism*, ed. Matthew Beaumont (Chichester: Wiley-Blackwell, 2010). Realism has been approached in distinctly different ways within the fields of postcolonialism and ecocriticism; in contrast to the celebration of realist aesthetics especially in first-wave ecocriticism, scholars in postcolonial literary studies have tended to focus on experimental novels while downplaying or denigrating realist texts. For discussion of realism in relation to postcolonial texts see Monika Fludernik, "The Narrative Forms of Postcolonial Fiction," in *The Cambridge History of Postcolonial Literature*, ed. Ato Quayson (Cambridge: Cambridge University Press, 2011), 903–37 and Warwick Research Collective, *Combined and Uneven Development*, 67.

55 Esty, "Realism Wars," 317.

56 Ghosh, *Great Derangement*, 71.

57 Brian Richardson distinguishes antimimetic strategies from nonmimetic strategies, clarifying that "by antimimetic, I mean representations that contravene the presuppositions of nonfictional narratives, violate mimetic expectations and the practices of realism, and defy conventions of existing, established genres," while nonmimetic refers to "nonrealist works, such as a fairy tale" that "employs a consistent, parallel storyworld and follows established conventions, or in some cases, merely adds supernatural components to its otherwise mimetic depiction of the actual world" (3–4). He acknowledges that many works mix mimetic and antimimetic features and he includes discussion of postcolonial texts that expand plots to cover centuries or deploy collective narrators in his discussions of the formal innovations that should be studied in association with an unnatural narrative theory that embraces antimimetic strategies (144, 160). *Unnatural Narrative: Theory, History, and Practice* (Columbus, OH: Ohio State University Press, 2015).

58 Ibid., 165.
59 Jan Alber, Stefan Iversen, Henrik Skov Nielsen, and Brian Richardson, "Unnatural Narrative, Unnatural Narratology: Beyond Mimetic Models," *Narrative* 18, no. 2 (2010): 114, 115.
60 Esther Peeren, "Everyday Ghosts and the Ghostly Everyday in Amos Tutuola, Ben Okri, and Achille Mbembe," in *Popular Ghosts: The Haunted Spaces of Everyday Culture*, ed. Maria dle Pilar Blanco and Esther Peeren (New York, NY: Continuum, 2010), 110.
61 Ibid., 131.
62 Phillips, *Truth of Ecology*, 182.
63 Warwick Research Collective, *Combined and Uneven Development*, 62.
64 Ibid., 70.
65 Mary Louise Pratt, "Coda," in *Arts of Living on a Damaged Planet*, ed. Anna Tsing, Heather Swanson, Elaine Gan, and Nils Bubandt (Minneapolis, MN: University of Minnesota Press, 2017), G173.
66 Haraway, *Staying with the Trouble*, 57.
67 See Stacy Alaimo, *Exposed: Environmental Politics and Pleasures in Posthuman Times* (Minneapolis, MN: University of Minnesota Press, 2016).
68 Neimanis, Asberg, and Hedren, "Four Problems," 67.
69 Alaimo, *Exposed*, 144.
70 Ibid., 145.
71 Ibid., 146.
72 Ibid.
73 Dipesh Chakrabarty, "Foreword," in *Global Ecologies and the Environmental Humanities: Postcolonial Approaches*, ed. Elizabeth DeLoughrey, Jill Didur, and Anthony Carrigan (New York, NY: Routledge, 2015), xiii–xvi.
74 Haraway, *Staying with the Trouble*, 55.
75 Jason W. Moore, *Capitalism in the Web of Life: Ecology and the Accumulation of Capital* (New York, NY: Verso, 2015), 4, 3.
76 Arundhati Roy, *The Ministry of Utmost Happiness* (New York, NY: Knopf, 2017), 404.
77 Thom Van Dooren, *Flight Ways: Life and Loss at the Edge of Extinction* (New York, NY: Columbia University Press, 2016), 3.
78 Paul Carter, *Dark Writing: Geography, Performance, Design* (Honolulu, HI: University of Honolulu Press, 2008).

Chapter 1

1 Alexander Greer Hartwiger invokes the uncanny in analyzing *GraceLand*, but focuses on a more literal dissolution of home: "I explore the disintegration of the

home, as manifested in psychological and physical terms, and the subsequent search for affiliation and community" ("Strangers in/to the World: The Unhomely in Chris Abani's *GraceLand*," *Matatu: Journal for African Culture and Society* 45, no. 1 [2014]: 236). Madhu Krishnan engages extensively with the spirit world in terms of Igbo mythology of the obanje, but uses this framework inventively to direct attention to division and relation between the United States and Nigeria rather than human–spirit worlds ("Mythopoetics and Cultural Re-Creation," in *Contemporary African Literature in English: Global Locations, Postcolonial Identifications* [New York, NY: Palgrave Macmillan, 2014]). Danica Savonick comes closest to considering ghosts as environmental agents in the novel, analyzing road ghosts in relation to her project of thinking automobility in contemporary Nigerian novels ("'The Problem of Locomotion': Infrastructure and Automobility in Three Postcolonial Urban Nigerian Novels," *Modern Fiction Studies* 61, no. 4 [2015]: 669–89).

2   For examples see Ashley Dawson, "Surplus City: Structural Adjustment, Self-Fashioning, and Urban Insurrection in Chris Abani's *GraceLand*," *Interventions* 11, no. 1 (2009): 16–34 and Sarah K. Harrison, "'Suspended City': Personal, Urban, and National Development in Chris Abani's *GraceLand*," *Research in African Literatures* 43, no. 2 (2012): 95–114.

3   For instance see Robert D. Bullard, *Dumping in Dixie: Race, Class, and Environmental Quality* (New York, NY: Routledge, 1990).

4   Gordon McGranahan and Peter Marcotullio, *Scaling Urban Environmental Challenges: From Local to Global and Back* (New York, NY: Routledge, 2007), 19. See also Wilson Akpan, "Between Ethnic Essentialism and Environmental Racism: Oil and the 'Glocalisation' of Environmental Justice Discourse in Nigeria," *African Sociological Review/Revue Africaine de Sociologie* 10, no. 2 (2006): 18–42. Akpan provides an important reminder to critically examine ways that environmental justice discourse is applied to local contexts, noting that it can provide a useful framework for approaching intersections of social and environmental justice, but it also might limit thinking, for instance to a focus on racial inequality, which he notes is not the most appropriate metric in the context of Nigeria. Scholars must be selective in using the framework and not let it dictate approaches that obscure local conditions.

5   UN Habitat, *United Nations Slum Almanac 2015–2016: Tracking Improvement in the Lives of Slum Dwellers*, https://unhabitat.org/slum-almanac-2015-2016/

6   Saleh Ahmed and Mahbubur Meenar, "Just Sustainability in the Global South: A Case Study of the Megacity of Dhaka," *Journal of Developing Societies* 34, no. 4 (2018): 402.

7   Timothy Morton, *Hyperobjects: Philosophy and Ecology after the End of the World* (Minneapolis, MN: University of Minnesota Press, 2013), 1.

8   McGranahan and Marcotulio, *Scaling*, 41.
9   Avery Gordon, *Ghostly Matters: Haunting and the Sociological Imagination* (Minneapolis, MN: University of Minnesota Press, 2008), xix.
10 Rob Nixon, *Slow Violence and the Environmentalism of the Poor* (Cambridge, MA: Harvard University Press, 2011), 16.
11 Ibid., 14.
12 Chris Abani, *GraceLand* (London: Picador, 2004), 7.
13 For a related discussion see Lauren Mason, "Leaving Lagos: Intertextuality and Images in Chris Abani's *GraceLand*," *Research in African Literatures* 45, no. 3 (2014): 223. Mason notes, "The postcard image of Lagos illuminates and reveals the city in ways that a singular narrative view cannot because it gives readers an additional Lagos that is still in need of further articulation and still open to interpretation." While Mason pursues the consequences for validating new modes of narrative including visual media, I suggest that the shifting between views operates to advance Abani's critique of capitalist models of vision.
14 Tundae Agbola and A.M. Jinadu, "Forced Eviction and Forced Relocation in Nigeria: The Experience of Those Evicted From Maroko in 1990," *Environment and Urbanization* 9, no. 2 (1997): 272.
15 Odia Ofiemun, "Daring Visions," review of *Invisible Chapters*, by Maik Nwosu, *English in Africa* 32, no. 1 (2005): 137.
16 Agbola and Jinadu, "Forced Eviction," 272.
17 Abani, *GraceLand*, 248.
18 Ibid., 247.
19 Torras and Boyce qtd. in McGranahan and Marcotulio, *Scaling*, 39–40.
20 Abani discusses his conception of Nigeria as haunted territory, indicating both a positive relation with ghosts enabled by Igbo cultural beliefs and a sense of haunting attending on the colonial destruction of indigenous culture. For example see Chris Abani, "Interview with Colm Toibin," *BOMB Magazine*, Summer 2006, http://bombmagazine.org/article/2840/chris-abani and Hope Wabuke, "Chris Abani: 'The Middle-Class View of Africa Is a Problem,'" *The Guardian*, July 27, 2016, https://www.theguardian.com/books/2016/jul/27/chris-abani-writer-nigeria-memoir-africa
21 Wabuke, "Chris Abani."
22 Achille Mbembe, "Life, Sovereignty, and Terror in the Fiction of Amos Tutuola," *Research in African Literatures* 34, no. 4 (2003): 1.
23 Jacques Derrida, *Specters of Marx*, trans. Peggy Kamuf (New York, NY: Routledge, 1994), 5.
24 Daniel Punday, "A Corporeal Narratology?" *Style* 34, no. 2 (2000): 233.
25 Ibid., 236.
26 Abani, *GraceLand*, 14.

27 Ibid., 95.
28 Dawson, "Surplus City," 20 and Harrison, "Suspended City," 97.
29 Abani, *GraceLand*, 6.
30 Ibid.
31 Ibid., 7.
32 John Scanlan, *On Garbage* (London: Reaktion Books, 2005), 13–14.
33 Ibid., 14.
34 Abani, *GraceLand*, 77.
35 Ibid.
36 Ibid., 294.
37 Ibid., 242.
38 Ibid., 137.
39 Ahmed and Meenar, "Just Sustainability," 405.
40 Abani, "Interview with Colm Toibin."
41 Cajetan Iheka, *Naturalizing Africa: Ecological Violence, Agency, and Postcolonial Resistance in African Literature* (Cambridge: Cambridge University Press, 2018), 22–3.
42 Esther Peeren, "Everyday Ghosts and the Ghostly Everyday in Amos Tutuola, Ben Okri, and Achille Mbembe," in *Popular Ghosts: The Haunted Spaces of Everyday Culture*, ed. Maria Del Pilar Blanco and Esther Peeren (New York, NY: Continuum, 2010), 106–17.
43 See Mike Davis, *Planet of Slums* (London: Verso, 2007). Davis discusses the social and environmental justice issues created through motor vehicle use and lack of urban planning in slums worldwide: "The result of this collision between urban poverty and traffic congestion is sheer carnage" (132). Davis supports this claim with a study by the World Health Organization (WHO) which concludes that traffic constitutes "one of the worst health hazards facing the urban poor" and the WHO also predicts that by 2020 road accidents will be the third leading cause of death for the urban poor (133).
44 Ibid., 132. Davis documents the ways that this banalization of death is reflected through the language for buses known locally as danfos and molues, "flying coffins" and "moving morgues."
45 Abani, *GraceLand*, 57.
46 Ibid., 9.
47 AbdouMaliq Simone, "Ghostly Cracks and Urban Deceptions: Jakarta," in *In the Life of Cities: Parallel Narratives of the Urban*, ed. Moshen Mostafavi (Zurich: Lars Muller, 2012), 121.
48 Ibid.
49 Abani, *GraceLand*, 21.
50 Matthew Gandy, "Learning from Lagos," *New Left Review* 33 (2005): 45.
51 Savonick, "The Problem of Locomotion," 680.

52 Abani, *GraceLand*, 287.
53 Ibid., 305.
54 Ibid.
55 Ibid., 186.
56 Ibid., 188.
57 Gerard Genette, *Narrative Discourse: An Essay in Method*, trans. Jane E. Lewin (Ithaca, NY: Cornell University Press, 1980), 56.
58 Gordon, *Ghostly Matters*, xvi.
59 Jacques Derrida and Bernard Stiegler, "Spectrographies," in *The Spectralities Reader: Ghosts and Haunting in Contemporary Cultural Theory*, ed. Maria Del Pilar Blanco and Esther Pereen (New York, NY: Bloomsbury, 2013), 42.
60 The ending of the novel has sparked much commentary with some critics reading it as a subversion of the bildungsroman that comments on the failure of Western models of development or provides a verdict on the hopelessness of postcolonial cities while others interpret it as a failure on Abani's part, an inability to imagine a fitting resolution to his tale. For instance, see Susan Z. Andrade, "Representing Slums and Home: Chris Abani's *GraceLand*," in *The Legacies of Modernism: Historicising Postwar and Contemporary Fiction*, ed. David James (Cambridge: Cambridge University Press, 2012), 225–42. Andrade finds fault with the ending, seeing the "magical" rescue of Elvis from the slums and the self-sacrifice of Redemption that makes Elvis's flight possible inconsistent with Abani's blending of the bildungsroman and picaresque, a resort to a deus ex machina that achieves an unbelievable display of upward mobility that "appears to be narratively unmotivated" and "certainly narratively unsatisfying" (239). I argue, however, that Elvis's mobility is consistent throughout the novel and his travel to America does not promise a simplified happy ending or completely avoid the complex social issues Abani has raised. Instead, it documents how movement participates in networks of visibility.
61 Zygmunt Bauman, *Wasted Lives: Modernity and Its Outcasts* (Cambridge: Polity Press, 2004), 27.
62 Maria Mies and Veronika Bennholdt-Thomsen, *The Subsistence Perspective: Beyond the Globalised Economy* (New York, NY: Zed Books, 1999), 155.
63 Simone, "Ghostly Cracks," 132, emphasis added.
64 Abani, *GraceLand*, 4–5.
65 Gandy, "Learning from Lagos," 52.
66 Movement collaborates in keeping garbage out of view when it comes to shuffling "superfluous" bodies from one nation to another or unloading the refuse of the Global North on the Global South. A 2011 United Nations report on electrical and electronic waste or e-waste in Africa documents, "Lagos has developed into West Africa's main entry point" for e-waste, an issue with social, economic, and

environmental consequences that began to draw increasing public attention after the release of the film *The Digital Dump*. For additional discussion, see Andreas Manhart, Oladele Osibanjo, Adeyinka Aderinto, and Siddharth Prakash, *Informal E-Waste Management in Lagos, Nigeria: Socio-Economic Impacts and Feasibility of International Recycling Co-Operations* (Lagos and Frieburg: Oko-Institut e.V., 2011), http://www.basel.int/Portals/4/Basel%20Convention/docs/eWaste/E-waste_Africa_Project_Nigeria.pdf. This example illustrates how movement can serve the interests of global capitalism by keeping waste invisible, but also suggests that the work of artists in bringing specters into view can provide a catalyst for action and combat the illusion that the consequences of waste production can be endlessly deferred by denying waste visibility.

67 Discussing *GraceLand* with Colm Toibin, Abani admits, "There are references in the book—the books that Elvis is reading—that talk about the way the book is made." Abani focuses on the mix of realism and the fabulous in the books that he read as a child and in the books that Elvis reads within the novel, suggesting that these influence and comment on the style of the novel. I expand this consideration to support my claims that texts such as Beatrice's journal and Baldwin's novel perform hauntings that allow absent voices to make their presence felt.

68 Dawson, "Surplus City," 20.

69 Hilary Dannenberg, "Narrating the Postcolonial Metropolis in Anglophone African Fiction: Chris Abani's *GraceLand* and Phaswane Mpe's "Welcome to Our Hillbrow," *Journal of Postcolonial Writing* 48, no. 1 (2012): 48.

70 Abani, *GraceLand*, 320.

71 Ibid., 319, 321.

72 Ibid., 321.

73 "Redemption," *Oxford English Dictionary*, 2nd ed. 20 vols. (Oxford: Oxford University Press, 1989), 1a, 2a. Also available at http://www.oed.com/

74 Janice Radway, foreword to *Ghostly Matters: Haunting and the Sociological Imagination*, by Avery Gordon (Minneapolis, MN: University of Minnesota Press, 2008), xiii, emphasis original.

75 Chris Abani, "Telling Stories from Africa," filmed 2007, video, 17:36, http://www.chrisabani.com/posts/2007/06/29/ted-video-telling-stories-from-africa/

Chapter 2

1 Shirley Toland-Dix, "Re-Negotiating Racial Identity: The Challenge of Migration and Return in Michelle Cliff's *No Telephone to Heaven*," *Studies in the Literary Imagination* 37, no. 2 (Fall 2004): 48. Cliff also discusses Clare in relation to a quest for wholeness in Michelle Cliff, "Clare Savage as Crossroads Character,"

in *Caribbean Women Writers: Essays from the First International Conference*, ed. Selwyn Reginald Cudjoe (Amherst, MA: University of Massachusetts Press, 1990).
2   Amitav Ghosh, *The Great Derangement: Climate Change and the Unthinkable* (Chicago, IL: University of Chicago Press, 2016), 79.
3   Wendy Walters, "Michelle Cliff's *No Telephone to Heaven*: Diasporic Displacement and the Feminization of the Landscape," in *Borders, Exiles, Diasporas*, ed. Elazar Barkan and Marie-Denise Shelton (Stanford, CA: Stanford University Press, 1998), 217.
4   See Elizabeth DeLoughrey and George B. Handley, eds., *Postcolonial Ecologies: Literatures of the Environment* (New York, NY: Oxford University Press, 2011) and Elizabeth DeLoughrey, Renee K. Gosson, and George B. Handley, eds., *Caribbean Literature and the Environment: Between Nature and Culture* (Charlottesville, VA: University of Virginia Press, 2005).
5   Edouard Glissant, *Caribbean Discourse: Selected Essays*, trans. J. Michael Dash (Charlottesville, VA: University of Virginia Press, 1999), 149.
6   Ibid., 105–6.
7   Wilson Harris, "Theater of the Arts," in *Theater of the Arts: Wilson Harris and the Caribbean*, ed. Hena Maes-Jelinek and Benedicte Ledent (Amsterdam: Brill Rodopi, 2002), 4.
8   Helen Tiffin, "'Man Fitting the Landscape': Nature, Culture and Colonialism," in *Caribbean Literature and the Environment: Between Nature and Culture*, ed. Elizabeth DeLoughrey, Renee K. Gosson, and George B. Handley (Charlottesville, VA: University of Virginia Press, 2005), 201.
9   Michelle Cliff, "Caliban's Daughter: The Tempest and the Teapot," *Frontiers: A Journal of Women's Studies* 12, no. 2 (1991): 37.
10 Harris recounts his experience of revelation, reporting that his contact with the land awakened in him a realization of "a *living* unpredictable planet. I found it impossible to write what I felt, but persisted … there was *something else*, something akin to a bloodstream or spirit that ran everywhere with astonishing momentum that made my former activities pale into fixity or immobility … a rhythm that awakens spaces within the passivities we take for granted." Harris explains further that "the language of conventional, linear fiction which seems so strong becomes an illusion and is broken by quantum holes." Wilson Harris, "Wilson Harris by Fred D'Aguiar," interview by Fred D'Aguiar, *BOMB*, January 1, 2003, https://bombmagazine.org/articles/wilson-harris/
11 Lin Knutson, "Michelle Cliff and the Feminization of Space: *No Telephone to Heaven* as Female Limbo Gateway into History," *Journal of Caribbean Studies* 11, no. 3 (1996): 278.
12 Ibid., 276. See also Monika Elbert, "Retrieving the Language of the Ghostly Mother: Displaced Daughters and the Search for Home in Amy Tan and Michelle Cliff,"

in *Ghosts, Stories, Histories: Ghost Stories and Alternative Histories*, ed. Sladja Blazan (Newcastle: Cambridge Scholars Publishing, 2007), 170 and Toland-Dix, "Renegotiating," 48.
13 Michelle Cliff, *No Telephone to Heaven* (New York, NY: Penguin, 1987), 1.
14 Ibid., 8.
15 Glissant, *Caribbean Discourse*, 154.
16 Timothy Morton, *Humankind: Solidarity with Nonhuman People* (London: Verso, 2017), 2.
17 Ibid., 12–13.
18 Ibid., 27.
19 Cliff, *No Telephone*, 8.
20 Ibid., 11.
21 Ibid., 87.
22 Ibid., 91.
23 Stacy Alaimo, *Bodily Natures: Science, Environment, and the Material Self* (Bloomington, IN: Indiana University Press, 2010), 2.
24 Linda Nash, *Inescapable Ecologies: A History of Environment, Disease, and Knowledge* (Berkeley, CA: University of California Press, 2007).
25 Nancy Tuana, "Viscous Porosity: Witnessing Katrina," in *Material Feminisms*, ed. Stacy Alaimo and Susan Hekman (Bloomington, IN: Indiana University Press, 2008), 198, 200.
26 Jacques Derrida, *Specters of Marx*, trans. Peggy Kamuf (New York, NY: Routledge, 1994), 5.
27 Elizabeth Freeman, *Time Binds: Queer Temporalities, Queer Histories* (Durham, NC: Duke University Press, 2010), 10.
28 Cliff, *No Telephone*, 156.
29 Ibid., 195.
30 Christopher Hitchens, "The Vietnam Syndrome," *Vanity Fair*, August 2006, https://www.vanityfair.com/news/2006/08/hitchens200608
31 Stacy Alaimo, *Exposed: Environmental Politics and Pleasures in Posthuman Times* (Minneapolis, MN: University of Minnesota Press, 2016), 72.
32 Derrida, *Specters*, xvii.
33 Cliff, *No Telephone*, 156–7.
34 Knutson, "Feminization," 286.
35 Jennifer J. Smith, "Birthed and Buried: Matrilineal History in Michelle Cliff's *No Telephone to Heaven*," *Meridians: Feminism, Race, Transnationalism* 9, no. 1 (2009): 142.
36 Anne McClintock, *Imperial Leather: Race, Gender, and Sexuality in the Colonial Contest* (New York, NY: Routledge, 1995), 24.
37 Cliff, *No Telephone*, 145.
38 Ibid., 146.

39 Ibid., 129–30.
40 Alaimo, *Exposed*, 4.
41 Ibid., 5.
42 Ibid.
43 Morton, *Humankind*, 14.
44 Ghosh, *Great Derangement*, 23, 84.
45 Glissant, *Caribbean Discourse*, 105.
46 Ibid., 106–7.
47 Cliff, *No Telephone*, 143.
48 Esther Pereen, "The Ghost as a Gendered Chronotope," in *Ghosts, Stories, Histories: Ghost Stories and Alternative Histories*, ed. Sladja Blazan (Newcastle: Cambridge Scholars Publishing, 2007), 90.
49 Cliff, *No Telephone*, 5.
50 Michelle Cliff, *Abeng* (New York, NY: Penguin, 1984), 21.
51 Cockpit Country Stakeholders Group and Jamaica Environmental Advocacy Network, *Save Cockpit Country Fact Sheet* 2007, http://www.jamaicancaves.org/Save_Cockpit_Country_Fact_Sheet_2007.pdf
52 Karyl Walker, "Dust, Stench and Claim of Impotence: Pollution Killing Us, Say Communities near Bauxite Plants—Firms Insist Waste Not Toxic," *Jamaica Observer*, February 11, 2007. See also Southern Trelawny Environmental Agency, "Bauxite Mining in Cockpit Country," December 3, 2011, http://stea.net/wp/?page_id=96
53 Ibid.
54 Cliff, *No Telephone*, 195.
55 Derrida, *Specters*, 50–60.
56 Hershini Bhana Young, *Haunting Capital: Memory, Text and the Black Diasporic Body* (Hanover, NH: Dartmouth College Press, 2005), 40–1.
57 Edwin A. Martini, *Agent Orange: History, Science, and the Politics of Uncertainty* (Amherst, MA: University of Massachusetts Press, 2012), 2.
58 Ibid., 3.
59 Ibid.
60 David Zierler, *The Invention of Ecocide: Agent Orange, Vietnam, and the Scientists Who Changed the Way We Think about the Environment* (Athens, GA: University of Georgia Press, 2011), 14.
61 Cliff, *No Telephone*, 146.
62 Ibid., 173.
63 Avery Gordon, *Ghostly Matters: Haunting and the Sociological Imagination* (Minneapolis, MN: University of Minnesota Press, 2008), 8.
64 Derrida, *Specters*, 67.
65 Jacques Derrida, *Du droit a la philosophie* (Paris: Galilee, 1990), 82.
66 Cliff, *Abeng*, 127.

67 Ibid., 129.
68 Ibid., 129, 130.
69 Ibid., 128.
70 Cliff, *No Telephone*, 193.
71 Ibid.
72 Nicole Seymour, *Strange Natures: Futurity, Empathy, and the Queer Ecological Imagination* (Urbana, IL: University of Illinois Press, 2013), 10–11.
73 Cliff, "Clare Savage," 266.
74 Walters, "Michelle Cliff's *No Telephone*," 232.
75 Smith, "Birthed and Buried," 144.
76 Peeren, "The Ghost," 87.
77 Morton, *Humankind*, 27.

Chapter 3

1 PanMacmillan Australia, "Kim Scott," https://www.panmacmillan.com.au/author/kim-scott/
2 Ibid.
3 Kim Scott and Hazel Brown, *Kayang and Me* (Fremantle: Fremantle Arts Centre Press, 2005), 14.
4 Ibid., 29.
5 Ibid., 28.
6 Kim Scott, *That Deadman Dance* (New York, NY: Bloomsbury, 2013), 147.
7 *That Deadman Dance* was first published in Australia in 2010. Among numerous awards, it was recognized for the 2011 Miles Franklin Award, the Victorian Prize for Literature, a regional Commonwealth Writers' Prize, and the Australian Literature Society Gold Medal.
8 Kim Scott, "Can You Anchor a Shimmering Nation State via Regional Indigenous Roots?" interview with Anne Brewster, *Cultural Studies Review* 18, no. 1 (2012): 230.
9 Avery Gordon, *Ghostly Matters: Haunting and the Sociological Imagination* (Minneapolis, MN: University of Minnesota Press, 2008), xvi.
10 Janice Radway, "Foreword," to Gordon, *Ghostly Matters*, x.
11 Nicolas Abraham and Maria Torok, *The Shell and the Kernel*, trans. Nicholas T. Rand (Chicago, IL: University of Chicago Press, 1994), 188. See also Colin Davis, "Etat Present: Hauntology, Spectres and Phantoms," in *The Spectralities Reader: Ghosts and Haunting in Contemporary Critical Theory*, ed. Maria del Pilar Blanco and Esther Peeren (New York, NY: Bloomsbury, 2013), 55–6.
12 Gordon, *Ghostly Matters*, 18.

13 David Crouch, "National Hauntings: The Architecture of Australian Ghost Stories," *Journal of the Association for the Study of Australian Literature* (2007): 101, https://openjournals.library.sydney.edu.au/index.php/JASAL/article/view/9642/9532
14 Ibid.
15 Scott, "Can You Anchor," 235.
16 See Anne Brewster, "Whiteness and Indigenous Sovereignty in Kim Scott's *That Deadman Dance*," *Journal of the European Association of Studies on Australia* 2, no. 2 (2011): 60–71; Sue Kossew, "Recovering the Past: Entangled Histories in Kim Scott's *That Deadman Dance*," in *Decolonizing the Landscape: Indigenous Cultures in Australia*, ed. Beate Neumeier and Kay Schaffer (Amsterdam: Rodopi, 2014), 169–84; Caterina Colomba, "History as Sharing Stories: Crossing the Cultural Divide through Kim Scott's Fiction," *Journal of Commonwealth and Postcolonial Studies* 17, no. 2 (2011): 39–56.
17 Jane Gleeson-White, "Capitalism versus the Agency of Place: An Ecocritical Reading of *That Deadman Dance* and *Carpentaria*," *Journal of the Association for the Study of Australian Literature* 13, no. 2 (2013), https://openjournals.library.sydney.edu.au/index.php/JASAL/article/view/9867/9756
18 Rosanne Kennedy, "Orbits, Mobilities, Scales: Kim Scott's *That Deadman Dance* as Transcultural Remembrance," *Australian Humanities Review* 59 (2016): 116.
19 Kate Rigby, "The Poetics of Decolonization: Reading *Carpentaria* in a Feminist Ecocritical Frame," in *International Perspectives in Feminist Ecocriticism*, ed. Greta Gaard, Simon Estok, and Serpil Opperman (New York, NY: Routledge, 2013), 125.
20 Alexis Wright, quoted in Ibid., 125.
21 Alison Ravenscroft, "The Strangeness of the Dance: Kate Grenville, Rohan Wilson, Inga Clendinnen and Kim Scott," *Meanjin* 72, no. 4 (2013), https://meanjin.com.au/essays/the-strangeness-of-the-dance-kate-grenville-rohan-wilson-inga-clendinnen-and-kim-scott/
22 Sue Kossew discusses the terminology of recovery, exploring the resonances of the word "recovery" in relationship to language work, and in relationship to Scott's fiction, since "recovery narrative" is the terminology he chooses to describe his novel *That Deadman Dance*, rejecting other labels such as "post-reconciliation novel" in "Recovering the Past," 170.
23 Kim Scott, "From Drill to Dance," in *Decolonizing the Landscape: Indigenous Cultures in Australia*, ed. Beate Neumeier and Kay Schaffer (Amsterdam: Rodopi, 2014), 12–13.
24 Ibid., 11.
25 Ibid., 3.
26 Kim Scott, "A Noongar Voice, an Anomalous History," *Westerly* 53 (2008): 93–106.
27 Scott, "Can You Anchor," 232.
28 Edward Said, *Culture and Imperialism* (New York, NY: Vintage, 1994), 69–71.

29 See Ngugi wa Thiong'o, *Decolonising the Mind: The Politics of Language in African Literature* (Portsmouth: Heinemann, 2011) and Graham Huggan, *The Postcolonial Exotic: Marketing the Margins* (New York, NY: Routledge, 2001).
30 Scott, "Can You Anchor," 232.
31 See Rob Nixon, *Slow Violence and the Environmentalism of the Poor* (Cambridge, MA: Harvard University Press, 2011).
32 Scott, *That Deadman Dance*, 1.
33 Ibid., 83.
34 Ibid., 85.
35 Ibid., 312.
36 Gordon, *Ghostly Matters*, xvi.
37 Scott, *That Deadman Dance*, 313.
38 Ibid., 313.
39 Ibid., 119.
40 Arnold Zable, "Language and Politics in Indigenous Writing," *Overland* 205 (2011): 55.
41 Scott, "Can You Anchor," 244.
42 David Abram, *The Spell of the Sensuous* (New York, NY: Vintage, 1996), 80.
43 Scott, *That Deadman Dance*, 3.
44 Ibid., 314.
45 Ibid., 55.
46 Ibid., 294–5.
47 Ibid., 114.
48 Ibid., 43.
49 Ibid.
50 William J. Lines, *Taming the Great South Land, a History of the Conquest of Nature in Australia* (Oakland, CA: University of California Press, 1991), 28.
51 Val Plumwood, "Decolonizing Relationships with Nature," in *Decolonizing Nature: For Conservation in a Post-Colonial Era*, ed. William M. Adams and Martin Mulligan (New York, NY: Earthscan, 2004), 65.
52 Scott, *That Deadman Dance*, 325.
53 Michael R. Griffiths, "Winton's Spectralities or What Haunts *Cloudstreet*?" in *Tim Winton: Critical Essays*, ed. Lyn McCredden and Nathanael O'Reilly (Crawley: UWA Publishing, 2014), 91.
54 Anthony Vidler, *The Architectural Uncanny* (Cambridge, MA: MIT Press, 1992), 17. See also Ken Gelder and Jane M. Jacobs, *Uncanny Australia: Sacredness and Identity in a Postcolonial Nation* (Melbourne: Melbourne University Publishing, 1998).
55 Cathy Carruth, *Explorations in Memory* (Baltimore, MD: Johns Hopkins University Press, 1995), 153.
56 Gordon, *Ghostly Matters*, xvi.
57 Scott, "Can You Anchor," 231.

58 Ibid., 232.
59 Scott, *That Deadman Dance*, 349.
60 Scott, "Can You Anchor," 233.
61 Scott, *That Deadman Dance*, 71.
62 Said, *Culture and Imperialism*, 71.
63 Ibid., 79.
64 Scott, *That Deadman Dance*, 311.
65 Ibid., 313.
66 Ibid., 315.
67 Ibid., 315.
68 Amitav Ghosh, *The Great Derangement: Climate Change and the Unthinkable* (Chicago, IL: University of Chicago Press, 2016), 61.
69 Ibid., 60
70 Ibid., 61.
71 Stephen Romei, "Forever Beginning," *The Australian*, July 22, 2017, https://www.theaustralian.com.au/arts/review/aboriginal-identity-in-the-here-and-now-in-kim-scotts-noveltaboo/news-story/ef04673ac974460c91ecffd41f874290
72 Darren Gray, "Traditional Owners Win Native Title Fight with Fortescue," *Sydney Morning Herald*, July 20, 2017, https://www.smh.com.au/business/companies/native-title-win-for-wa-fortescue-land-20170720-gxf78m.html
73 See Jane Bennett, *Vibrant Matter: A Political Ecology of Things* (Durham, NC: Duke University Press, 2010); Serenella Iovino and Serpil Oppermann, "Material Ecocriticism: Materiality, Agency and Models of Narrativity," *Ecozon@* 3, no. 1 (2012): 75–91; Serenella Iovino, "Steps to a Material Ecocriticism: The Recent Literature about the 'New Materialisms' and Its Impact on Ecocritical Theory," *Ecozon@* 3, no. 1 (2012): 134–45; Val Plumwood, "Nature in the Active Voice," *Australian Humanities Review* 46 (2009): 13–129.
74 Plumwood, "Nature in the Active Voice," 128.
75 Ghosh, *Great Derangement*, 63–4.
76 Scott, "A Noongar Voice," 93–106.
77 Deborah Bird Rose, *Wild Dog Dreaming: Love and Extinction* (Charlottesville, VA: University of Virginia Press, 2011), 18.

Chapter 4

1 Rural Development and Land Reform. *Land Audit Report 2017*, February 2018, http://www.ruraldevelopment.gov.za/publications/land-audit-report/file/6126
2 Lindsay Frederick Braun, *Colonial Survey and Native Landscapes in Rural South Africa, 1850–1913: The Politics of Divided Space in the Cape and Transvaal* (Boston, MA: Brill, 2014), 11.

3   Ibid., 12.
4   Leah Temper, Daniela Del Bene, and Joan Martinez-Alier, "Mapping the Frontiers and Front Lines of Global Environmental Justice: The EJ Atlas," *Journal of Political Ecology* 22, no. 1 (2015): 259.
5   See, for example, David Turnbull, *Maps Are Territories: Science Is an Atlas* (Chicago, IL: University of Chicago Press, 1994); J.B. Harley, *The New Nature of Maps: Essays in the History of Cartography* (Baltimore, MD: Johns Hopkins University Press, 2001); Denis Cosgrove, *Geography and Vision: Seeing, Imagining, and Representing the World* (New York, NY: I.B. Tauris, 2008); John Pickles, *Ground Truth: The Social Implications of Geographic Information Systems* (New York, NY: The Guilford Press, 1994); and Denis Wood, *The Power of Maps* (New York, NY: The Guilford Press, 1991).
6   Paul Carter, *Dark Writing: Geography, Performance, Design* (Honolulu, HI: University of Hawaii Press, 2008), 19.
7   Doreen Massey, *For Space* (Thousand Oaks, CA: Sage, 2005), 4.
8   See Harley, *The New Nature,* where Harley characterizes cartographic omissions as political silences.
9   Rose-Innes's *The Rock Alphabet* has not yet drawn substantial attention from literary critics. Pat Louw has analyzed interactions between characters and the Cederberg Mountains to explore how the human and the nonhuman leave imprints on one another, while Jack Kearney includes attention to the representation of parentless children in the novel as part of a larger discussion of parent–child relationships in contemporary African novels. See Pat Louw, "Imprinting the Self: Mountain Presencing, Place and Identity in *The Rock Alphabet* by Henrietta Rose-Innes," *Scrutiny 2* 19, no. 2 (2014): 30–9 and Jack Kearney, "The Representation of Child Deprivation in Three Contemporary African Novels: An Exploration," *English in Africa* 39, no. 1 (2012): 125–44. Since publishing *The Rock Alphabet*, Rose-Innes won the 2008 Caine Prize for African Writing for her short story "Poison" and her novels *Nineveh* (2011) and *Green Lion* (2016) have been drawing positive attention from reviewers and postcolonial and ecocritical scholars.
10 Byron Caminero-Santangelo, *Different Shades of Green: African Literature, Environmental Justice, and Political Ecology* (Charlottesville, VA: University of Virginia Press, 2014).
11 "History: Historical Mapping Background," *NGI: National Geo-Spatial Information*, Rural Development and Land Reform, http://www.ngi.gov.za/index.php/home/history
12 Ibid.
13 Ibid.
14 Although the images were also dismissed by early settlers and scientists as the "primitive," "incomprehensible," and "ugly" work of "a degraded race," they have since become a lucrative focus for tourism, and their meaning continues to be a

subject of enthusiastic debate. J.D. Lewis-Williams, *San Rock Art* (Columbus, OH: Ohio University Press, 2013), 18–19, 30.
15 Braun, *Colonial Survey*, 10–11.
16 Carter, *Dark Writing*, 17.
17 See A.J. Christopher, *The Atlas of Changing South Africa* (New York, NY: Routledge, 2000) and Rita Barnard, *Apartheid and Beyond: South African Writers and the Politics of Place* (New York, NY: Oxford University Press, 2007).
18 Barnard, *Apartheid*, 7.
19 Thomas Bassett, "Signs of the Times: Commercial Road Mapping and National Identity in South Africa," in *Decolonizing the Map: Cartography from Colony to Nation*, ed. James R. Akerman (Chicago, IL: University of Chicago Press, 2017), 347–8.
20 In the epigraph to this chapter, Rose-Innes discusses her interest in human connection with the land. See Henrietta Rose-Innes, "An Interview with Henrietta Rose-Innes," interview by Mildred K. Barya, *Pambazuka News*, June 11, 2009, https://www.pambazuka.org/governance/interview-henrietta-rose-innes
21 Jan Alber, *Unnatural Narrative: Impossible Worlds in Fiction and Drama* (Lincoln, NE: University of Nebraska Press, 2016).
22 Marie-Laure Ryan, Kenneth Foote, and Maoz Azaryahu, *Narrating Space/Spatializing Narrative: Where Narrative Theory and Geography Meet* (Columbus, OH: Ohio State University Press, 2016), 9.
23 Ibid., 8–9. Ryan, Foote, and Azaryahu apply the terms map and tour to describe narrative organization of space in terms of intersections with geography, and they credit narratological scholars Charlotte Linde and William Labov with originally developing the terms in their essay, "Spatial Networks as a Site for the Study of Language and Thought," *Language* 51, no. 4 (December 1975): 924–39.
24 Ibid., 30.
25 Henrietta Rose-Innes, *The Rock Alphabet* (Cape Town: Kwela, 2004), 11.
26 Ibid., 13.
27 "Rock Art," Cederberg Tourism, 2019, https://www.cederberg.com/info.php?id=29
28 Paul Carter, *Ground Truthing: Explorations in a Creative Region* (Perth: UWA Publishing, 2010), 21.
29 Rose-Innes, *Rock Alphabet*, 13.
30 Ibid., 12.
31 Deborah Bird Rose, "Multispecies Knots of Ethical Time," *Environmental Philosophy* 9, no. 1 (2012): 130.
32 Rose-Innes, *Rock Alphabet*, 67–8.
33 Massey, *For Space*, 189.
34 Jacques Derrida, *Specters of Marx*, trans. Peggy Kamuf (New York, NY: Routledge, 1994), xvii.
35 Rose, "Multispecies Knots," 135.
36 Ibid., 131.

37 Ibid., 136.
38 Jacques Derrida, *Writing and Difference*, trans. Alan Bass (Chicago, IL: University of Chicago Press, 1978), 292.
39 Rose-Innes, *Rock Alphabet*, 83.
40 Ibid., 82.
41 David Abram, *Becoming Animal: An Earthly Cosmology* (New York, NY: Vintage Books, 2010), 177.
42 Jacques Derrida, *Archive Fever: A Freudian Impression*, trans. Eric Prenowitz (Chicago, IL: University of Chicago Press, 1997), 2.
43 Ibid.
44 Jacques Derrida, "Archive Fever in South Africa," in *Refiguring the Archive*, ed. Carolyn Hamilton, et al. (New York, NY: Springer, 2002), 54.
45 Achille Mbembe, "The Power of the Archive and Its Limits," in *Refiguring the Archive*, ed. Carolyn Hamilton, et al. (New York, NY: Springer, 2002), 22.
46 Rose-Innes, *Rock Alphabet*, 31–2.
47 Rose, "Multispecies Knots," 128.
48 Rose-Innes, *Rock Alphabet*, 44.
49 Mishuana Goemen, *Mark My Words: Native Women Mapping Our Nations* (Minneapolis, MN: University of Minnesota Press, 2013), 3.
50 Rose-Innes, *Rock Alphabet*, 45.
51 Ibid., 43.
52 Scientists have debated a variety of possibilities to explain the birds' navigational feats from olfactory cues to electromagnetic fields to infrasound to visual landmarks. See Cordula V. Mora, Jeremy D. Ross, Peter V. Gorsevski, Budhaditya Chowdhury and Verner P. Bingman, "Evidence for Discrete Landmark Use by Pigeons during Homing," *Journal of Experimental Biology* 215 (2012): 3379–87; Ingo Schiffner and Roswitha Wiltschko, "Development of the Navigational System in Homing Pigeons: Increase in Complexity of the Navigational Map," *Journal of Experimental Biology* 216 (2013): 2675–81; Jonathan T. Hagstrum, "Atmospheric Propagation Modeling Indicates Homing Pigeons Use Loft-Specific Infrasonic 'Map' Cues," *Journal of Experimental Biology* 216 (2013): 687–99.The reference to homing pigeons also demands attention to what makes land a home to human and nonhuman inhabitants. An intersecting story involves Noor Ebrahim who was evicted from his home in Cape Town's District Six when it was declared a neighborhood for whites only in the 1960s. Noor relocated, along with his treasured pigeons, and when he released them from his new lodging, the pigeons failed to return. The following day, Noor found the pigeons at the site of his bulldozed former home; he reports, "My house was gone. I stopped my car, and when I got out of my car, guess what? All my pigeons were sitting on the empty lane. This was unbelievable. I tip toed behind them. Slowly, they looked at me to

ask, "Where is our home?" (qtd. in Sarah Darby, "Personal Story: Noor Ebrahim," *Center for the Digital Globe* University of Missouri, http://cdig.missouri.edu/personal-story-noor-ebrahim/).

Noor tells his story to visitors to the District Six Museum as a way of depicting the personal impacts of apartheid legislation, and Henrietta Rose-Innes also reflects on ways that urban development impacts people and pigeons in her short story "Homing" in *Homing: Short Stories* (Cape Town: Umuzi, 2010); across these contexts, pigeons push audiences to consider combined impacts of human and nonhuman displacement as well as the impetus to return to places that bear the mark of home, which endures as a relationship to place that cannot be erased by laws or bulldozers.

53 Anthony Vidler, *The Architectural Uncanny* (Cambridge, MA: MIT Press, 1992), 17.
54 While Rose-Innes's approach is distinctive for the way it aligns play with haunting to enable awareness of more-than-human communities that include a range of others from ancestors to animals, drawing on the motif of the haunted house aligns her with other South African writers such as Ivan Vladislavic, Zoe Wicomb, Zakes Mda, Marlene van Niekerk, and Nadine Gordimer. Literary scholars have analyzed South African writers' fascination with architectural forms, including ways that representations of houses serve to convey fears and hopes about the future of the post-apartheid nation and to manifest a haunting of the nation by the past of apartheid and imperial history. See, for example, Jack Shear, "Haunted House, Haunted Nation: *Triomf* and the South African Postcolonial Gothic," *Journal of Literary Studies* 22, no. 1–2 (2006): 70–95; Shameem Black, "Fictions of Rebuilding: Reconstruction in Ivan Vladislavic's South Africa," *Ariel* 39, no. 4 (2009): 5–30; Elizabeth S. Anker, "Rebuilding the Nation: On Architecture and the Aesthetics of Constitutionalism in South African Literature," *Cambridge Journal of Postcolonial Literary Inquiry* 2, no.1 (2015): 73–91. I suggest that *The Rock Alphabet* participates in this literary interrogation of South Africa's spatial history, but I also contend that Rose-Innes offers a particular contribution in calling attention to the human and ecological consequences of the repression of alternate ways of representing and relating to home; she powerfully illustrates the consequences of arresting the play of meanings to control and distinguish a space as a human habitation. For Rose-Innes, home includes more than architecture and human history; it also includes a living community of ecological others, a dimension of haunting that is not fully explored by many of the existing studies of South Africa's haunted houses.
55 Rose-Innes, *Rock Alphabet*, 68.
56 Ibid., 92.
57 Ibid., 91.
58 Ibid., 74.

59 Scott's ideas about sharing recovered knowledge through expanding circuits that keep the local community at the center are discussed in depth in Chapter 3 of this work.
60 Rose-Innes, *Rock Alphabet*, 159.
61 Ibid., 175.
62 Ibid., 160.
63 Ibid., 20.
64 Ibid., 190.
65 Ibid., 106.
66 See David Abram, *The Spell of the Sensuous* (New York, NY: Vintage, 1996), 95–6.
67 Ibid., 190–1.
68 Michiel Heyns, review of *The Rock Alphabet*, by Henrietta Rose-Innes, http://www.michielheyns.co.za/documents/The%20Rock%20Alphabet.pdf
69 Caminero-Santangelo, *Different Shades*, 78.
70 See Henrietta Rose-Innes, "Semiprecious," *Granta*, August 5, 2010, https://granta.com/semiprecious/
71 Greg Ruiters, "Race, Place, and Environmental Rights: A Radical Critique of Environmental Justice Discourse," in *Environmental Justice in South Africa*, ed. David A. McDonald (Athens, OH: Ohio University Press, 2002), 112.
72 Ibid., 112–13.
73 Ibid., 120, 123.
74 David Scholsberg, *Defining Environmental Justice: Theories, Movements, and Nature* (New York, NY: Oxford University Press, 2009), 79.
75 Temper, del Bene, and Martinez-Alier, "Mapping the Frontiers," 261–2.
76 See Stacy Alaimo, *Exposed: Environmental Politics and Pleasures in Posthuman Times* (Minneapolis, MN: University of Minnesota Press, 2016). As I discuss in the introduction to this project, Alaimo cites examples from popular and scientific discourse to demonstrate how an epistemology of overseeing vision dominates representations of the Anthropocene, a claim that she supports by providing multiple examples of ways that visual tropes and tactics such as zooming out are deployed in attempts to visualize planetary scales, but at the cost of making other scales invisible and perpetuating the detached vision of the imperial eye that places viewers outside the scene and removed from any consequences.
77 See *Environmental Justice Atlas*, https://ejatlas.org
78 Ra'eesa Pather, "District Six Claimants Take on Land Reform Minister in Restitution Fight," *Mail and Guardian*, April 24, 2018, https://mg.co.za/article/2018-04-24-district-six-claimants-take-on-land-reform-minister-in-restitution-fight
79 District Six Museum, http://districtsix.co.za/index.php
80 Ibid.
81 Ibid.

82 Ibid.
83 Capeetc, "Water Crisis: Cape Town Water Map Goes Live," *Cape{town}etc*, January 16, 2018, www.capetownetc.com/news/green-light-for-cape-town-water-map-despite-objections/

Life in the Graveyard

1 See Amitav Ghosh, *The Great Derangement: Climate Change and the Unthinkable* (Chicago, IL: University of Chicago Press, 2016).
2 Parul Sehgal, "Arundhati Roy's Fascinating Mess," *The Atlantic*, July/August 2017, https://www.theatlantic.com/magazine/archive/2017/07/arundhati-roys-fascinating-mess/528684/
3 Alex Clark, "*The Ministry of Utmost Happiness* by Arundhati Roy Review: A Patchwork of Narratives," *The Guardian*, June 11, 2017, https://www.theguardian.com/books/2017/jun/11/ministry-utmost-happiness-arundhati-roy-review
4 Caroline Moore, "Arundhati Roy's New Big Cause: The Conflict in Kashmir," *The Spectator*, June 3, 2017, https://www.spectator.co.uk/2017/06/arundhati-roys-new-big-cause-the-conflict-in-kashmir/
5 "Delightful Listening: A Conversation between Viet Thanh Nguyen with Arundhati Roy," *Los Angeles Review of Books*, July 31, 2018, https://lareviewofbooks.org/article/delightful-listening-a-conversation-between-viet-thanh-nguyen-with-arundhati-roy/#!
6 Ibid.
7 Pablo Mukherjee, "Arundhati Roy: Environment and Uneven Form," in *Postcolonial Green*, ed. Bonnie Roos and Alex Hunt (Charlottesville, VA: University of Virginia Press, 2010), 18.
8 Zac O'Yeah, "Writing Fiction Is a Prayer, A Song: Arundhati Roy," *The Hindu*, June 2, 2017, https://www.thehindu.com/books/arundhati-roy-on-the-ministry-of-utmost-happiness-writing-fiction-is-a-prayer-a-song/article18701769.ece
9 Ziya Us Salam, "We Are All Living in a Graveyard of Sorts: Interview with Arundhati Roy," *Frontline*, August 4, 2017, https://frontline.thehindu.com/arts-and-culture/literature/we-are-all-living-in-a-graveyard-ofsorts/article9775128.ece
10 Arundhati Roy, *Field Notes on Democracy: Listening to Grasshoppers* (Chicago, IL: Haymarket Books, 2009), 5–6.
11 Edward Said, *Beginnings: Intention and Method* (New York, NY: Columbia University Press, 1985), xiii.
12 Niels Buch Leander, "To Begin with the Beginning: Birth, Origin, and Narrative Inception," in *Narrative Beginnings: Theories and Practices*, ed. Brian Richardson (Lincoln, NE: University of Nebraska Press, 2008), 16.

13 Catherine Romagnolo, *Opening Acts: Narrative Beginnings in Twentieth Century Feminist Fiction* (Lincoln, NE: University of Nebraska Press, 2015), xiv, xv.
14 Ibid., xxii.
15 Roy in Jeremy Scahill, "Arundhati Roy: 'I Need to Know the Place Where I Stand,'" *The Intercept*, April 17, 2018, https://theintercept.com/2018/04/17/arundhati-roy-intercepted-jeremy-scahill/
16 Said, *Beginnings*, 141.
17 Greg Ruiters, "Race, Place, and Environmental Rights: A Radical Critique of Environmental Justice Discourse," *Environmental Justice in South Africa*, ed. David A. McDonald (Athens, OH: Ohio University Press, 2002), 124.
18 Roy, *Field Notes*, 14.
19 Ashgar Ali Engineer, "Gujarat Riots in the Light of the History of Communal Violence," *Economic and Political Weekly* 37, no. 50 (2002): 5047.
20 Arundhati Roy, *The Ministry of Utmost Happiness* (New York, NY: Knopf, 2017), 105, 107.
21 Ibid., 118.
22 Ibid., 120–1.
23 Michelle Murphy, "Against Population, towards Alterlife," in *Making Kin Not Population*, ed. Adele E. Clarke and Donna Haraway (Chicago, IL: University of Chicago Press, 2018), 110.
24 Michelle Murphy, *Seizing the Means of Reproduction: Entanglements of Feminism, Health And Technoscience* (Durham, NC: Duke University Press, 2012), 8.
25 Jacques Derrida, *Specters of Marx*, trans. Peggy Kamuf (New York, NY: Routledge, 1994), 11. emphasis in original.
26 Susan Winnett, "Macculate Reconceptions," in *Narrative Beginnings: Theories and Practices*, ed. Brian Richardson (Lincoln, NE: University of Nebraska Press, 2008), 246–62.
27 Roy, *Ministry*, 432.
28 Ibid.
29 Timothy Morton, *Humankind: Solidarity with Nonhuman People* (London: Verso, 2017).
30 Roy, *Ministry*, 35.
31 Ibid., 18.
32 Paulla Ebron, and Anna Tsing. "Feminism and the Anthropocene: Assessing the Field through Recent Books," *Feminist Studies* 43, no. 3 (2017): 666.
33 Roy, *Ministry*, 21.
34 Ibid., 29.
35 Ibid.
36 Said, *Beginnings*, xii.
37 Jed Esty and Colleen Lye, "Peripheral Realisms Now," *Modern Language Quarterly* 73, no. 3 (2012): 285.

38 Nicholas Robinette, *Realism, Form and the Postcolonial Novel* (New York, NY: Palgrave, 2014), 5.
39 Esty and Lye, "Peripheral," 277.
40 Roy, *Ministry*, 31–2.
41 Ibid., 53.
42 Ibid., 55.
43 Ibid., 57.
44 See Roy, *Field Notes*, which contains an essay about the killings in Gujarat. See also "History of Communal Violence in Gujarat," *Outlook India*, November 22, 2002, https://www.outlookindia.com/website/story/history-of-communal-violence-in-gujarat/217988, which provides an extended history that traces patterns of violence in Gujarat that include violence against Muslims in the decade of 1961–71, a shift to violence based on caste and violence directed at Christians, and a return to violence against Muslims in late 1990s. See also Ashgar Ali Engineer, "Gujarat Riots," which offers analysis of a range of political and economic factors that have contributed to a history of violence in Gujarat.
45 Roy, *Field Notes*, 147.
46 Ibid., xxi.
47 Susanne Kappeler, "Speciesism, Racism, Nationalism ... or the Power of Scientific Subjectivity," in *Animals and Women: Feminist Theoretical Explorations*, ed. Carol J. Adams and Josephine Donovan (Durham, NC: Duke University Press, 1995), 323.
48 Ibid., 326.
49 Ibid., 348.
50 Roy, *Ministry*, 365.
51 Ibid., 351.
52 Ibid., 377.
53 Ibid., 399, 404.
54 Avery Gordon, *Ghostly Matters: Haunting and the Sociological Imagination* (Minneapolis, MN: University of Minnesota Press, 2008), 27.
55 Roy, *Ministry*, 7.
56 Ibid., 6.
57 Ibid.
58 Roy references diclofenac directly in the novel. For additional information about diclofenac as the cause of vulture deaths see Ministry of Environment and Forests, Government of India, "Action Plan for Vulture Conservation in India," April 2006, http://www.moef.nic.in/sites/default/files/vulture_plan.pdf
59 Roy, *Ministry*, 6.
60 Ibid.
61 Thom Van Dooren, *Flight Ways: Life and Loss at the Edge of Extinction* (New York, NY: Columbia University Press, 2016), 50.
62 Ibid., 51.

63 Ibid., 55.
64 Ibid., 58.
65 Ashley Dawson, *Extinction: A Radical History* (New York, NY: OR Books, 2016), 13.
66 Ibid., 98–9.
67 Deborah Bird Rose, "Multispecies Knots of Ethical Time," *Environmental Philosophy* 9, no. 1 (2012): 128.
68 For discussion of burial ground controversies see Atul Sethi, "Grave Crisis Hits Cemeteries," *The Times of India*, April 5, 2009, https://timesofindia.indiatimes.com/home/sunday-times/deep-focus/Grave-crisis-hits-cemeteries/articleshow/4360271cms. See also Mallica Joshi "Grave Concerns: As Population Increases, Space to Bury the Dead Is Fast Shrinking," *The Indian Express*, June 25, 2018, https://indianexpress.com/article/cities/delhi/grave-concerns-5024790/
69 Scahill, "Arundhati Roy."
70 Roy, *Ministry*, 77.
71 Ibid., 90.
72 Ibid., 92–3.
73 Ibid., 33.
74 Ibid., 62–3.
75 Ibid., 62.
76 Ibid., 70.
77 It is also worth briefly noting that this approach to time marks a point of difference between my approach and other critics who have considered Roy in relation to peripheral realism or a "realist impulse." Those discussions focus on the novel's setting in the present rather than the past and note its contemporary focus as a shift from earlier postcolonial writers' attention to the past. While I am suggesting that Roy challenges divisions of past/present/future, I contend that separating the contemporary from the past does not reflect the novel's deep engagement with India's past or reflect Roy's desires to work across categories. In fact, I would reiterate the need to think across categories in order to achieve social and environmental justice: focusing on the contemporary alone does not allow for the accountability to past and future generations required for inclusive justice. For discussion of the novel in relation to realism see Ulka Anjaria, "The Realist Impulse and the Future of Postcoloniality," *Novel: A Forum on Fiction* 49, no. 2 (2016): 278–94 and Filippo Menozzi, "'Too Much Blood for Good Literature': Arundhati Roy's *The Ministry of Utmost Happiness* and the Question of Realism," *Journal of Postcolonial Writing* (2018). DOI: 10.1080/17449855.2018.1507919.
78 Roy, *Ministry*, 87.
79 Ibid., 444.

80 Arundhati Roy, *Capitalism: A Ghost Story* (Chicago, IL: Haymarket Books, 2014), 37.
81 Patrick Colm Hogan, "Stories, Wars, and Emotions: The Absoluteness of Narrative Beginnings," in *Narrative Beginnings: Theories and Practices*, ed. Brian Richardson (Lincoln, NE: University of Nebraska Press, 2008), 55.
82 Ibid., 57–8.

Conclusion

1 Ursula Heise, *Imagining Extinction: The Cultural Meanings of Endangered Species* (Chicago, IL: University of Chicago Press, 2016), 12.
2 Amitav Ghosh, *The Great Derangement: Climate Change and the Unthinkable* (Chicago, IL: University of Chicago Press, 2016), 128–9.
3 Ibid., 72.
4 Alexis Wright, *The Swan Book* (New York, NY: Atria Books, 2013), 297.
5 Ibid., 298.
6 Ibid., 301.
7 Edward Said, *Culture and Imperialism* (New York, NY: Vintage, 1994), 17.
8 Chris Abani, "Telling Stories from Africa," filmed 2007, 17: 36, http://www.chrisabani.com/posts/2007/06/29/ted-video-telling-stories-from-africa/
9 Avery Gordon, *Ghostly Matters: Haunting and the Sociological Imagination* (Minneapolis, MN: University of Minnesota Press, 2008), 8.
10 Henrietta Rose-Innes, *The Rock Alphabet* (Cape Town: Kwela, 2004), 74.
11 Greg Ruiters, "Race, Place, and Environmental Rights: A Radical Critique of Environmental Justice Discourse," *Environmental Justice in South Africa*, ed. David A. McDonald (Athens, OH: Ohio University Press, 2002), 124.
12 Nicole Seymour, *Strange Natures: Futurity, Empathy, and the Queer Ecological Imagination* (Urbana, IL: University of Illinois Press, 2013), 7.
13 David Wallace-Wells, "Why Do We Fail When We Try to Tell the Story of Climate Change?" *Slate*, February 19, 2019, https://slate.com/technology/2019/02/climate-change-storytelling-hollywood-failure-imagination.html
14 Claire Colebrook, "Anti-Catastrophic Time," *New Formations* 92 (2017): 106.
15 Timothy Morton, *Humankind: Solidarity with Nonhuman People* (London: Verso, 2017), 12–13.

Bibliography

Abani, Chris. *GraceLand*. London: Picador, 2004.

Abani, Chris. "Interview with Colm Toibin." *BOMB Magazine*, Summer 2006. http://bombmagazine.org/article/2840/chris-abani

Abani, Chris. "Telling Stories from Africa." Filmed, 2007. TED video, 17: 36. http://www.chrisabani.com/posts/2007/06/29/ted-video-telling-stories-from-africa/

Abraham, Nicolas, and Maria Torok. *The Shell and the Kernel*. Translated by Nicholas T. Rand. Chicago, IL: University of Chicago Press, 1994.

Abram, David. *Becoming Animal: An Earthly Cosmology*. New York, NY: Vintage Books, 2010.

Abram, David. *The Spell of the Sensuous*. New York, NY: Vintage, 1996.

Adisa, Opal. "Journey into Speech: A Writer between Two Worlds: An Interview with Michelle Cliff." *African American Review* 28, no. 2 (1994): 273–82.

Agbola, Tundae, and A.M. Jinadu "Forced Eviction and Forced Relocation in Nigeria: The Experience of Those Evicted from Maroko in 1990." *Environment and Urbanization* 9, no. 2 (1997): 271–88.

Ahmed, Saleh, and Mahbubur Meenar. "Just Sustainability in the Global South: A Case Study of the Megacity of Dhaka." *Journal of Developing Societies* 34, no. 4 (2018): 401–24.

Akpan, Wilson. "Between Ethnic Essentialism and Environmental Racism: Oil and the 'Glocalisation' of Environmental Justice Discourse in Nigeria." *African Sociological Review/Revue Africaine de Sociologie* 10, no. 2 (2006): 18–42.

Alaimo, Stacy. *Bodily Natures: Science, Environment, and the Material Self*. Bloomington, IN: Indiana University Press, 2010.

Alaimo, Stacy. *Exposed: Environmental Politics and Pleasures in Posthuman Times*. Minneapolis, MN: University of Minnesota Press, 2016.

Alber, Jan. *Unnatural Narrative: Impossible Worlds in Fiction and Drama*. Lincoln, NE: University of Nebraska Press, 2016.

Alber, Jan, Stefan Iversen, Henrik Skov Nielsen, and Brian Richardson. "Unnatural Narrative, Unnatural Narratology: Beyond Mimetic Models." *Narrative* 18, no. 2 (2010): 113–36.

Andrade, Susan Z. "Representing Slums and Home: Chris Abani's *GraceLand*." In *The Legacies of Modernism: Historicising Postwar and Contemporary Fiction*, edited by David James, 225–42. Cambridge: Cambridge University Press, 2012.

Anjaria, Ulka. "The Realist Impulse and the Future of Postcoloniality." *Novel: A Forum on Fiction* 49, no. 2 (2016): 278–94.

Anker, Elizabeth S. "Rebuilding the Nation: On Architecture and the Aesthetics of Constitutionalism in South African Literature." *Cambridge Journal of Postcolonial Literary Inquiry* 2, no. 1 (2015): 73–91.

Barnard, Rita. *Apartheid and Beyond: South African Writers and the Politics of Place.* New York, NY: Oxford University Press, 2007.

Barya, Mildred K. "An Interview with Henrietta Rose-Innes." *Pambazuka News*, June 11, 2009. https://www.pambazuka.org/governance/interview-henrietta-rose-innes

Bassett, Thomas. "Signs of the Times: Commercial Road Mapping and National Identity in South Africa." In *Decolonizing the Map: Cartography from Colony to Nation*, edited by James R. Akerman, 339–76. Chicago, IL: University of Chicago Press, 2017.

Bauman, Zygmunt. *Wasted Lives: Modernity and Its Outcasts.* Cambridge: Polity Press, 2004.

Beaumont, Matthew, ed. *A Concise Companion to Realism.* Chichester: Wiley-Blackwell, 2010.

Bennett, Jane. *Vibrant Matter: A Political Ecology of Things.* Durham, NC: Duke University Press, 2010.

Bennholdt-Thomsen, Veronika, and Maria Mies. *The Subsistence Perspective: Beyond the Globalised Economy.* London: Zed Books, 1999.

Black, Shameem. "Fictions of Rebuilding: Reconstruction in Ivan Vladislavic's South Africa." *Ariel* 39, no. 4 (2009): 5–30.

Blanco, Maria del Pilar, and Esther Peeren. "Introduction: Conceptualizing Spectralities." In *The Spectralities Reader: Ghosts and Haunting in Contemporary Cultural Theory*, edited by Maria del Pilar Blanco and Esther Peeren, 1–27. London: Bloomsbury, 2013.

Braun, Lindsay Frederick. *Colonial Survey and Native Landscapes in Rural South Africa, 1850–1913: The Politics of Divided Space in the Cape and Transvaal.* Boston, MA: Brill, 2014.

Brewster, Anne. "Whiteness and Indigenous Sovereignty in Kim Scott's *That Deadman Dance*." *Journal of the European Association of Studies on Australia* 2, no. 2 (2011): 60–71.

Buell, Lawrence. *The Environmental Imagination: Thoreau, Nature Writing, and the Formation of American Culture.* Cambridge, MA: Harvard University Press, 1995.

Buell, Lawrence. *The Future of Environmental Criticism: Environmental Crisis and Literary Imagination.* Oxford: Blackwell Publishing, 2005.

Bullard, Robert D. *Dumping in Dixie: Race, Class, and Environmental Quality.* New York, NY: Routledge, 1990.

Caminero-Santangelo, Byron. *Different Shades of Green: African Literature, Environmental Justice, and Political Ecology.* Charlottesville, VA: University of Virginia Press, 2014.

Capeetc. "Water Crisis: Cape Town Water Map Goes Live." *Cape{town}etc*, January 16, 2018. www.capetownetc.com/news/green-light-for-cape-town-water-map-despite-objections/

Carrigan, Anthony. "'Justice Is on Our Side'? *Animal's People*, Generic Hybridity, and Eco-Crime." *The Journal of Commonwealth Literature* 47, no. 2 (2012): 159–74.

Carruth, Cathy. *Explorations in Memory.* Baltimore, MD: Johns Hopkins University Press, 1995.

Carter, Paul. *Dark Writing: Geography, Performance, Design*. Honolulu, HI: University of Hawaii Press, 2008.

Carter, Paul. *Ground Truthing: Explorations in a Creative Region*. Perth: UWA Publishing, 2010.

Chakrabarty, Dipesh. "Foreword." In *Global Ecologies and the Environmental Humanities: Postcolonial Approaches*, edited by Elizabeth DeLoughrey, Jill Didur, and Anthony Carrigan, xiii–xv. New York, NY: Routledge, 2015.

Christopher, A.J. *The Atlas of Changing South Africa*. New York, NY: Routledge, 2000.

Cilano, Cara, and Elizabeth DeLoughrey. "Against Authenticity: Global Knowledges and Postcolonial Ecocriticism." *Interdisciplinary Studies in Literature and Environment* 14, no. 1 (2007): 71–87.

Clark, Alex. "*The Ministry of Utmost Happiness* by Arundhati Roy Review: A Patchwork of Narratives." *The Guardian*, June 11, 2017. https://www.theguardian.com/books/2017/jun/11/ministry-utmost-happiness-arundhati-roy-review

Cliff, Michelle. *Abeng*. New York, NY: Penguin, 1984.

Cliff, Michelle. "Caliban's Daughter: The Tempest and the Teapot." *Frontiers: A Journal of Women's Studies* 12, no. 2 (1991): 36–51.

Cliff, Michelle. "Clare Savage as Crossroads Character." In *Caribbean Women Writers: Essays from the First International Conference*, edited by Selwyn Reginald Cudjoe, 263–8. Amherst, MA: University of Massachusetts Press, 1990.

Cliff, Michelle. *No Telephone to Heaven*. New York, NY: Penguin, 1987.

Cockpit Country Stakeholders Group and Jamaica Environmental Advocacy Network. *Save Cockpit Country Fact Sheet*, 2007. http://www.jamaicancaves.org/Save_Cockpit_Country_Fact_Sheet_2007.pdf

Colebrook, Claire. "Anti-Catastrophic Time." *New Formations* 92 (2017): 102–19.

Colebrook, Claire. *Death of the Post Human: Essays on Extinction, Volume I*. London: Open Humanities Press, 2014.

Colomba, Caterina. "History as Sharing Stories: Crossing the Cultural Divide through Kim Scott's Fiction." *Journal of Commonwealth and Postcolonial Studies* 17, no. 2 (2011): 39–56.

Cosgrove, Denis. *Geography and Vision: Seeing, Imagining, and Representing the World*. New York, NY: I.B. Tauris, 2008.

Crouch, David. "National Hauntings: The Architecture of Australian Ghost Stories." *Journal of the Association for the Study of Australian Literature* (2007): 94–105.

Dannenberg, Hilary. "Narrating the Postcolonial Metropolis in Anglophone African Fiction: Chris Abani's *GraceLand* and Phaswane Mpe's *Welcome to Our Hillbrow*." *Journal of Postcolonial Writing* 48, no. 1 (2012): 39–50.

Darby, Sarah. "Personal Story: Noor Ebrahim." *Center for the Digital Globe*. University of Missouri. http://cdig.missouri.edu/personal-story-noor-ebrahim/

Davidson, Tonya, Ondine Park, and Rob Shields. *Ecologies of Affect: Placing Nostalgia, Desire and Hope*. Waterloo: Wilfrid Laurier University Press, 2011.

Davis, Colin. "Etat Present: Hauntology, Spectres and Phantoms." In *The Spectralities Reader: Ghosts and Haunting in Contemporary Critical Theory*, edited by Maria del Pilar Blanco and Esther Peeren, 53–60. New York, NY: Bloomsbury, 2013.

Davis, Mike. *Planet of Slums*. London: Verso, 2007.

Dawson, Ashley. *Extinction: A Radical History*. New York, NY: OR Books, 2016.

Dawson, Ashley. "Surplus City: Structural Adjustment, Self-Fashioning, and Urban Insurrection in Chris Abani's *GraceLand*." *Interventions* 11, no. 1 (2009): 16–34.

Del Principe, David, ed. "The EcoGothic in the Long Nineteenth Century." Special Issue, *Gothic Studies* 16, no. 1 (May 2014): 1–8.

"Delightful Listening: A Conversation between Viet Thanh Nguyen with Arundhati Roy." *Los Angeles Review of Books*, July 31, 2018. https://lareviewofbooks.org/article/delightful-listening-a-conversation-between-viet-thanh-nguyen-with-arundhati-roy/#!

DeLoughrey, Elizabeth, and George B. Handley, eds. *Postcolonial Ecologies: Literatures of the Environment*. New York, NY: Oxford University Press, 2011.

DeLoughrey, Elizabeth, Jill Didur, and Anthony Carrigan, eds. *Global Ecologies and the Environmental Humanities: Postcolonial Approaches*. New York, NY: Routledge, 2015.

DeLoughrey, Elizabeth, Renee K. Gosson, and George B. Handley, eds. *Caribbean Literature and the Environment: Between Nature and Culture*. Charlottesville, VA: University of Virginia Press, 2005.

Derrida, Jacques. *Archive Fever: A Freudian Impression*. Translated by Eric Prenowitz. Chicago, IL: University of Chicago Press, 1997.

Derrida, Jacques. "Archive Fever in South Africa." In *Refiguring the Archive*, edited by Carolyn Hamilton, et al., 38–60. New York, NY: Springer, 2002.

Derrida, Jacques. *Du droit a la philosophie*. Paris: Galilee, 1990.

Derrida, Jacques. *Specters of Marx*. Translated by Peggy Kamuf. New York, NY: Routledge, 1994.

Derrida, Jacques. *Writing and Difference*. Translated by Alan Bass. Chicago, IL: University of Chicago Press, 1978.

Derrida, Jacques, and Bernard Stiegler. "Spectrographies." In *The Spectralities Reader: Ghosts and Haunting in Contemporary Cultural Theory*, edited by Maria Del Pilar Blanco and Esther Peeren, 37–51. New York, NY: Bloomsbury, 2013.

District Six Museum. http://districtsix.co.za/index.php

Easterlin, Nancy. *A Biocultural Approach to Literary Theory and Interpretation*. Baltimore, MD: Johns Hopkins University Press, 2012.

Ebron, Paulla, and Anna Tsing. "Feminism and the Anthropocene: Assessing the Field through Recent Books." *Feminist Studies* 43, no. 3 (2017): 658–83.

Elbert, Monika. "Retrieving the Language of the Ghostly Mother: Displaced Daughters and the Search for Home in Amy Tan and Michelle Cliff." In *Ghosts, Stories, Histories: Ghost Stories and Alternative Histories*, edited by Sladja Blazan, 159–72. Newcastle: Cambridge Scholars Publishing, 2007.

Engineer, Asghar Ali. "Gujarat Riots in the Light of the History of Communal Violence." *Economic and Political Weekly* 37, no. 50 (2002): 5047–54.

Environmental Justice Atlas. https://ejatlas.org

Estok, Simon. *The Ecophobia Hypothesis.* New York, NY: Routledge, 2018.

Estok, Simon. "Hollow Ecology and Anthropocene Scales of Measurement." *Mosaic* 51, no. 3 (2018): 37–49.

Estok, Simon. "Theorizing in a Space of Ambivalent Openness: Ecocriticism and Ecophobia." *Interdisciplinary Studies in Literature and Environment* 16, no. 2 (2009): 203–25.

Esty, Jed. "Realism Wars." *Novel* 49, no. 2 (2016): 316–42.

Esty, Jed, and Colleen Lye. "Peripheral Realisms Now." *Modern Language Quarterly* 73, no. 3 (2012): 269–88.

Fanon, Frantz. *The Wretched of the Earth.* Translated by Richard Philcox. New York, NY: Grove Press, 2005.

Freeman, Elizabeth. *Time Binds: Queer Temporalities, Queer Histories.* Durham, NC: Duke University Press, 2010.

"Full Extended Interview: Arundhati Roy on *Democracy Now!*" *Democracy Now!*, June 20, 2017. https://www.democracynow.org/2017/6/20/full_extended_interview_arundhati_roy_on

Gan, Elain, Anna Tsing, Heather Swanson, and Nils Bubandt. "Introduction: Haunted Landscapes of the Anthropocene." In *Arts of Living on a Damaged Planet*, edited by Anna Tsing, Heather Swanson, Elaine Gan, and Nils Bubandt, G1–14. Minneapolis, MN: University of Minnesota Press, 2017.

Gandy, Matthew. "Learning from Lagos." *New Left Review* 33 (2005): 37–52.

Gelder, Ken, and Jane M. Jacobs. *Uncanny Australia: Sacredness and Identity in a Postcolonial Nation.* Melbourne: Melbourne University Publishing, 1998.

Genette, Gerard. *Narrative Discourse: An Essay in Method.* Translated by Jane E. Lewin. Ithaca, NY: Cornell University Press, 1980.

Ghosh, Amitav. *The Great Derangement: Climate Change and the Unthinkable.* Chicago, IL: University of Chicago Press, 2016.

Gleeson-White, Jane. "Capitalism versus the Agency of Place: An Ecocritical Reading of *That Deadman Dance* and *Carpentaria*." *Journal of the Association for the Study of Australian Literature* 13, no. 2 (2013). https://openjournals.library.sydney.edu.au/index.php/JASAL/article/view/9867/9756

Glissant, Edouard. *Caribbean Discourse: Selected Essays.* Translated by J. Michael Dash. Charlottesville, VA: University of Virginia Press, 1999.

Glissant, Edouard. *Poetics of Relation.* Translated by Betsy Wing. Ann Arbor, MI: University of Michigan Press, 1997.

Goemen, Mishuana. *Mark My Words: Native Women Mapping our Nations.* Minneapolis, MN: University of Minnesota Press, 2013.

Gordon, Avery. *Ghostly Matters: Haunting and the Sociological Imagination.* Minneapolis, MN: University of Minnesota Press, 2008.

Gray, Darren. "Traditional Owners Win Native Title Fight with Fortescue." *Sydney Morning Herald*, July 20, 2017. https://www.smh.com.au/business/companies/native-title-win-for-wa-fortescue-land-20170720-gxf78m.html

Griffiths, Michael R. "Winton's Spectralities or What Haunts *Cloudstreet*?" In *Tim Winton: Critical Essays*, edited by Lyn McCredden and Nathanael O'Reilly, 75–95. Crawley: UWA Publishing, 2014.

Hagstrum, Jonathan T. "Atmospheric Propagation Modeling Indicates Homing Pigeons Use Loft-Specific Infrasonic 'Map' Cues." *Journal of Experimental Biology* 216 (2013): 687–99.

Haraway, Donna J. *Staying with the Trouble: Making Kin in the Chthulucene*. Durham, NC: Duke University Press, 2016.

Harley, J.B. *The New Nature of Maps: Essays in the History of Cartography*. Baltimore, MD: Johns Hopkins University Press, 2001.

Harris, Wilson. "Interview with Fred D'Aguiar." *BOMB*, January 1, 2003. https://bombmagazine.org/articles/wilson-harris/

Harris, Wilson. "Theater of the Arts." In *Theater of the Arts: Wilson Harris and the Caribbean*, edited by Hena Maes-Jelinek and Benedicte Ledent, 1–10. Amsterdam: Brill Rodopi, 2002.

Harrison, Sarah K. "'Suspended City': Personal, Urban, and National Development in Chris Abani's *GraceLand*." *Research in African Literatures* 43, no. 2 (2012): 95–114.

Hartwiger, Alexander Greer. "Strangers in/to the World: The Unhomely in Chris Abani's *GraceLand*," *Matatu: Journal for African Culture and Society* 45, no. 1 (2014): 233–50.

Heise, Ursula. "Afterword: Postcolonial Ecocriticism and the Question of Literature." In *Postcolonial Green: Environmental Politics and World Narratives*, edited by Bonnie Roos, Alex Hunt, and John Tallmadge, 251–8. Charlottesville, VA: University of Virginia Press, 2010.

Heise, Ursula. *Imagining Extinction: The Cultural Meanings of Endangered Species*. Chicago, IL: University of Chicago Press, 2016.

Heyns, Michiel. Review of *The Rock Alphabet*, December 2004. http://www.michielheyns.co.za/documents/The%20Rock%20Alphabet.pdf

Hillard, Tom. "Deep into That Darkness Peering: An Essay on Gothic Nature." *ISLE: Interdisciplinary Studies in Literature and Environment* 16, no. 4 (2009): 685–95.

"History of Communal Violence in Gujarat." *Outlook India*, November 22, 2002. https://www.outlookindia.com/website/story/history-of-communal-violence-in-gujarat/217988

"History: Historical Mapping Background." *NGI: National Geo-spatial Information*, Rural Development and Land Reform. 2013. http://www.ngi.gov.za/index.php/home/history

Hitchens, Christopher. "The Vietnam Syndrome." *Vanity Fair*, August 2006. https://www.vanityfair.com/news/2006/08/hitchens200608

Hogan, Patrick Colm. "Stories, Wars, and Emotions: The Absoluteness of Narrative Beginnings." In *Narrative Beginnings: Theories and Practices*, edited by Brian Richardson, 44–62. Lincoln, NE: University of Nebraska Press, 2008.

Huggan, Graham. *The Postcolonial Exotic: Marketing the Margins*. New York: Routledge, 2001.

Huggan, Graham, and Helen Tiffin. *Postcolonial Ecocriticism: Literature, Animals, Environment*. New York, NY: Routledge, 2010.

Iheka, Cajetan. *Naturalizing Africa: Ecological Violence, Agency, and Postcolonial Resistance in African Literature*. Cambridge: Cambridge University Press, 2018.

Iovino, Serenella. "Steps to a Material Ecocriticism: The Recent Literature about the 'New Materialisms' and Its Impact on Ecocritical Theory." *Ecozon@* 3, no. 1 (2012): 134–45.

Iovino, Serenella, and Serpil Oppermann. "Material Ecocriticism: Materiality, Agency and Models of Narrativity." *Ecozon@* 3, no. 1 (2012): 75–91.

James, Erin. *The Storyworld Accord: Econarratology and Postcolonial Narratives*. Lincoln, NE: University of Nebraska Press, 2015.

Joshi, Mallica. "Grave Concerns: As Population Increases, Space to Bury the Dead Is Fast Shrinking." *The Indian Express*, June 25, 2018. https://indianexpress.com/article/cities/delhi/grave-concerns-5024790/

Kaiser, Nick. "Arundhati Roy: I Feel Like All the Human Race Is in a Graveyard." *Dpa International*.com. http://www.dpa-international.com/topic/arundhati-roy-feel-like-human-race-graveyard-170820-99-711824

Kappeler, Susanne. "Speciesism, Racism, Nationalism ... or the Power of Scientific Subjectivity." In *Animals and Women: Feminist Theoretical Explorations*, edited by Carol J. Adams and Josephine Donovan, 320–52. Durham, NC: Duke University Press, 1995.

Kearney, Jack. "The Representation of Child Deprivation in Three Contemporary African Novels: An Exploration." *English in Africa* 39, no. 1 (2012): 125–44.

Kennedy, Rosanne. "Multidirectional Eco-memory in an Era of Extinction." In *The Routledge Companion to the Environmental Humanities*, edited by Ursula Heise, Jon Christensen, and Michelle Niemann, 268–77. New York, NY: Routledge, 2017.

Kennedy, Rosanne. "Orbits, Mobilities, Scales: Kim Scott's *That Deadman Dance* as Transcultural Remembrance." *Australian Humanities Review* 59 (2016): 114–35. Accessed June 15, 2018. http://australianhumanitiesreview.org/wp-content/uploads/2016/08/AHR59_Kennedy.pdf

Knutson, Lin. "Michelle Cliff and the Feminization of Space: *No Telephone to Heaven* as Female Limbo Gateway into History." *Journal of Caribbean Studies* 11, no. 3 (1996): 276–300.

Kossew, Sue. "Recovering the Past: Entangled Histories in Kim Scott's *That Deadman Dance*." In *Decolonizing the Landscape: Indigenous Cultures in Australia*, edited by Beate Neumeier and Kay Schaffer, 169–82. Amsterdam: Rodopi, 2014.

Krishnan, Madhu. "Mythopoetics and Cultural Re-Creation." In *Contemporary African Literature in English: Global Locations, Postcolonial Identifications*, 96–129. New York, NY: Palgrave Macmillan, 2014.

Leander, Niels Buch. "To Begin with the Beginning: Birth, Origin, and Narrative Inception." In *Narrative Beginnings: Theories and Practices*, edited by Brian Richardson, 15–28. Lincoln, NE: University of Nebraska Press.

Lewis-Williams, J.D. *San Rock Art*. Columbus, OH: Ohio University Press, 2013.

Lines, William J. *Taming the Great South Land: A History of the Conquest of Nature in Australia*. Oakland, CA: University of California Press, 1991.

Louw, Pat. "Imprinting the Self: Mountain Presencing, Place and Identity in The Rock Alphabet by Henrietta Rose-Innes." *Scrutiny 2* 19, no. 2 (2014): 30–9.

Manhart, Andreas, Oladele Osibanjo, Adeyinka Aderinto, and Siddharth Prakash. *Informal E-Waste Management in Lagos, Nigeria: Socio-Economic Impacts and Feasibility of International Recycling Co-Operations*. Lagos and Frieburg: Oko-Institute.V., 2011. http://www.basel.int/Portals/4/Basel%20Convention/docs/eWaste/E-waste_Africa_Project_Nigeria.pdf

Martini, Edwin A. *Agent Orange: History, Science, and the Politics of Uncertainty*. Amherst, MA: University of Massachusetts Press, 2012.

Mason, Lauren. "Leaving Lagos: Intertextuality and Images in Chris Abani's *GraceLand*." *Research in African Literatures* 45, no. 3 (2014): 206–26.

Massey, Doreen. *For Space*. Thousand Oaks, CA: Sage, 2005.

Mbembe, Achille. "Life, Sovereignty, and Terror in the Fiction of Amos Tutuola." *Research in African Literatures* 34, no. 4 (2003): 1–26.

Mbembe, Achille. "The Power of the Archive and Its Limits." In *Refiguring the Archive*, edited by Carolyn Hamilton, et al., 19–28. New York, NY: Springer, 2002.

McGranahan, Gordon, and Peter Marcotullio. *Scaling Urban Environmental Challenges: From Local to Global and Back*. New York, NY: Routledge, 2007.

Menozzi, Filippo. "'Too Much Blood for Good Literature': Arundhati Roy's *The Ministry of Utmost Happiness* and the Question of Realism." *Journal of Postcolonial Writing* (2018). DOI: 10.1080/17449855.2018.1507919

Mies, Maria and Veronika Bennholdt-Thomsen, *The Subsistence Perspective: Beyond the Globalised Economy*. New York, NY: Zed Books, 1999.

Ministry of Environment and Forests, Government of India, "Action Plan for Vulture Conservation in India," April 2006. http://www.moef.nic.in/sites/default/files/vulture_plan.pdf

Moore, Caroline. "Arundhati Roy's New Big Cause: The Conflict in Kashmir." *The Spectator*, June 3, 2017. https://www.spectator.co.uk/2017/06/arundhati-roys-new-big-cause-the-conflict-in-kashmir/

Moore, Jason W. Moore. *Capitalism in the Web of Life: Ecology and the Accumulation of Capital*. New York, NY: Verso, 2015.

Mora, Cordula V., Jeremy D. Ross, Peter V. Gorsevski, Budhaditya Chowdhury, and Verner P. Bingman. "Evidence for Discrete Landmark Use by Pigeons during Homing." *Journal of Experimental Biology* 215 (2012): 3379–87.

Morton, Timothy. *Humankind: Solidarity with Nonhuman People*. London: Verso, 2017.

Morton, Timothy. *Hyperobjects: Philosophy and Ecology after the End of the World*. Minneapolis, MN: University of Minnesota Press, 2013.

Mukherjee, Pablo. "Arundhati Roy: Environment and Uneven Form." In *Postcolonial Green*, edited by Bonnie Roos and Alex Hunt, 17–31. Charlottesville, VA: University of Virginia Press, 2010.

Murphy, Michelle. "Against Population, towards Alterlife." In *Making Kin Not Population*, edited by Adele E. Clarke and Donna Haraway, 101–24. Chicago, IL: University of Chicago Press, 2018.

Murphy, Michelle. *Seizing the Means of Reproduction: Entanglements of Feminism, Health and Technoscience*. Durham, NC: Duke University Press, 2012.

Neimanis, Astrida, Cecilia Asberg, and Johan Hedren. "Four Problems, Four Directions for Environmental Humanities: A Critical Posthumanities for the Anthropocene." *Ethics and Environment* 20, no. 1 (2015): 67–97.

Ngugi wa Thiong'o. *Decolonising the Mind: The Politics of Language in African Literature*. Portsmouth: Heinemann, 2011.

Ngugi wa Thiongo. *Something Torn and New: An African Renaissance*. New York, NY: Civitas Books, 2009.

Nixon, Rob. "Environmentalism and Postcolonialism." In *Postcolonial Studies and Beyond*, edited by Ania Loomba, Suvir Kaul, Matti Bunzl, Antoinette Burton, and Jed Esty, 233–51. Durham, NC: Duke University Press, 2005.

Nixon, Rob. *Slow Violence and the Environmentalism of the Poor*. Cambridge, MA: Harvard University Press, 2011.

Ofiemun, Odia. "Daring Visions." Review of *Invisible Chapters*, by Maik Nwosu. *English in Africa* 32, no. 1 (2005): 135–41.

O'Yeah, Zac. "Writing Fiction Is a Prayer, a Song: Arundhati Roy." *The Hindu*, June 2, 2017. https://www.thehindu.com/books/arundhati-roy-on-the-ministry-of-utmost-happiness-writing-fiction-is-a-prayer-a-song/article18701769.ece

Pan Macmillan Australia. "Kim Scott." 2019. https://www.panmacmillan.com.au/author/kim-scott/

Pather, Ra'eesa. "District Six Claimants Take on Land Reform Minister in Restitution Fight." *Mail and Guardian*, April 24, 2018. https://mg.co.za/article/2018-04-24-district-six-claimants-take-on-land-reform-minister-in-restitution-fight

Peeren, Esther. "Everyday Ghosts and the Ghostly Everyday in Amos Tutuola, Ben Okri, and Achille Mbembe." In *Popular Ghosts: The Haunted Spaces of Everyday Culture*, edited by Maria del Pilar Blanco and Esther Peeren, 106–17. New York, NY: Continuum, 2010.

Pereen, Esther. "The Ghost as a Gendered Chronotope." In *Ghosts, Stories, Histories: Ghost Stories and Alternative Histories*, edited by Sladja Blazan, 81–96. Newcastle: Cambridge Scholars Publishing, 2007.

Phillips, Dana. *The Truth of Ecology: Nature, Culture, and Literature in America*. New York, NY: Oxford University Press, 2003.

Pickles, John. *Ground Truth: The Social Implications of Geographic Information Systems*. New York, NY: The Guilford Press, 1994.

Plumwood, Val. "Decolonizing Relationships with Nature." In *Decolonizing Nature: Strategies for Conservation in a Post-Colonial Era*, edited by William M. Adams and Martin Mulligan, 51–78. New York, NY: Earthscan, 2004.

Plumwood, Val. "Nature in the Active Voice." *Australian Humanities Review* 46 (2009): 113–29.

Pratt, Mary Louise. "Coda." In *Arts of Living on a Damaged Planet*, edited by Anna Tsing, Heather Swanson, Elaine Gan, and Nils Bubandt, G169–174. Minneapolis, MN: University of Minnesota Press, 2017.

Punday, Daniel. "A Corporeal Narratology?" *Style* 34, no. 2 (2000): 227–42.

Radway, Janice. Foreword to *Ghostly Matters: Haunting and the Sociological Imagination*, edited by Avery Gordon, vii–xiii. Minneapolis, MN: University of Minnesota Press, 2008.

Ravenscroft, Alison. *The Postcolonial Eye: White Australian Desire and the Visual Field of Race*. New York, NY: Routledge, 2012.

Ravenscroft, Alison. "The Strangeness of the Dance: Kate Grenville, Rohan Wilson, Inga Clendinnen and Kim Scott." *Meanjin* 72, no. 4 (2013). Accessed February 12, 2019. https://meanjin.com.au/essays/the-strangeness-of-the-dance-kate-grenville-rohan-wilson-inga-clendinnen-and-kim-scott/

Richardson, Brian. *Unnatural Narrative: Theory, History, and Practice*. Columbus, OH: Ohio State University Press, 2015.

Rigby, Kate. "The Poetics of Decolonization: Reading *Carpentaria* in a Feminist Ecocritical Frame." In *International Perspectives in Feminist Ecocriticism*, edited by Greta Gaard, Simon Estok, and Serpil Opperman, 120–36. New York, NY: Routledge, 2013.

Robinette, Nicholas. *Realism, Form and the Postcolonial Novel*. New York, NY: Palgrave, 2014.

"Rock Art." Cederberg Tourism, 2019. https://www.cederberg.com/info.php?id=29

Romagnolo, Catherine. *Opening Acts: Narrative Beginnings in Twentieth Century Feminist Fiction*. Lincoln, NE: University of Nebraska Press, 2015.

Romei, Stephen. "Forever Beginning." *The Australian*, July 22, 2017. https://www.theaustralian.com.au/arts/review/aboriginal-identity-in-the-here-and-now-in-kim-scotts-novel-taboo/news-story/ef04673ac974460c91ecffd41f874290

Rose, Deborah Bird. "Multispecies Knots of Ethical Time." *Environmental Philosophy* 9, no. 1 (2012): 127–40.

Rose, Deborah Bird. *Wild Dog Dreaming: Love and Extinction*. Charlottesville, VA: University of Virginia Press, 2011.

Rose-Innes, Henrietta. *Homing: Short Stories*. Cape Town: Umuzi, 2010.

Rose-Innes, Henrietta. *The Rock Alphabet*. Cape Town: Kwela, 2004.

Rose-Innes, Henrietta. "Semiprecious." *Granta*, August 5, 2010. https://granta.com/semiprecious/

Roy, Arundhati. *Capitalism: A Ghost Story*. Chicago, IL: Haymarket Books, 2014.

Roy, Arundhati. *Field Notes on Democracy: Listening to Grasshoppers*. Chicago, IL: Haymarket Books, 2009.

Roy, Arundhati. *The Ministry of Utmost Happiness*. New York, NY: Knopf, 2017.

Rural Development and Land Reform. *Land Audit Report 2017*, February 2018. http://www.ruraldevelopment.gov.za/publications/land-audit-report/file/6126

Ruiters, Greg. "Race, Place, and Environmental Rights: A Radical Critique of Environmental Justice Discourse." In *Environmental Justice in South Africa*, edited by David A. McDonald, 112–26. Athens, OH: Ohio University Press, 2002.

Ryan, Marie-Laure, Kenneth Foote, and Maoz Azaryahu. *Narrating Space/Spatializing Narrative: Where Narrative Theory and Geography Meet*. Columbus, OH: Ohio State University Press, 2016.

Said, Edward. *Beginnings: Intention and Method*. New York, NY: Columbia University Press, 1985.

Said, Edward. *Culture and Imperialism*. New York, NY: Vintage, 1994.

Savonick, Danica. "'The Problem of Locomotion': Infrastructure and Automobility in Three Postcolonial Urban Nigerian Novels." *Modern Fiction Studies* 61, no. 4 (2015): 669–89.

Scahill, Jeremy. "Arundhati Roy: 'I Need to Know the Place Where I Stand.'" *The Intercept*, April 17, 2018. https://theintercept.com/2018/04/17/arundhati-roy-intercepted-jeremy-scahill/

Scanlan, John. *On Garbage*. London: Reaktion Books, 2005.

Schiffner, Ingo, and Roswitha Wiltschko. "Development of the Navigational System in Homing Pigeons: Increase in Complexity of the Navigational Map." *Journal of Experimental Biology* 216 (2013): 2675–81.

Scholsberg, David. *Defining Environmental Justice: Theories, Movements, and Nature*. New York, NY: Oxford University Press, 2009.

Scott, Kim. "Can You Anchor a Shimmering Nation State via Regional Indigenous Roots?" Interview with Anne Brewster. *Cultural Studies Review* 18, no. 1 (2012): 228–46.

Scott, Kim. "From Drill to Dance." In *Decolonizing the Landscape: Indigenous Cultures in Australia*, edited by Beate Neumeier and Kay Schaffer, 3–22. Amsterdam: Rodopi, 2014.

Scott, Kim. "A Noongar Voice, an Anomalous History." *Westerly* 53 (2008): 93–106.

Scott, Kim. *That Deadman Dance*. 2010. New York, NY: Bloomsbury, 2013.

Scott, Kim, and Hazel Brown. *Kayang and Me*. Fremantle: Fremantle Arts Centre Press, 2005.

Sehgal, Parul. "Arundhati Roy's Fascinating Mess." *The Atlantic*, July/August 2017. https://www.theatlantic.com/magazine/archive/2017/07/arundhati-roys-fascinating-mess/528684/

Sethi, Atul. "Grave Crisis Hits Cemeteries." *The Times of India*, April 5, 2009. https://timesofindia.indiatimes.com/home/sunday-times/deep-focus/Grave-crisis-hits-cemeteries/articleshow/4360271.cms

Seymour, Nicole. *Strange Natures: Futurity, Empathy, and the Queer Ecological Imagination*. Urbana, IL: University of Illinois Press, 2013.

Shear, Jack. "Haunted House, Haunted Nation: *Triomf* and the South African Postcolonial Gothic." *Journal of Literary Studies* 22, no. 1–2 (2006): 70–95.

Simone, AbdouMaliq. "Ghostly Cracks and Urban Deceptions: Jakarta." In *In the Life of Cities: Parallel Narratives of the Urban*, edited by Moshen Mostafavi, 121–39. Zurich: Lars Muller, 2012.

Sinha, Indra. *Animal's People*. New York, NY: Simon & Schuster, 2008.

Smith, Andrew, and William Hughes. *EcoGothic*. Manchester: Manchester University Press, 2013.

Smith, Jennifer J. "Birthed and Buried: Matrilineal History in Michelle Cliff's *No Telephone to Heaven*." *Meridians: Feminism, Race, Transnationalism* 9, no. 1 (2009): 141–62.

Southern Trelawny Environmental Agency. "Bauxite Mining in Cockpit Country." December 3, 2011. http://stea.net/wp/?page_id=96

Temper, Leah, Daniela del Bene, and Joan Martinez-Alier, "Mapping the Frontiers and Front Lines of Global Environmental Justice: The EJ Atlas," *Journal of Political Ecology* 22, no. 1 (2015): 255–78.

Tiffin, Helen. "'Man Fitting the Landscape': Nature, Culture and Colonialism." In *Caribbean Literature and the Environment: Between Nature and Culture*, edited by Elizabeth DeLoughrey, Renee K. Gosson, and George B. Handley, 199–212. Charlottesville, VA: University of Virginia Press, 2005.

Toland-Dix, Shirley. "Re-Negotiating Racial Identity: The Challenge of Migration and Return in Michelle Cliff's *No Telephone to Heaven*." *Studies in the Literary Imagination* 37, no. 2: (Fall 2004): 37–52.

Tuana, Nancy. "Viscous Porosity: Witnessing Katrina." In *Material Feminisms*, edited by Stacy Alaimo and Susan Hekman, 188–213. Bloomington, IN: Indiana University Press, 2008.

Turnbull, David. *Maps Are Territories: Science Is an Atlas*. Chicago, IL: University of Chicago Press, 1994.

UN Habitat. *United Nations Slum Almanac 2015–2016: Tracking Improvement in the Lives of Slum Dwellers*. https://unhabitat.org/slum-almanac-2015-2016/

Us Salam, Ziya. "We Are All Living in a Graveyard of Sorts: Interview with Arundhati Roy." *Frontline*, August 4, 2017. https://frontline.thehindu.com/arts-and-culture/literature/we-are-all-living-in-a-graveyard-of-sorts/article9775128.ece

Van Dooren, Thom. *Flight Ways: Life and Loss at the Edge of Extinction*. New York, NY: Columbia University Press, 2016.

Vidler, Anthony. *The Architectural Uncanny*. Cambridge, MA: MIT Press, 1992.

Vital, Anthony. "Toward an African Ecocriticism: Postcolonialism, Ecology and *Life and Times of Michael K*." *Research in African Literatures* 39, no. 1 (2008): 87–106.

Wabuke, Hope. "Chris Abani: 'The Middle-Class View of Africa Is a Problem.'" *The Guardian*, July 27, 2016. https://www.theguardian.com/books/2016/jul/27/chris-abani-writer-nigeria-memoir-africa

Walker, Gordon. *Environmental Justice: Concepts, Evidence and Politics*. New York, NY: Routledge, 2012.

Walker, Karyl. "Dust, Stench and Claim of Impotence: Pollution Killing Us, Say Communities near Bauxite Plants—Firms Insist Waste not Toxic." *Jamaica Observer*, February 11, 2007.

Wallace-Wells, David. "Why Do We Fail When We Try to Tell the Story of Climate Change?" *Slate*, February 19, 2019. https://slate.com/technology/2019/02/climate-change-storytelling-hollywood-failure-imagination.html

Walters, Wendy. "Michelle Cliff's *No Telephone to Heaven*: Diasporic Displacement and the Feminization of the Landscape." In *Borders, Exiles, Diasporas*, edited by Elazar Barkan and Marie-Denise Shelton, 217–33. Stanford, CA: Stanford University Press, 1998.

Warwick Research Collective. *Combined and Uneven Development: Towards a New Theory of World-Literature*. Liverpool: Liverpool University Press, 2015.

Winnett, Susan. "Macculate Reconceptions." In *Narrative Beginnings: Theories and Practices*, edited by Brian Richardson, 246–62. Lincoln, NE: University of Nebraska Press.

Wright, Alexis. *The Swan Book*. New York, NY: Atria Books, 2013.

Wood, Denis. *The Power of Maps*. New York, NY: Guilford Press, 1991.

Young, Hershini Bhana. *Haunting Capital: Memory, Text and the Black Diasporic Body*. Hanover: Dartmouth College Press, 2005.

Zable, Arnold. "Language and Politics in Indigenous Writing." *Overland* 205 (2011): 55.

Zierler, David. *The Invention of Ecocide: Agent Orange, Vietnam, and the Scientists Who Changed the Way We Think about the Environment*. Athens, GA: University of Georgia Press, 2011.

Index

Abani, Chris 22, 27–8, 30, 32–3, 35–51, 162, 173 n.13, 173 n.20, 175 n.60, 176 n.67. *See also GraceLand* (Abani)
Abeng (Cliff) 63, 68, 74
Abraham, Nicolas 83, 167 n.6
Abram, David 91, 116
Akpan, Wilson 172 n.4
Alaimo, Stacy 19, 60–2, 65, 188 n.76
Andrade, Susan Z. 175 n.60
Anglo-American ecocriticism 14, 168 n.19
Animal's People (Sinha) 4–5
Anthropocene 18–21, 159, 164, 188 n.76
antimimetic narrative strategies 17, 170 n.57
Archive Fever (Derrida) 117
Arts of Living on a Damaged Planet (Gan, Tsing, Swanson, and Bubandt) 7, 19

Barnard, Rita 107–8
Bauman, Zygmunt 46
Beginnings: Intention and Method (Said) 134, 136, 142
Bennholdt-Thomsen, Veronika 46–7
Braun, Lindsay Frederick 103, 107
Brewster, Anne 94
Brown, Hazel 81–2
Buell, Lawrence 168 n.19

Caminero-Santangelo, Byron 10, 12, 106
capitalism 18, 20, 29, 46–8, 54, 151, 164, 176 n.66
Capitalism: A Ghost Story (Roy) 155
Capitalocene 20, 151
Caribbean Literature and the Environment (DeLoughrey, Handley and Gosson) 10
Carrigan, Anthony 15, 167 n.11
Carruth, Cathy 94
Carter, Paul 23, 104–5, 107, 109, 111
cartography 104–5, 107, 109. *See also* maps/mapping
Christopher, A. J. 107

Cliff, Michelle 22, 53–9, 61–9, 71–4, 76–7, 176 n.1. *See also No Telephone to Heaven* (Cliff)
Cloudstreet (Winton) 93
Colebrook, Claire 7, 164
Crouch, David 83, 93
Culture and Imperialism (Said) 15, 88, 95, 162

Dannenberg. Hilary 49
Davis, Mike 39, 174 nn.43–4
Dawson, Ashley 49, 151
DeLoughrey, Elizabeth 10, 15
Derrida, Jacques 8, 11, 39, 46, 61–2, 67, 69, 73, 83, 114, 117–18, 128, 138
Didur, Jill 15
Different Shades of Green: African Literature, Environmental Justice, and Political Ecology (Caminero-Santangelo) 10, 12, 106
District Six Museum 127–8
duppies 3, 57, 74

Easterlin, Nancy 14
ecocriticism 7, 10, 14, 20, 170 n.54
    Anglo-American 14, 168 n.19
    postcolonial 12, 14–15, 168 n.19
ecogothic 3–4, 166–7 n.5
ecospectral approach 3–4, 6, 8, 10, 12, 18, 21, 22, 23, 39, 84–5, 94, 100, 140, 157, 159
environmental humanities 7, 14, 20
Environmental Justice Atlas (EJ Atlas) 127, 129
environmental justice scholarship 10–14, 21–2, 28, 30
environmental literature 10, 14
environmental threats 2–3, 6–7, 13, 16, 22, 24, 28, 51, 156, 164
    climate change 13, 16, 28, 160, 166 n.1
Estok, Simon 166 n.1, 166–7 n.5
Esty, Jed 16

Euro-American gothic tradition 3
Exposed: Environmental Politics and Pleasures in Posthuman Times (Alaimo) 65

Fanon, Frantz 11
Field Notes on Democracy: Listening to Grasshoppers (Roy) 132, 136, 145–6, 191 n.44
Freeman, Elizabeth 61

Genette, Gerard 45
Ghosh, Amitav 6, 16–17, 54, 66–7, 72, 98–9, 101, 131, 160, 166 n.1
ghosts 9, 11–12, 20–4, 33–6, 67, 75, 83–4, 86, 94, 99 101, 159, 163–5. *See also* specters
Glissant, Edouard 15, 55, 58, 66, 72, 170 n.48
Global Ecologies and the Environmental Humanities: Postcolonial Approaches (DeLoughrey, Didur, and Carrigan) 15
The God of Small Things (Roy) 133
Gordon, Avery 8–9, 11, 29, 72–3, 82–4, 89, 94, 149, 162, 165
GraceLand (Abani) 22, 27, 30, 32, 171–2 n.1, 176 n.67. *See also* Abani, Chris
  demolition of Maroko 32–3, 36
  Elvis Oke (fictional character) 27, 30–1, 33–5, 37–40, 43–50, 61
  environmental justice/injustice 22, 27–8, 30, 33, 38–9, 43, 45–6, 50–1
  environmental threats 28–9
  ghosts of Lagos 33–46
  haunting 35–8, 44–5, 49
  justice and slum conditions 22, 27–8, 32
  postcard image of Lagos 30–1, 40, 173 n.13
  Redemption (fictional character) 35, 37, 49–50
  slum clearance 27–32, 42–4
  social invisibility 31, 35–8, 46
  urban violence 44, 46
The Great Derangement: Climate Change and the Unthinkable (Ghosh) 6, 16–17, 54, 66–7, 72, 98–9, 101, 131, 160, 166 n.1
Green Lion (Rose-Innes) 129
Griffiths, Michael R. 93

Handley, George B. 10
Haraway, Donna 9, 19
Harley, J. B. 107
Harris, Wilson 55–6, 177 n.10
haunting 4, 6, 8–9, 11, 13–14, 16, 33, 35, 37–8, 54, 67–8, 71–2, 83–4, 86, 148–9, 159–60, 167 n.6, 167 n.11, 187 n.54
  Anthropocene 18–21
  literary 2–3, 6–7, 14–15, 21, 30, 67
Heise, Ursula 14–15, 159–60
Hillard, Tom 166 n.5
Hitchens, Christopher 62
Hogan, Patrick Colm 155–6
Huggan, Graham 88, 168 n.19
human 6–7, 10–12, 14, 20, 24, 28, 39–41, 54, 84–5, 89, 91, 129, 148–51, 155, 159–61, 163. *See also* nonhuman
human emotion system 156

Iheka, Cajetan 38
The Invention of Ecocide: Agent Orange, Vietnam, and the Scientists Who Changed the Way We Think about the Environment (Zierler) 70

James, Erin 15

Kappeler, Susanne 146–7
Kayang and Me (Brown and Scott) 81–2
Kearney, Jack 184 n.9
Kennedy, Rosanne 84–5
Kossew, Sue 181 n.22
Krishnan, Madhu 172 n.1

Lauren, Mason, 173 n.13
Leander, Niels Buch 134
Leopold, Aldo 29
Lines, William J. 93
literary hauntings 2–3, 6–7, 14–15, 21, 30, 67
Louw, Pat 184 n.9

maps/mapping 103, 107, 127, 185 n.23
  colonial maps 103–4
  critical cartography 104
  EJ Atlas 127, 129
  European map 104
  imperial/touristic mapping 111
  Water Usage Map, Cape Town's 128–9

Martinez-Alier, Joan 13, 104, 127
Martini, Edwin 70
Massey, Doreen 104, 113
Mbembe, Achille 34, 38, 117–18, 128
Mies, Maria 46–7
The Ministry of Utmost Happiness (Roy) 21, 23, 131, 134
    Aftab (fictional character) 140–2, 153
    Anjum (fictional character) 137, 140–3, 145, 153–4
    graveyards (India) 148–57
    multispecies communities 140–8
    Miss Udaya Jebeen (fictional character) 139–40, 155
modernism 16, 142–3
Moore, Jason W. 20
Morton, Timothy 6, 28, 58, 63, 66, 75–6, 140, 164
Mukherjee, Pablo 133
multispecies communities 2, 24, 28, 140–8
Murphy, Michelle 138

Narrative Beginnings: Theories and Practices (Richardson) 134
National Geo-spatial Information (NGI) 106–7
navigational feats of birds 186 n.52
Ngugi wa Thiongo 15, 88, 169 n.48
Nineveh (Rose-Innes) 129
Nixon, Rob 10, 29–30, 88
nonhuman 3, 6–7, 10–12, 14, 20, 24, 28, 38–9, 84–5, 89–93, 101, 129, 135, 140, 149–50, 154–5, 160–1. *See also* human
nonmimetic narrative strategies 170 n.57
Noongar 3, 23, 84–5, 98. *See also That Deadman Dance* (Scott)
    cultural inheritance 81, 98
    Indigenous knowledge 87, 100–1
    language 86–7, 90–1, 93–4
    "mitjal" 90–1
    repression of Noongar knowledge 88–9, 94
    settler-colonial notion 93–4
No Telephone to Heaven (Cliff) 22, 53, 67, 73. *See also* Cliff, Michelle
    Agent Orange 53, 61–2, 70, 72–3
    Bobby (fictional character) 53, 61–4, 67–9, 71–3, 75

    Clare Savage (fictional character) 22, 53–5, 57, 59–61, 63, 67–9, 71–7
    conjuring 66–73
    human and land 56–60
    individual protagonist 54–60, 76
    solidarity 58, 60
    spectral legacies 73–7
    toxins 60–4, 66, 72
    transcorporeality 60–1

Opening Acts: Narrative Beginnings in Twentieth Century Feminist Fiction (Romagnolo) 135

Peeren, Esther 17, 39, 67, 71, 76
Phillips, Dana 14, 17
Plumwood, Val 93, 100
Postcolonial Ecologies: Literatures of the Environment (DeLoughrey and Handley) 10
The Postcolonial Exotic (Huggan) 88
The Postcolonial Eye: White Australian Desire and the Visual Field of Race (Ravenscroft) 85
postcolonialism/postcolonial 10–15, 35, 42, 50, 57, 59, 65–6, 87–8, 94, 142–3, 170 n.54, 170 n.57, 192 n.77
    ecocriticism 10, 12, 14–15, 168 n.19
    postcolonial gothic 3
Pratt, Mary Louise 19
Punday, Daniel 34, 38

Radway, Janice 50, 83
Ravenscroft, Alison 85–6
realism 14–18, 66, 170 n.51, 170 n.54, 192 n.77
"recovery" 181 n.22
Renee, Gosson 10
Richardson, Brian 17, 134, 170 n.57
The Rock Alphabet (Rose-Innes) 23, 105, 129, 184 n.9, 187 n.54. *See also* maps/mapping
    Beatrice Faro (fictional character) 105, 108, 110, 112–13, 116–17, 119
    Bernard Faro (fictional character) 105, 108–9, 112–13, 115–16, 118
    environmental justice 126–9
    Flin (fictional character) 108, 113, 116–17
    inheritance 119–26

Ivy (fictional character) 105, 108–9, 111–12, 115, 118
Jean (fictional character) 105, 108–9, 111–15, 119
legacies of mapping 115–19
locating Cederberg 106–8
mapping 108–14
Romagnolo, Catherine 135–6
Rose, Deborah Bird 21, 101, 113–14, 117–18, 151
Rose-Innes, Henrietta 23, 105–6, 108–10, 112–13, 115, 117–19, 129, 162, 184 n.9, 185 n.20, 187 n.54
Roy, Arundhati 21, 23–4, 131–3, 191 n.58, 192 n.77. *See also The Ministry of Utmost Happiness* (Roy)
  forms of narration 134–40
  graveyards (India) 148–57
  multispecies communities 140–8
Ruiters, Greg 126, 128, 136, 162

Said, Edward 15, 88, 95–7, 134, 136, 138, 162
Salam, Ziya Us 134
Savonick, Danica 41–2, 172 n.1
scale 1–2, 7, 19–20, 24, 28–30, 37, 48, 50–1, 55, 66–9, 71–2, 77, 84–8, 98–9, 127, 131, 155–6, 159–61, 166 n.1, 188 n.76
Scholsberg, David 13
Scott, Kim 23, 81–2, 84–8, 90–2, 94–101, 188 n.59. *See also That Deadman Dance* (Scott)
Seizing the Means of Reproduction (Murphy) 138
Seymour, Nicole 75, 163
Simone, AbdouMaliq 41, 47
Sinha, Indra 4–5, 13, 167 n.11
social invisibility 31, 35–8, 46
social visibility 4, 8, 12, 27–30, 46–7
South Africa 103, 108, 110, 113, 117, 120, 126, 187 n.54. *See also* maps/mapping
  in colonial mapmaking 107
  NGI 106–7
specters 2, 4–5, 7, 9, 12, 18, 21, 30, 42, 45, 67, 75. *See also* ghosts
  of environmental justice scholarship 10–14
  of literary form 14–18

of permeable bodies 60–6
return of spirits 4, 6, 8–9
spectrality 3, 6–7, 9, 12, 33–8, 42, 61, 69, 94, 157
Specters of Marx (Derrida) 8, 34, 73, 114
The Spectralities Reader: Ghosts and Haunting in Contemporary Cultural Theory (Blanco and Peeren) 8
The Spell of the Sensuous and *Becoming Animal* (Abram) 116
The Storyworld Accord: Econarratology and Postcolonial Narratives (James) 15
Strange Natures (Seymour) 75
supernatural 6, 33, 170 n.57
The Swan Book (Wright) 160, 164

That Deadman Dance (Scott) 23, 84, 94, 180 n.7. *See also* Noongar
  Bobby Wabalanginy (fictional character) 82, 88–9, 92, 95–6, 98
  Dr. Cross (fictional character) 89, 92, 95–8
  ghosts 99–101
  haunting 89–94
  repression of Noongar knowledge 88–9
  Wunyeran (fictional character) 90, 95–8
Tiffin, Helen 56
Torok, Maria 83, 167 n.6
"transformation" 162–3

unnatural narratives 17, 170 n.57

Van Dooren, Thom 150
Van Riebeeck, Jan 107

Wallace-Wells, David 163
"Why Do We Fail When We Try to Tell the Story of Climate Change?" (Wallace-Wells) 163
Winnett, Susan 138–9
Winton, Tim 93
Wirlomin Noongar Language and Stories Project 86–7
The Wretched of the Earth (Fanon) 11
Wright, Alexis 160–1

Young, Hershini Bhana 11–14, 69

Zierler, David 70–1

www.ingramcontent.com/pod-product-compliance
Lightning Source LLC
Chambersburg PA
CBHW072234290426
44111CB00012B/2094